W9-CTD-420

KYOTO

A CULTURAL GUIDE

to Japan's Ancient Imperial City

京都

KYOTO

A CULTURAL GUIDE

to Japan's Ancient Imperial City

John H. and Phyllis G. Martin

CHARLES E. TUTTLE COMPANY

Rutland, Vermont & Tokyo, Japan

Published by the Charles E. Tuttle Company, Inc.
of Rutland, Vermont & Tokyo, Japan
with editorial offices at
2-6 Suido 1-chome, Bunkyo-ku, Tokyo 112

© 1994 by Charles E. Tuttle Publishing Co., Inc.

All rights reserved

LCC Card No. 93-61749
ISBN 0-8048-1955-6

First edition, 1994

Printed in Singapore

Contents

**TOUR 4: The Realms of the Dead, the Dancing Saint,
and Zen Beginnings**

**TOUR 5: The Pleasure Quarters, the Floating World,
and the Gion Shrine**

TOUR 6: Awata Palace, Fine Arts and Crafts,
and the Martial Arts

TOUR 12: Temples, Palaces, and Pavilions of Delight

TOUR 13: **Brocades, Samurai Movies, and the Contemplative Bodhisattva**

TOUR 14: The Old Imperial Palace

ILLUSTRATIONS

PHOTOGRAPHS *follow page* 128

MAPS

MAP OF KYOTO CITY *follows page* 344

Introduction
Kyoto and Its Heritage

TO EXPERIENCE the essence of Kyoto, one should walk its avenues and its streets, its alleys and its byways. Only in this manner can one appreciate the spirit of the place—its quiet lanes, its bustling main thoroughfares, and its juxtaposition of houses and shops, temples and shrines, gardens and industries.

Such an approach may seem to offer difficulties since many cities in Japan are centuries old and have streets laid out in a winding and seemingly incoherent pattern. Unlike many cities in Japan, however, Kyoto has a very orderly city plan based on streets that intersect at right angles. This systematic, rectangular plan reflects the fascination of the founders of Kyoto with the ancient Chinese capital of Ch'ang-an (present day Sian) whose orderly street plan it copied. Specific main streets as well as the major rivers further subdivided this plan so that the grid pattern of Kyoto streets makes it an easy city in which to roam.

Kyoto was established in 794 after the Emperor Kammu moved the capital, first from Nara in 784 to Nagaoka (a suburb of Kyoto today), and then to Kyoto itself ten years later. Its orderly street plan laid out on the plain within the encircling hills to the west, north, and east, and its two main rivers, the Kamogawa river to the east and the Katsuragawa river to the west, are the enduring physical vestiges of those early years. The other enduring elements of the earlier city are of a more spiritual and cultural nature. These elements can be seen in the zest for life of Kyoto residents as manifested in the city's great festivals, the continuing artistic sophistication as represented in its crafts and arts, and the appreciation of Kyoto's special architectural treasures which have been preserved or rebuilt after each disaster suffered by the traditional capital and its inhabitants.

A city composed of wood is prey to earthquake, fire, and flood—and to the destruction occasioned by war. Although some of the major sites in Kyoto have their roots in the city's ancient past, the present buildings are usually later reconstructions along traditional lines. The glory that was Kyoto in its golden age in the years between 800 and 1200 was to disappear in the next three centuries. In particular, the later era known as Sengoku Jidai (Period of the Warring States, 1467–1568) in the 1400s and the 1500s saw the virtual destruction of the city and its population. Two opposing Japanese armies were camped to the north and to the south of the city, Kyoto itself being the battlefield for a war which went on endlessly until both sides were exhausted and the city was devastated.

The return of peace, under Oda Nobunaga and Toyotomi Hideyoshi in the second half of the sixteenth century, saw a gradual resurgence of life in Kyoto. When Francis Xavier, one of the first Europeans to visit Kyoto, arrived in the city in 1551, he described it in a letter: ". . . formerly it had 18,000 houses . . . Now, in fact, it is destroyed." Xavier was simply reporting what a Japanese official had said in a more poetic way years previously when he described the capital as "an empty field from which the evening skylark rises with song and descends among tears."

Conditions had sunk to so deplorable an economic level in the mid-1500s that a contemporary Japanese document describes the imperial palace in terms that could well fit a peasant's hut. The imperial income itself had declined to a point where the

emperor was reduced to selling the imperial household treasures—as well as his autograph to anyone who would pay for it.

It was under the dictatorial but benevolent rule of Toyotomi
Hideyoshi from 1582 to 1598 that Kyoto was rebuilt and began to
prosper once more. With peace and with the movement of many
of the peasants from the countryside to the cities, the population
of Kyoto was quickly restored. These newcomers soon became
involved in commerce and in the crafts, and within a brief few
years a cultural and economic renaissance was under way. Temples
and shrines were rebuilt, palaces and castles of unparalleled
splendor were erected, commerce flourished, and the citizens of
Kyoto came to view their political ruler, Hideyoshi, almost as a
god. The thirty-five years from the death of Hideyoshi's predecessor Nobunaga in 1582 to the death in 1616 of Tokugawa Ieyasu
(who succeeded Hideyoshi) mark the height of Kyoto's revival as
well as the flourishing of the ostentatious Momoyama period.

Though Kyoto's glory shone less brightly once the capital of
the shogun was moved to Edo (Tokyo) in the early 1600s, Kyoto
remained the center of traditional culture for the nation as well
as the home of the emperor and his court. The city retained the
aura of sophistication that had been its heritage; the sensibility to
beauty for which it had always been noted was never lost—a
sensibility its brasher successor in Edo could never achieve. Even
the departure of the imperial court to Tokyo after 1868 has not
dimmed the importance of Kyoto. Its ability to retain the essence
of Japanese culture is the element for which Kyoto has always
been noted, and the multifaceted artistic heritage of its many
centuries continues to flourish despite the modern sprawl of a
major world city beset with all the problems of the twentieth
century. Thus it is that millions of visitors continue to come to
Kyoto to enjoy the traditions, the arts, the crafts, and the
inspiration offered by its Buddhist temples and Shinto shrines, its
many private and public museums, and its aesthetically satisfying
gardens, palaces, and villas.

There are various ways in which one can approach a city with treasures as varied as those of Kyoto: one can search out its heritage chronologically from its earliest surviving buildings to its most modern structures; its religious edifices can be visited according to their affiliation (Amida temples, Zen monasteries, Shinto shrines in their amazing variety), or one can concentrate on palaces or gardens or literary associations. All are valid approaches. In *Kyoto: A Cultural Guide* we have, instead, used Kyoto's grid pattern of streets as the basis of an approach, since, with the city's fine transportation network, the city can easily be explored segment by segment on foot.

Although Kyoto spreads from the Higashiyama mountains on its eastern perimeter to the mountains of Arashiyama and the Saga area on the west, it is easiest to divide the city at the Kamogawa river. It can be argued that this places a disproportionate area of the city to the west of the river. While geographically this is true, it is a fact that the wealth of important temples, shrines, and gardens are preponderantly to be found to the east of the Kamogawa river. Thus, as a demarcation line, the river divides the cultural treasures more equitably than would a point midway between the eastern and western mountain ranges which encompass Kyoto. Accordingly, this guide to Kyoto starts with sites to the east of the Kamogawa river, with sites to the west of the river following in due course. Each chapter begins with a brief introduction to the major sites in the area under consideration. Then the temples, shrines, or villas that follow are described. Directions for reaching the sites, the days and hours they are available to the visitor, and whether or not a fee is charged for entry are listed before the description of each site. Directions are given from the bus stop nearest the site to be visited, and a map of bus routes can be obtained from the Tourist Information Office. Although this volume is set up primarily for walking tours, occasionally a bus ride between some sites is indicated if one does not wish a long walk. Naturally, taxis provide the easiest means of travel within the city, and they can provide the most expeditious transportation to the various sites of interest.

TOUR
1

Ancient Lanes
to Kiyomizu-dera

清水寺

I N THE years since the Second World War, Kyoto has changed greatly. The city of one-story traditional houses has seen modern buildings of extraordinary height rise within its midst. Travelers often come to Kyoto looking for a traditional Japanese city of low buildings and an architecture of past centuries. Instead, they are amazed by the modern steel, glass, and brick structures they find. Kyoto, as with every other city in the world, continues to grow and to change, for it cannot remain a museum frozen in time. Yet there is an active concern within Kyoto itself about the continuing danger to the city's historic natural and architectural heritage. There are ongoing attempts, therefore, to preserve the best of the past both in temples and shrines as well as in Kyoto's traditional housing. Thus, this initial walk takes place in an area that has been designated as a historic section worthy of preservation, and it ends at one of the most venerable of Kyoto's temples, Kiyomizu-dera (Clear Water Temple). Accordingly, this walk offers a partial glimpse of the city as it existed prior to the modernization of Japan in the twentieth century.

Bus 18, 202, 206, or 207 can be taken from various points in Kyoto to the Kiyomizu-michi bus stop which lies between Gojo-dori and Shijo-dori (Gion) on Higashi-oji-dori. One could walk straight up Kiyomizu-zaka from the bus stop to the temple, but a deviation two streets to the north of Kiyomizu-zaka along Higashi-oji-dori (the main north-south street) offers a worthwhile diversion. Here, one turns to the right on to Kodai Minami Monzen-dori. At the second street on the right one turns again to the right and up the steps to Ninen-zaka (Two-Year Slope).

NINEN-ZAKA, SANNEN-ZAKA

Ninen-zaka begins a walk into the past and offers a picture of the city of Kyoto as it once was. Fires have destroyed so much of old Kyoto through the centuries that it is unusual to find an area which still provides the appearance of a Japanese city before the modern age. Fortunately, Ninen-zaka (Two-Year Slope) and

Sannen-zaka (Three-Year Slope) offer just such a remembrance of times past. Concerned over the disappearance of the two-story shops and homes that were typical of Kyoto city life, the city government created a few historical preservation districts in areas that have remained comparatively unchanged. One such area is that which encompasses Ninen-zaka and Sannen-zaka.

For centuries, pilgrims labored up the Two-Year Slope and the Three-Year Slope on their way to Kiyomizu-dera. (The strange names for the two streets have their basis in a superstition: to stumble on Ninen-zaka brought two years of misfortune, while a fall on Sannen-zaka could result in three years of bad luck.) Here on these streets, pilgrims found small restaurants which offered food, inns which provided a place to sleep, and shops which sold Kiyomizu-yaki and Awata-yaki pottery as souvenirs of a visit to the temple, pottery made in the stepped *noborigama* kilns which were formerly ubiquitous on this hillside.

Pilgrims still climb these slopes, as do thousands of tourists. The narrow, two-story wood-and-plaster row houses one finds along the way once covered all of Kyoto, and although frequently destroyed by fire, they were always rebuilt in the traditional style with the shop at the front and the family living quarters behind the sales area. Normally only 26 feet wide, the buildings often extended as much as 131 feet to the rear. Some of them were two-story structures which had narrow slatted windows at the front of the second floor. Since commoners were forbidden to look down upon passing samurai or daimyo, the narrow, slatted windows helped to hide the faces and eyes of curious merchant families who dared to peer at their betters passing below. The great fire of 1864 destroyed eighty percent of Kyoto; thus, these buildings represent the latest rebuilding of the traditional cityscape prior to modern times.

Today's shops, with perhaps one or two exceptions, have modern storefronts and interiors. In the past, the shop consisted of a raised platform on which the merchant sat and perhaps even created the wares he sold. The would-be purchaser was always welcomed with a cup of tea so that a proper mood could be established before the merchant's wares were brought forth and displayed. Modern life seldom permits such polite amenities; thus, the present shops are more oriented toward a contemporary display of chinaware or whatever is currently desired by the public.

Ninen-zaka and Sannen-zaka are lined with old buildings which still serve as purveyors to the pilgrim and the tourist, although one must admit that tourists seem to be the main clientele to whom the shopkeepers now appeal. But then, weren't pilgrims of past centuries souvenir seekers as well? Here for sale are small Buddhas, iron lanterns, scarves—all the paraphernalia of an ephemeral trade which the visitor cannot resist. A few restaurants tempt the famished with the variety of noodles that such Japanese establishments offer, and, of course, the soft drinks of the modern age are ever present. One enterprising shopkeeper on Ninen-zaka even has a rickshaw in which one can be photographed or transported, the latter, naturally, for an appropriate fee. A few rickshaws do still exist, but their day is past, and those that remain appear primarily at festival times.

KIYOMIZU-ZAKA

Ninen-zaka bends gracefully, as a proper traditional Japanese street should, and it ends in a short flight of steps which leads into Sannen-zaka. In turn, Sannen-zaka also ends in a steeper set of steps which leads up to Kiyomizu-zaka (Clear Water Slope). As has been the case for the number of centuries past, pottery can be found for sale along both Ninen-zaka and Sannen-zaka, but the full panoply of chinaware is not encountered until one mounts the steps at the southern end of Sannen-zaka and enters Kiyomizu-zaka which leads uphill from Higashi-oji-dori to Kiyomizu-dera at the top of the street. Here, one can find shops that sell Kiyomizu-yaki and other chinaware. Souvenir shops line the street cheek by jowl, and the street is always crowded with visitors heading to the temple, many in groups led by their banner-waving leader. It is always a street of excitement and color in the daytime.

The making of porcelain was a craft and an art that began to flourish in Kyoto as a result of the incursions into Korea in 1592 and 1597 by the Japanese troops under the command of Toyotomi Hideyoshi, the then civil and military ruler of Japan. The Koreans, of course, had learned the craft from the Chinese, and such products were appropriately summed up in one word in English-speaking countries as "chinaware." Among the prizes of war brought back to Japan in the 1590s were Korean ceramic craftsmen and artists, and a fascination with their work led in time to the development of fine Japanese porcelains. The cult of tea which developed with Sen-no-Rikyu under the patronage of Hideyoshi also encouraged the development of the Japanese ceramic craft. Once there were ten different schools or styles of pottery; today only Kiyomizu-yaki remains—and it is no longer made in Kyoto but in the outskirts of the city due to the anti-pollution laws of the last one-third of the twentieth century which have restricted industrial fires.

Once the attractions (or distractions) of Kiyomizu-yaki have been experienced, the top of Kiyomizu-zaka is reached, and Kiyomizu-dera is before one.

KIYOMIZU-DERA

The Kiyomizu-dera temple is open from 6:00 a.m. to 6:00 p.m., although a number of the temple buildings are closed after 4:00 p.m. There is an entry fee to the main portion of the complex during open hours.

The Kiyomizu-dera is one of the oldest temples in Kyoto, its establishment even predating the founding of the city. It was first founded in 788, six years before the emperor Kammu decided to move his capital to Kyoto. Legend recounts that Enchin, a priest at a temple in Nara, had a vision that he would find a fountain of pure or clear water *(kiyomizu)* at which he could build a temple. At the Otawa-no-taki (Sound of Feathers Waterfall) on the hillside where Kiyomizu-dera now stands, he came upon the hermit Gyo-ei. To Enchin's surprise, the hermit announced that he had been awaiting Enchin's arrival, and now that the priest from Nara had arrived, he could move on to a less settled area.

He gave Enchin a log of sacred wood and instructed him to carve the log into an image of Kannon, the Bodhisattva of Mercy. With that, the hermit disappeared. Later, Enchin found the hermit's sandals atop the mountain, leading him to the realization that he had been speaking with a manifestation of Kannon who had since ascended from the mountain crest. Enchin carved the image of the Eleven-faced Kannon (Juichimen Senju Sengen Kannon), and created a small, crude temple building to house the image—the beginning of the Kiyomizu-dera.

Kannon was obviously pleased by Enchin's act, and soon another miraculous event occurred. Sakenoue-no-Tamuramaro, the emperor's leading general, went deer hunting one day near the temple. Having shot a deer, he was immediately reproved by Enchin, who happened to come upon him with the dead animal, for, in the Buddhist faith, killing creatures is forbidden. The warrior, according to tradition, repented of his action and, as an act of contrition, had his house disassembled and given to Enchin for a proper temple building in which to house his sacred Kannon image.

Enchin's good fortune did not stop there. In 794 the emperor had his palace buildings at his capital of Nagaoka (now a Kyoto suburb) disassembled prior to the move to his new capital at Kyoto. Deciding to erect an entirely new structure, he gave his Shishin-den (Throne Hall) to Tamuramaro as a gift in recognition of his military service to the nation. Tamuramaro, in turn, gave the huge structure to Enchin as a new main hall for his temple since Tamuramaro had become a devotee of Kannon. That original building lasted until 1629, when it was destroyed by fire, and the main hall of the temple today is a reconstruction of what was originally an imperial palace building. As such, it is one of the few major Buddhist temples with a *hinoki* (cypress) bark roof instead of the traditional tiled roof, in remembrance of its original condition as a portion of the emperor's palace.

At the head of Kiyomizu-zaka, Kiyomizu-dera commands the top of this portion of the mountainside. On the left of the initial set of steps is a rare remainder of past times, the Uma-todome from the 1400–1550s, the horse stalls at which samurai and daimyo once left their horses when visiting the temple. By contrast, to the right of the steps leading into the temple grounds is a modern attraction, a twentieth-century solar clock.

Nio-mon   To the right of the Uma-todome are steps which lead to the two-story Nio-mon (Gate of the Deva Kings) with its cypress-bark roof. Two Deva Kings (Nio) stand guard, as do two *koma-inu* (Korean lion-dogs), to protect the temple from the possible entry of evil forces. Alone of the many temple structures, this gateway escaped destruction in the 1478 conflagration. The twelve-foot-tall Nio on the right has his mouth open to pronounce the Sanskrit "A" while the one on the left has his lips closed so as to pronounce the "UN" sound: the two sounds, being the alpha and omega of Buddhist lore, symbolize the all-inclusiveness of Buddhist teachings.

Sai-mon   A second flight of steps leads up to the Sai-mon (West Gateway), another two-story gate whose large cypress-bark roof is held up by eight pillars. The elaborately carved gateway reflects the grandiose architectural taste of the Momoyama period in which it was created in 1607. The elephant heads decorating its end beams are said to be a detail brought back from Korea after the military incursions by Japan into that country in the 1590s. Two more Nio guardians stand on either side of the passageway through the gate as additional protectors of the temple. The Shoro (Bell Tower) is to the left of the Sai-mon, and although the tower dates from 1596, its bell was cast in 1478.

Sanju-no-to   The Sanju-no-to, the three-storied pagoda of 1633, rises behind the Sai-mon to the east. It is the tallest three-story pagoda in Japan. In 1987 the pagoda was repainted in the traditional vermilion for the first time in a number of years, and this has made it stand out against the weathered brown color of the other buildings of the temple. The pride of early Buddhist temples was to have their structures enhanced with the brilliant vermilion color which reflected the grandeur of their Chinese heritage.

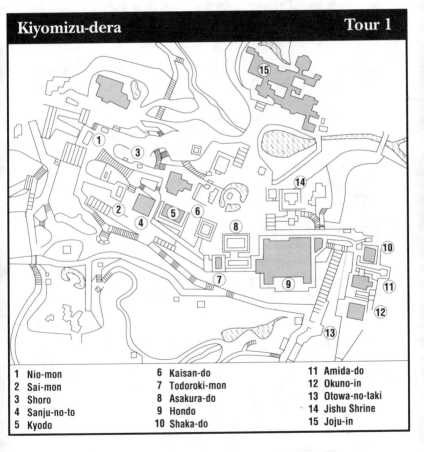

Kiyomizu-dera   Tour 1

1	Nio-mon	6	Kaisan-do	11	Amida-do
2	Sai-mon	7	Todoroki-mon	12	Okuno-in
3	Shoro	8	Asakura-do	13	Otowa-no-taki
4	Sanju-no-to	9	Hondo	14	Jishu Shrine
5	Kyodo	10	Shaka-do	15	Joju-in

Kyodo   A series of small temple buildings follow, buildings that usually are not open to the public. The first one, beyond the pagoda, is the Kyodo (Sutra Library) which holds the sacred Buddhist texts. The building is large enough to serve as a lecture hall for the monks as well, and it contains a Shaka Nyorai as its main image with a Monju, the Buddhist deity of wisdom, and a Fugen image, the Buddhist deity of virtue, on either side. The ceiling of the Kyodo is decorated with the painting of a coiled dragon. Behind it is the Jishin-in (Temple of Mercy) which is said to have been the favorite place of worship in the late 1500s for Toyotomi Hideyoshi, the military and civil ruler of Japan, and some of his belongings are still retained within.

Kaisan-do   Next beyond the Kyodo is the Kaisan-do (Founder's Hall), which is also known as the Tamura-do in honor of the general who donated the Hondo (Main Hall) to Priest Enchin back in the 700s. The Kaisan-do holds four multicolored images: that of Gyo-ei, the hermit who was practicing austerities on the mountainside when Priest Enchin first appeared here; of Priest Enchin; of Tamuramaro; and of his wife Takako. These finely colored images, each 2.5 feet tall, are seated on multicolored platforms.

Todoroki-mon   Next, one comes to the Todoroki-mon or Chu-mon (Middle Gate). Temples have traditionally had a main gateway and then a middle gate before one arived at the Hondo. This 1633 middle gate was given the name Todoroki-mon, "Gate Resounding to the Call of the Buddha's Teachings," due to the fact that the chants of the priests should resound to the benefit of all believers. The gate has two more Deva Kings who serve as protectors of the innermost areas of Kiyomizu-dera.

Benten-jima   In the distance to the left is the Benten-jima (Benten Island). A small pond has in its center a tiny island on which stands a shrine to the Shinto goddess Benten. Most

Buddhist temples have one or more Shinto shrines attached to them to offer the protection of the native Shinto gods to the Buddhist deities. Japanese religion, except in the period from 1868 to 1945, has always been able to offer reverence to the original native gods as well as the Buddhist deities who first were accepted in the early seventh century.

Asakura-do To the left, beyond the Todoroki-mon is the Asakura-do, a 1633 replacement for the original building (later destroyed by fire) which was a gift of Asakura Sadakaga (1473–1512), a son of the emperor Temmu. It has an Eleven-faced Kannon with an image of Bishamon-ten (god of wealth) and Jizo (guardian deity of children) on either side. Ahead to the east is a stone with the traditional impress of the Buddha's feet and an eight-spoked "Wheel of the True Law" imprinted on the heel. Custom decrees that by looking on such a memorial footprint one is forgiven of all one's sins. In the early years of Buddhism in India, images were not created of the Buddha and bodhisattvas. (A bodhisattva is an individual who can achieve nirvana but who chooses instead to remain active in this world in order to assist others toward the state of nirvana; thus, a bodhisattva serves as a living mediator between humans and ultimate reality.) In time, the influence of Hindu and Greek representations of their deities caused Buddhism to personify its sacred beings in human form. In the earliest centuries, however, before such iconography developed, the representation of the Buddha's footprints sufficed as reminders of the way of the Buddha's law.

One of the effects that the native religion of Shinto had upon Buddhism was the physical concern for purity at holy places and the need for individual purification before approaching the gods; thus, Buddhist temples, as do Shinto shrines, always have a water basin with a running fountain where one can purify one's hands (of deeds and actions) and one's mouth (of thoughts or spirit) before entering upon sacred ground. The Kiyomizu-dera fountain has been created in the form of a delightfully ferocious-looking dragon which spews forth clear water instead of the traditional breath of flame. The basin which receives the dragon's stream is known as the Owl Washing Basin from the owl motif on the foundation stone beneath the basin.

Faith, myth, and legend have a delightful way of becoming intertwined in all cultures, and Japan is no exception. The Japanese have always been attracted to tragic heroes as well as to their devoted followers, and none are better known than Minamoto-no-Yoshitsune and Benkei, Yoshitsune's faithful companion in arms. In the late 1100s, Benkei was a monk of an unusual combative nature. Much given to uproarious conduct, he was a lover of duels, and he once vaingloriously swore to fight and to defeat one thousand warriors and to deprive them of their swords. Having conquered 999 such unfortunates, he chanced upon the armed sixteen-year-old Yoshitsune, crossing the Gojo (Fifth Street) Bridge at the Kamogawa river below Kiyomizu-dera. He challenged this easy mark of a youngster to conflict, not knowing that the lad had been taught the art of swordsmanship by a *tengu*, a long-nosed goblin learned in the arts of war. Since he wished to be fair to the young man, Benkei weighted himself down with iron geta (sandals) as well as with a cumbersome sword. To his amazement, he was defeated by the youth. As a result, he pledged to become Yoshitsune's devoted companion, and thereafter accompanied the handsome, courageous, and able Yoshitsune in his many victorious battles and to his tragic end.

Benkei is remembered today at Kiyomizu-dera, for representations of his oversized geta and staff stand just before the Hondo of the temple. (The items are oversized since Benkei is said to have been almost eight feet tall.) In the latter quarter of the nineteenth century, a blind blacksmith regained his sight after repeated prayers at Kiyomizu-dera; thus, he created these versions in iron of Benkei's geta and staff as a thanksgiving offering to the temple for the return of his vision. One other remembrance of this legendary monk and his failure to win his one thousandth sword can be found at Gojo Bridge. Today a modern statue of Benkei has been placed at the western end of the bridge in a mid-traffic park. Here Benkei stands in miniature, sword in hand, ready to take on all comers as they cross the Kamogawa river as Yoshitsune once did. He stands unchallenged today, no doubt due to the heavy traffic which creates a barrier no modern Kyoto pedestrian would ever defy.

Hondo   The Hondo (Main Hall), looming grandly beyond the Asakura-do and the purification fountain, is the main attraction of Kiyomizu-dera. Its original structure before the 1629 fire was the Shishin-den, the throne hall, of Emperor Kammu. The 190-foot-long by 88-foot-deep building of seven bays stands on the side of a cliff, and it is supported by 139 pillars some 49 feet tall. Its huge *hinoki,* hip-ridged roof rises 53 feet high and is skirted with *mokoshi* (smaller and lower false roofs) on its east, west, and north sides, these extra roofs providing covered, open corridors on these three sides. The Hondo's front (southern) veranda juts out by 25 feet over the valley below. This large *butai* (dancing stage) is flanked by the two wings of the roofed *gakuya* (orchestra). These two units are so named since religious music and dance took place on this veranda. A fine view over a portion of the city of Kyoto and to the south can be obtained from the platform which sits high above the valley.

The interior of the Hondo has an outer sanctuary *(gejin)* and an inner sanctuary *(naijin).* The outer sanctuary is striking in its simplicity with its plain, massive unfinished columns and unfinished floor. Some thirty wooden tablets or paintings are hung high up on the walls, and they thus enrich the simple structure. These are votive gifts of tradesmen at the time of the 1633 rebuilding of the temple after its last disastrous fire. Among the most noted of these gifts are the four paintings of ships, three commissioned by the merchant-trading family of the Sumiyoshi and one by the Suminokura family, all from 1633–34. The Suminokura gift is particularly interesting since it shows a festival on board a ship. Represented among its figures are European sailors and an African servant or slave. It stands 8.8 feet tall by 11.8 feet wide.

In contrast to the simplicity of the outer sanctuary, the inner sanctuary of the Hondo is of great splendor. At the center of the inner sanctuary *(naijin)* is a sunken, stone-floored innermost sanctuary *(nainaijin)* where the sacred, hidden image is kept. The major gold-leaf-covered images on public view stand behind vermilion wooden railings on a raised black lacquer platform with gold decorations hanging from the roof of the unit.

The primary image of the Hondo is the Eleven-faced Kannon (Juichimen Senju Sengen Kannon) said to have been carved by Enchin in the 700s. It is a *hibutsu,* a hidden image, which is only brought forth every thirty-three years, its last appearance being in 1977. (The number thirty-three has religious significance since Kannon is said to have taken thirty-three vows to save mankind.) This 5.16-foot-tall image is unique in that two of its arms extend over its head, its hands almost touching each other and seemingly supporting a topmost tiny Buddha image. Each of this Kannon's many hands holds a different religious symbol.

To the right and left of the Kannon's case are the Nijuhachibu-shu, the 28 supernatural followers of Kannon, each approximately 4.6 feet tall. At each corner of the black lacquer platform stand the Shitenno, the four Deva Kings, protecting all the images from evil. In a shrine at the east end is an image of Bishamon-ten, while at the west end is the Jizo image. These and the Kannon are said to have been carved by Priest Enchin. Pictures of these three images hang at the end of the inner shrine, so they can be seen even when their cases are closed.

Nishi-muki Jizo   On leaving the Hondo and walking toward the hillside, one should bypass the grand stairway leading down to the Otowa Falls in order that the four small buildings that close the temple grounds on the east can be visited. The first of these

houses the minor Nishi-muki Jizo (Westward-Facing Jizo) dedicated to the bodhisattva who protects children, travelers, and the
dead. To the right of the Jizo Shrine is the thatch-roofed Shaka-
do (Buddha's Hall). Within is a three-foot-tall smiling image of
the Shaka Buddha seated on a golden lotus flower. A
nimbus appears behind his head, and a magnificent lacelike
aureole behind the full image is enriched with flying angels
(apsaras) carrying musical instruments. On either side of the
Shaka stands a thirteen-inch-tall Fugen and a Monju, the Buddhist
deities of virtue and wisdom. Between the Shaka-do and its
neighboring Amida-do (Amida Hall) are some 180 small Jizo
images sitting under an open, roofed structure known as the Hall
of One Hundred Jizo (Hyakutai Jizo). One folk tale holds that
bereaved parents can view these images and, if they find one that
resembles their dead child, can rest assured that the child is at
peace.

Amida-do   The Amida-do to the south of the Shaka-do has the
traditional tiled roof of Buddhist temples. The building is divided into three sections: the first portion holds many *ihai,*
memorial tablets to the dead; the middle section holds the
Amida Nyorai image which is 6.25 feet tall, its hands arranged in
the *mudra* (the symbolic position of the hands) indicating contemplation. Amida is the Buddha of the Western Paradise, and
the golden aureole behind his image has the traditional one
thousand Buddha figures in relief as well as a number of larger
such images also in raised relief. It was here that the doctrine of
the *nenbutsu (Namu Amida Butsu*—Praise to the Buddha Amida)
was proclaimed in 1188 by Priest Honen, thereby creating the
cult of Amida and the Jodo sect of Buddhism. The repetition of
this phrase insures one of being received by Amida into his
western paradise after death. A special *nenbutsu* service takes
place here five times a year.

Okuno-in The last building in this row is the thatch-roofed Okuno-in (the Inner Temple). This was the site of the original grass hut of Gyo-ei, the hermit whom Enchin came upon at this spot. Here Enchin created the rude hut that housed the three images he had carved of Kannon, Bishamon-ten, and Jizo, and here later stood the house that Tamuramaro gave Enchin to replace the simple hut housing the sacred Kannon image. In front of the Okuno-in is a *butai* (a dancing stage similar to but much smaller than the one in front of the Hondo). Behind the Okuno-in is the Nurete Kannon (Water-soaked Kannon) image, a figure standing in a water-filled basin. It is an act of purification and piety to dip water from the basin and to pour it over the head of the Kannon.

Otowa-no-taki Below the Okuno-in, at the foot of the grand staircase bypassed earlier, lies the Otowa-no-taki (Sound of Feathers Waterfall). Water falling down the three-part waterfall is said to have a divine power which prevents illness; thus, many visitors will be seen using long, wooden-handled metal cups that enable them to reach out and partake of the curative waters of the falls. The most devout of devotees can be seen at times, clad all in white, standing under the icy waters of the falls as an ascetic practice—even in the coldest of winter weather. The deity of these falls is the Fudo Myo-o, a ferocious-looking deity who punishes evildoers. It is this Fudo, enshrined at the waterfall font, whom the devotees worship as they toss coins into the basin before drinking the sacred waters.

Jishu Shrine A most popular Shinto shrine exists right in the middle of Kiyomizu-dera Buddhist temple, a not unusual situation prior to 1868 when the government forcibly separated the two religions, often through destructive physical separation. Somehow the Jishu Shrine remained on the small hill just behind the Hondo of Kiyomizu-dera. As with many Shinto shrines, it has more than one resident god. In this case, it enshrines the tutelary

Shinto god of the land on which the temple and shrine sit. It also enshrines the wayward brother, Susa-no-o, of the imperial family's supposed ancestress Amaterasu Omikami.

If that were not enough, the shrine also reverences Okuninushi-no-Mikoto, and a statue of the god and a rabbit stand at the head of the steps leading up to this tightly packed set of Shinto buildings. The ancient *Kojiki,* the legendary account of Japanese history, tells of a deceitful rabbit who was punished by having its skin peeled from its body. Okuninushi is said to have taken pity on the rabbit, to have healed it, and to have led it to reform its ways; thus, they are both honored here. More important, however, and particularly to young women who can be found giggling at the shrine, is that the god of love and good marriages resides within.

The heart of the shrine is the Mekura-ishi (Blind Stones). These two stones are set some sixty feet apart. If one walks from the first stone to the second stone with eyes shut and arrives at the second stone (without opening the eyes while walking) repeating the loved one's name continuously en route, success in love and marriage is guaranteed. The unsteady walker, it is presumed, had best seek another lover. There are other alternatives for the unsteady, however, since the shrine has a most successful business in the sale of charms which can guarantee success in love, luck on examinations, easy delivery in childbirth, good luck, long life, wisdom, good fortune with money—and, just to prove that the gods are up-to-date, the shrine also can make available charms for safety in traffic. Little wonder that it is a popular shrine.

Joju-in A visit to the Kiyomizu-dera between November 1 and November 10 provides a special delight, for then the garden of the superior of the temple is open to the public. The Joju-in (Achievement Temple), the superior's residence, can be reached by a path to the north of the main entrance to the Kiyomizu-dera. Originally a private temple for the emperor Go-Kashiwabara (reigned 1500–26), it is noted for its exquisite garden usually attributed to two of Japan's most noted landscape gardeners: Soami (1455–1525) and Kobori Enshu (1579–1647).

The Superior's small garden on the edge of the Yuyadani valley seems much larger than when it is viewed from the veranda and rooms of the Joju-in's north-facing *shoin* (study). This seeming spaciousness is derived from the device of "borrowed scenery" whereby the plantings in the garden seem to merge with the neighboring hillside as though all in view were part of the garden itself. The garden is created around a pond which has two islands. A large stone in the pond, the Eboshi-ishi (Eboshi Stone), is so called from its resemblance to the formal hat *(eboshi)* worn by the nobility in the Heian period (794–1185); the angle of the stone suggests the head of a nobleman bowed in prayer. A water basin whose shape resembles the long sleeves of a young girl's kimono is called the Furisode (Sleeve Basin). This stone was donated to the temple by Toyotomi Hideyoshi in the 1590s. Noted as well are some of the garden's stone lanterns, particularly the one called Kagero (Dragonfly) on the larger island.

Daiko-do   Returning from the Joju-in toward the entrance to the temple, one passes a series of 500 small stone Buddha images surrounded by ferns on a hillside, the images having been placed about an Eleven-faced Kannon. Further toward the western end of the grounds is the Daiko-do, the Great Lecture Hall, which was built in 1978 on the 1,200th anniversary of the founding of the temple. The Tahokaku (Tower of Treasures) of the Daiko-do has a wing on either side, and the walls of the base of the tower hold a Buddha's footprint thirteen feet long while the walls surrounding the footprint have 4,076 images of the four major Buddhas. The seventy-nine-foot-long walls about the area have an image of these four Buddhas inscribed on them: the Taho Nyorai on the north wall, the Shaka Nyorai on the south wall, the Yakushi Nyorai on the east wall, and the Amida Nyorai on the west wall. The upper hall of the tower contains some of the ashes of the historic Buddha.

The walk down the hill to Higashi-oji-dori and the bus lines can be taken by the alternative street Kiyomizu-michi which parallels Kiyomizu-zaka one street to the south. Partway down the hill is the Tojiki Kaikan, the pottery hall, where one has yet another chance to purchase Kiyomizu-yaki or other ceramic wares before leaving this center of traditional and contemporary pottery.

NISHI OTANI CEMETERY

At the foot of the hill at Higashi-oji-dori lies the entry to the Nishi Otani Cemetery. The small double bridge over the waterway has been nicknamed the Spectacles Bridge since the reflection of its semicircular arches in the water makes for a complete circle and the circles and the structure of the bridge can be perceived as a pair of spectacles. A cemetery may seem to be an unusual place to visit, but this mortuary for the abbots of the Nishi Hongan-ji and the followers of the Jodo Shinshu sect of the great priest Shinran offers another aspect of Japanese life.

When Shinran died on November 28, 1262, his body was cremated, and, eventually, in 1694, his remains were moved from his original burial site to a hexagonal mausoleum at the Nishi Otani Cemetery, one of the two oldest cemeteries in Kyoto. (A portion of his ashes was also placed in the Higashi Otani Cemetery of the Higashi Hongan-ji temple, which is a branch of Shinran's faith.)

Taiko-do The path over the bridge leads to the main gate of the cemetery, and once past the gateway the Taiko-do (Drum Tower) is to the left. This two-story structure has been used as place of penance for refractory monks, and here they do penance beating a drum *(taiko)*. Behind the Taiko-do is the Shoro tower of the complex. Ahead is the Amida wor~ Amida-do, with its gilt image of Amida. To Amida-do are two structures: in the mod southwest a Japanese-style lunch may be c visitors may purchase flowers to place in the mortuary building; the building to the southeast of the Amida-do contains the office responsible for receiving the ashes of deceased members of the sect.

Haiden   Behind and to the left of the Amida-do is a two-story gateway, and beyond it is the Haiden (Oratory), which stands before Shinran's tomb. At the Haiden, the ashes of the dead are ceremonially received by a priest in a brief religious service before committal to the mortuary hall. In 1966 the Muryoju-do (Hall of Immeasurable Bliss) was erected to the south of the Haiden. This modern, concrete structure is a repository for the ashes of members of the sect. There is a large chapel on the second floor for services, its entry wall enriched with a gold screen and a golden image of Amida. Across the open courtyard is the columbarium building where the ashes of the deceased are placed in compartments.

To the right and left of Shinran's tomb, in an area not open to the public, are the graves of the abbots of the Nishi Hongan-ji. Old trees about the area add dignity and serenity to the site.

On leaving the Nishi Otani Cemetery, one is back at Higashi-oji-dori. Here bus 18, 202, 206, 207, or a taxi can be taken to one's next destination within the city.

TOUR
2

The 1,001 Golden Kannon
of Sanjusangen-do,
the General, and the Potter

T HE SANJUSANGEN-DO is one of the sights that all visitors to Kyoto wish to see, for its 1,001 golden images are remarkable. They are particularly unusual when one recalls the number of centuries they have survived despite the many fires, earthquakes, and even wars that Kyoto has suffered. While this walk begins with the spectacular golden Kannon of the Sanjusangen-do, there are other fascinating sites virtually across the street as well as a few streets away, places that the average visitor too often misses. These other attractions are connected with Toyotomi Hideyoshi who ruled Japan at the end of the 1500s and who brought prosperity back to the formerly war-ravaged city. In addition, the lovely house of one of the most distin-guished potters of the twentieth century, that of Kawai Kanjiro, is another site that few foreign visitors have heard of, and yet it offers an invitation into a traditional home right in the heart of Kyoto. It is the home of a man of taste and artistic ability, and the climbing kilns in which he made his pottery are one of the unusual sights seen during a visit to his home and workshop.

Of course, there is but little choice as to where one should start this particular tour, since the Sanjusangen-do with its golden Kannon will always head any visitor's list of places that must be experienced.

SANJUSANGEN-DO

The Sanjusangen-do is on the south side of Shichijo-dori at Yamato-oji-dori. Bus 206 or 208 to the Hakubutsukan/ Sanjusangen-do-mae bus stop on Shichijo-dori leaves one at the Kyoto National Museum opposite the Sanjusangen-do. Alterna-tively, bus 16, 202, or 207 to the Higashi-oji-dori/Shichijo bus stop leaves one just north of the temple. The temple is one street west on Shichijo-dori from this bus stop, just to the west Kyoto Park Hotel. The Sanjusangen-do is open f- 5:00 p.m. between March 16 and October 31 ai to 4:00 p.m. between November 1 and March 1.

The Sanjusangen-do is one of the most famous places in Kyoto because of its large main image of the Eleven-faced Kannon (Juichimen Senju Kannon) as well as the one thousand golden images that surround it. The temple's official name, Renge-o, means "Lotus King," the name given to the Senju Kannon who was regarded as the lord of all the other forms of Kannon. (Kannon can appear in thirty-three different incarnations.) The name Lotus King was appropriate for this temple since in the Sanjusangen-do the devotion to Kannon has been carried to an extravagant level with its 1,001 images of Kannon, the deity of mercy, each image standing on a golden lotus blossom.

The Renge-o-in (Sanjusangen-do) was created in 1164 at the request of ex-emperor Go-Shirakawa (1127–92), a devotee of Kannon, who wished to bring peace and prosperity to the country by promoting the spread of Buddhism and its doctrines. The emperor was assisted in the construction of the temple by Taira-no-Kiyomori (1118–81), the de facto civil ruler of Japan. The Taira leaders, as the actual political rulers of the state, identified themselves with the twenty-eight gods whose images appear at the rear of the temple. These deities protect the Buddhist universe—as the Taira leaders felt they protected and brought peace to Japan.

The temple sat amid the various imperial villas that existed in this eastern area of Kyoto. It had many buildings, including a five-story pagoda in the southeastern section of the grounds, a Shinto shrine in the northwest area, and an Amida hall, among other buildings. All these structures were destroyed in a fire in 1249. The temple was rebuilt at the order of the then emperor Go-Fukakusa (1243–1304) so as to appear just as it had been before the conflagration. However, only the Hondo (Main Hall) was reconstructed. Certain images had been saved from the fire, including the head of the main Kannon image, 156 of the 1,000 smaller Kannon, and the twenty-eight followers of Kannon. The Hondo (Main Hall) was reconstructed between 1251 and 1253, ʾd the leading artists of the day recreated the 1,001 images of

Kannon of which 125 of the smaller images are from the pre-fire temple. The temple was completed and rededicated in 1266.

The Sanjusangen-do, like most temples, has a tile-topped, plastered wall about the borders of its grounds. Its Nandai-mon (South Gate) was rebuilt about 1590 in the elegant style of the Momoyama period (1568–1603). On the eastern side of the property, the temple's outer wall is broken by a mid-twentieth century restoration of the vermilion To-mon (East Gate) and corridor in the style of the Kamakura period (1185–1336). A stone garden and a pond of the same period lie between the gate and its corridor and the Sanjusangen-do Hondo.

Hondo   The Sanjusangen-do Hondo is 390.4 feet long by 54 feet wide. The temple derives its common name (Sanjusangen-do) from the fact that it has thirty-three (*san-ju-san* = thirty-three) bays *(ken)* created by the thirty-four columns that sub-divide and support the gradually curving, tiled roof. (The word *do* in Sanjusangen-do means "hall.") Each bay has wood shutter-doors and behind them are moveable shoji panels. The thirty-three bays symbolize the thirty-three incarnations into which Kannon can transform himself in his merciful acts of saving mankind from the miseries of human existence.

Juichimen Senju Kannon   The central image of the Juichimen Senju Kannon has five hundred images of this deity on either side. The main image is an eleven-foot-tall (including the pedestal) gilded Kannon seated on a lotus blossom. This Kannon, with eyes of crystal, was created in the *yosegi* style; that is, composed of hollow wooden blocks which were put together and then roughly carved. Thereafter, the image was finely carved, lacquered, and then covered with gold leaf. The image was created between 1251 and 1254 by the most distinguished sculptor of Kamakura times, Tankei (1173–1256), in his eighty-second year. It and nine of the smaller Kannon images are the only works by Tankei that have been truly authenticated.

This central image, as with the one thousand other images, has eleven smaller heads about the crown of its head. Although the Kannon has only twenty pairs of arms, since each of the forty arms saves twenty-five worlds, figuratively there are one thousand arms represented. The image is seated on an octagonal lotus-blossom pedestal with seven rows of petals. A large, oval aureole behind it has small images of the thirty-three manifestations of Kannon amid an openwork pattern of clouds and sacred trees.

The smaller (5.4- to 5.5-foot-tall) images of Kannon were constructed with the same *yosegi* technique as is described above. This permitted several craftsmen to work on the same sculpture at one time, and the technique also created a lighter wooden image which was less likely to split. The images are in groups of five hundred on either side of the main Kannon, standing in ten rows of fifty each. The images were created not only by Tankei (1173–1256), but by seventy others under his direction. The 1,001 images of Kannon symbolize the 33,033 ways in which mankind can be helped by this deity of mercy (1,001 images multiplied by 33 possible incarnations = 33,033).

The God of Wind (Fujin) and the God of Thunder (Raijin) stand at either end and in front of the rows of the one thousand Kannon. The image of Fujin stands 3.8 feet tall and holds a large bag of wind over its shoulders. Raijin is 3.5 feet tall and is surrounded from behind by a circlet of drums which he beats with his drumsticks, thereby causing thunder to roll. Both deities are of a ferocious mien, and both were actively feared and placated by the people of earlier times.

In a corridor behind the one thousand Kannon are the statues of the twenty-eight followers (Nijuhachibu-shu) of Kannon, Buddhist deities with human or animal heads who protect mankind. The Nijuhachibu-shu were made during the Kamakura period or later and are approximately five feet in height. The twenty-eight images are spirits of deified wisdom, beauty, prosperity, relief for the poor, etc., and are lined up in a row along the rear corridor of the temple. Additional images of Nio, Fudo,

Jizo, and other deities are also located in the rear of the building.

The platform under the eaves at the rear of the Sanjusangen-do structure should be observed on leaving the building, for here is where the annual ancient Hikizome Matsuri (First Shooting of the Year Festival) takes place. The Hikizome Matsuri is held on the fifteenth of each January, and it represents the initial archery contest of the New Year. Since the arrows launched seemed to fly through the air one after another, the ceremony is also called Toshiya, or "Passing Arrows." These bow-and-arrow contests first began in 1606 on the west veranda of the temple, and they remained most popular among the samurai right through the Edo period (1603–1868). The archers had to shoot their arrows from a squatting position, aiming from the south end of the veranda to the target, one yard in diameter, at the north end, 196 feet away. (As a result, the pillars have had to be protected by metal coverings against stray arrows.) In former times, the contests began at 6:00 p.m. and continued for twenty-four hours. The 1686 champion, Wasa Daihachiro, at the age of twenty-two, sent a record 8,233 arrows out of 13,053 to the target at the north end of the veranda.

Today, the contest on January 15 begins in the morning at 9:00 a.m., but it is only a modest repetition of the Toshiya of former times. In truth, it no longer is a real contest, but it remains as a tradition worth retaining. As part of the tradition of this ceremony, a collection of bows and arrows is displayed on the south end of the interior of the hall.

Across Shichijo-dori from the Sanjusangen-do is the Kyoto National Museum, and it is worth a visit since it presents an excellent picture of the arts of Kyoto's past. It perhaps is best saved for a rainy day (as with other museums) when one does not wish to be traipsing between outdoor temples and shrines.

KYOTO NATIONAL MUSEUM

The Kyoto National Museum is entered from the Shichijo-dori side. It is open daily (except Monday) from 9:00 a.m. to 4:00 p.m.;

if a national holiday falls on a Monday, it remains open that Monday but is closed the next day. The museum is closed during the New Year holiday (December 26–January 3). Entry fee.

The Kyoto National Museum was founded in 1875 as an imperial museum, and in 1897 its original building was erected in the then current European style which can best be described as Victorian Neo-Renaissance. The museum was given to the city of Kyoto in 1924 and then was nationalized in 1952. In 1966 an addition in a modern architectural form (designed by Keiichi Morita) was opened.

Originally planned as a museum for important items of artistic or historic merit brought from temples and shrines, it has developed a collection of its own—as well as borrowing from private collections and religious institutions when mounting special exhibitions. As one of the major holdings of artifacts and historical art of early Japan, the exhibits cover the period from pre-history through the Edo period. Inasmuch as the collections are extensive, many of the objects in the museum's holdings are rotated; thus, it is not possible to indicate those items currently on view.

The collections include art, religious objects, and items of archeological and historical interest including sculpture, paintings, ceramics and pottery, metalwork, lacquer, toys, dolls of Japan, calligraphy, sutra scrolls (sacred writings), paintings, Buddhist images, and costumes. Chinese works of art are represented as well since they had a major influence on Japanese art and taste in the past. Special exhibitions are mounted in the spring and autumn in the original Meiji-era building. Labels are in Japanese and in English, and a guidebook to the collections (in English) is available in the museum shop. The museum also contains a research library and a photographic laboratory.

When one leaves the Kyoto National Museum and exits on to Shichijo-dori, one should walk to the right (west) to the corner of Yamato-oji-dori (the next cross-street) and turn to the right. On Yamato-oji-dori, one will then encounter the end of Japan's medieval period and become acquainted with the intriguing figure of Toyotomi Hideyoshi (1536–98), the military general and civil ruler of the late 1500s (he ruled from 1585 to 1598).

Toyotomi Hideyoshi, who brought peace and prosperity back to a devastated city, was one of the major personalities in the history of Japan and Kyoto. He was honored by the citizens of Kyoto in particular, for Kyoto was a city that had suffered the depredations of war and fire and the privations of starvation and disease, all caused by the country's internecine wars of the previous one hundred years. Hideyoshi's day in the sun was a comparatively brief but glorious one. By 1585 those who opposed him had been conquered and he ruled a pacified nation; by 1598 he was dead, leaving a memorable legacy which the thankful people of Kyoto could not forget. The fourteen years were important ones in Japan's history, and they are especially remembered as the glorious Momoyama period when art flourished, business and commercial enterprises revived, and Japan was at peace.

Hideyoshi is recalled in many places in Kyoto, but in the portion of the city covered in this walk one encounters some of the most memorable reminders of his life: the Hoko-ji temple, the site of the image of the Buddha which was meant, in a vainglorious moment, to outshine that of the Daibutsu (the Great Buddha image) of Nara and whose memorial bell, which was to herald an era of peace, led instead to the downfall of Hideyoshi's son and the eradication of his line; Mimizuka, the mound that commemorates his brutal wars in Korea; and the Hokoku Shrine, the restored Shinto shrine to his spirit.

HOKO-JI

It is best to begin with what remains of the Hoko-ji. The Hoko-ji is on the east side of Yamato-oji-dori just beyond the Hokoku Shrine whose main entrance faces Shomen-dori, a street heading downhill to the west. The entrance to the Hokoku Shrine should be bypassed, for the Hoko-ji grounds begin at the end of the shrine property. The Hoko-ji temple is open from 9:00 a.m. to 5:00 p.m. There is no entry fee.

The only historic unit extant in the Hoko-ji, the onetime site of the Great Buddha of Kyoto, is its infamous temple bell. There is no charge to see it, but if you wish to strike the bell with its beam, the attendant may collect a small fee for this privilege. Although the history of the temple is fascinating, other than seeing the bell it is not worth entering the remaining buildings which date from the 1970s after the latest of many fires that have plagued the temple.

The Hoko-ji was erected by Toyotomi Hideyoshi in part out of his own vanity and in part as a ploy to disarm all but the new warrior class which officially came into being as a result of the codification of rank and status which Hideyoshi began and which the Tokugawa shoguns would formulate definitively after 1600. If one thing need be said, it is that this "pious" act of creating the Hoko-ji temple was hardly based on religious zeal.

Determined to build a huge image of the Buddha which would outclass the Daibutsu (Great Buddha) of Nara, Hideyoshi boasted that his Great Buddha would be created in five years rather than the twenty years it had taken to build the Daibutsu of the emperor Shomu in the seventh century. The temple grounds, which held Hideyoshi's gigantic image, and its hall covered an area 780 feet from east to west by 822 feet north to south.

Hideyoshi's vassals (the daimyo or lords dependent upon him) were required to furnish the funds and the thousands of workers needed to bring this 160-foot-tall Buddha into being. Originally intended to be cast in bronze, difficulties with the casting led instead to the creation of the image in wood which was then lacquered. The Hondo (Main Hall), built in 1587 to house this gigantic image, stood 222 feet wide by 330 feet long and 200 feet high.

The creation of the Buddha image gave rise to the device of disarming the general populace. Many citizens had maintained their own weapons for defensive purposes or for use when impressed into military battles during the Sengoku Jidai (Period of the Warring States, 1467–1568). The armed monks who had also plagued the government before being crushed by Oda Nobunaga, Hideyoshi's predecessor, were also a target. Thus, a government decree ordered the surrender of "any sword, short sword, bows, spears, firearms, or other types of arms." The avowed purpose of this 1585 "Taiko's Sword Hunt" (as the campaign was known, Taiko [His Highness] being the title by which Hideyoshi was known by the public) was to melt down such metals in order to cast the fittings needed to erect the great hall that would house the Buddha at the Hoko-ji.

With the public deprived of arms, according to official pro-nouncements, the populace would have a double benefit: without arms, there would be less chance of death from armed conflict, and by surrendering their arms for the sake of the Buddha, donors would be granted peace not only in this life but in the next world as well. In the long run, this not only removed the danger of uprisings against the ruling authorities but also emphasized the class distinction between soldiers and farmers,

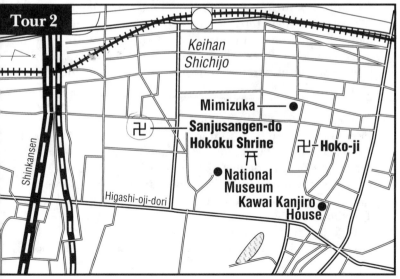

soldiers and merchants. It made the wearing of a sword a badge of rank, a privilege granted only to the samurai. The rigid stratification of society during the following 265 years of Tokugawa rule, after Hideyoshi's demise, was in process.

The Bukko-ji, which stood on the site of Hideyoshi's projected Great Buddha image, was conveniently moved across the river in order to provide sufficient land for the gigantic undertaking. Canals were dug and a new bridge was built, the Gojo-ohashi, the Great Bridge of Fifth Street, to facilitate the delivery of materials to the site. The temple was completed in 1589, with one thousand priests participating in the dedicatory ceremonies. Unhappily, the image was doomed to disaster. In 1596 a great earthquake damaged much of the Kyoto area and the Great Buddha was destroyed. Two years later, Hideyoshi was dead. The question of the successor to Hideyoshi lay open since his intended political heir, his son Hideyori, was only five years old.

The various lords who formed a regents' council had pledged to support Hideyoshi's son as the next political ruler when he came of age. Dissension among them, however, enabled Tokugawa Ieyasu (1543–1616) to gain control of the government by 1603 both by guile and by force. Concerned with creating a new ruling family, he determined to get rid of Hideyori in time. In order to weaken Hideyori financially as the years went by, Ieyasu encouraged him and his mother to melt ten million gold coins from Hideyoshi's estate to obtain the needed funds for a gigantic image which would replace the Great Buddha. For Hideyori's political supporters, this rebuilding of the Great Buddha provided an opportunity to restore the family's flagging political influence. Thus, the rebuilding began in 1603. Unfortunately, a fire in the nearly completed hall destroyed the work already done. Ieyasu convinced Hideyori and his mother once more that the project had to be completed, thereby further sapping the Toyotomi finances.

By 1609 the Buddha had been recreated (in wood), and by 1612 the temple was restored. This second hall was 272 feet long by 167.5 feet deep, and it rose 150 feet into the air. Ninety-two pillars supported the roof over the 58.5-foot-tall image of Buddha. In 1615, to mark the completion of the project, a huge bronze bell was cast and mounted in its own structure. It still stands, 14 feet tall and nine feet in diameter; it is 9 inches thick and weighs 82 tons. On it, Hideyori had inscribed the words *Kokka Anko,* "Security and Peace in the Nation."

Ieyasu, looking for a pretext to undermine Hideyori whom he found too handsome and too capable and thereby a political threat to his and his family's continued rule, had not only refused to contribute funds to the rebuilding of this popular memorial to Hideyoshi but also claimed that the second and fourth characters in the inscription on the bell could be read as "Ieyasu." The intent, he claimed, was to place a curse upon him.

In time, Ieyasu resorted to armed force, and in 1615 he besieged Hideyori in his castle in Osaka, a castle Hideyori had inherited from his father. The Toyotomi family was exterminated, and one of the justifications used by Ieyasu for this treacherous and brutal act was the supposed threat which had appeared on the great bell at the Hoko-ji. Afterwards, the head of Toyotomi Hideyori's seven-year-old son was displayed at the Sanjo (Third Street) Bridge in the same manner as were those of traitors and criminals.

The Hoko-ji today is a rather nondescript complex. The 1609 Buddha and its hall, which were restored at the expense of Hideyori and his mother, were destroyed by an earthquake in 1662, and the replacements of these were lost in a fire in 1798. The new image of 1843, which replaced the previous Buddha, was destroyed in a 1973 fire. Thus, the existing halls of the temple are not very important since all that was of consequence has been consumed by the flames of the centuries.

What remains of the original Hoko-ji is the Great Bell of 1615 which stands in a belfry rebuilt in 1884. The offending characters of *Kokka Anko* were removed at Hideyori's order soon after the bell was completed because of Ieyasu's pretended offense at the curse he claimed to have read. Today, one can have the experience of pulling the cord that sends the wooden beam of the belfry crashing against the side of the bell—to sound the praise of Hideyoshi or to curse Ieyasu, as one is so inclined.

One other item of note remains from the sixteenth-century temple: the huge stone walls along Yamato-oji-dori which served to hold the embankment on which the Hoko-ji was built. These gigantic stones were gifts from Hideyoshi's daimyo, many of these daimyo competing to see if they could send a larger stone from their fiefdom than could other donors. The stones are still in place, today encompassing the grounds of both the Hoko-ji temple and the Hokoku Shrine. The entrance to the present Hokoku Shrine at the head of Shomen-dori is approximately the entrance to the Great Buddha Hall of the past. Before leaving the Hoko-ji, one should be conscious of the Mimizuka mound which was created in front of the Great Buddha Hall of the Hoko-ji. It reflects the obverse side of the honor given to Hideyoshi in his own day, for it is illustrative of the cruelty of the wars waged by the warriors of that as well as of later times.

MIMIZUKA

The Mimizuka (Ear Mound) is on Shomen-dori just west of where that street intersects with Yamato-oji-dori (west of the entrance to the Hokoku Shrine) and immediately to the west of the children's playground.

The Mimizuka is a mound in which the ears and noses of defeated Koreans were buried after the Korean wars of Hideyoshi in 1592 and 1597. The mound originally stood in front of the gateway to the Daibutsu-den (Hall of the Great Buddha) of the Hoko-ji, a hall which has now been replaced by the Hokoku Shrine in honor of Toyotomi Hideyoshi. The mound is a tall hill surrounded by a fence and topped by a very tall five-tier memorial stone.

In 1592, Toyotomi Hideyoshi determined that he would conquer China, a part of his dream of ruling all of East Asia. He sent a massive army into Korea, penetrating to Pyongyang and to the Tumen River as far as the border of China. Ultimately forced by the Chinese to retreat to the south of Korea, Hideyoshi failed in his quest, and the war merely engendered many casualties on both sides as well as a continuing antagonism with Korea and China. In 1597 he launched a second attempt against Korea so as to reach China. Harassment of his supply lines by Korean armored boats and the combined military forces of Korea and China proved an overwhelming series of obstacles to his expansionist goals. His death in 1598 provided his successors with an excuse for a withdrawal from Korea—until the nineteenth and twentieth centuries.

The custom of victorious armies severing the heads of the defeated enemy for presentation to their commander as a proof of victory proved logistically impractical during these overseas military adventures. Therefore, in 1592, the ears of the defeated enemy were cut off and shipped back to Kyoto in barrels of brine. They were buried in a mound in front of the gateway to the Daibutsu-den of the Hoko-ji of Hideyoshi and marked by five large, circular stones. Again, in November 1598, the ears and, this time, the noses of 38,000 victims of the Japanese forces in Korea were buried in Mimizuka. The noses were hung up by threes for inspection, verification, and counting before they were pickled and shipped. According to some sources, the mound should be called Hanazuka (Nose Mound) since it was noses rather than ears that were shipped and buried.

A moat 12 feet broad was created around a mound 720 feet in circumference and 30 feet high. On top was placed a five-story, 21-foot-tall *sotoba* (Buddhist shrine) with a 15-foot-wide base. In earlier days, there was a bridge with railings which crossed the moat from the north side. The mound and *sotoba* were built at Hideyoshi's order, and on June 12, 1597, he had three hundred priests chant a requiem prayer for the Korean dead. In former times, when Korean embassies came to the court on official visits, they always worshipped at this mound.

The Mimizuka mound reflects the senseless military ardor of Hideyoshi, and today it remains, ironically, before the Hokoku Shrine, the Shinto memorial to his enshrined spirit.

HOKOKU SHRINE (TOYOKUNI SHRINE)

The Hokoku Shrine, also known as the Toyokuni Shrine, is on Yamato-oji-dori where Shomen-dori meets Yamato-oji-dori, north of the Kyoto National Museum. There is no admission charge to the shrine. Its treasury is open from 9:00 a.m. to 5:00 p.m.

The era of peace and a growing economy, after the devastation that had been visited on Kyoto by the century of civil war, endeared Hideyoshi to the public. His festival occasions, though sometimes brash, also warmed the citizens of Kyoto to his rule. Thus, after his death, one of the popular songs sung by the people at his shrine summarized these feelings:

> Who's that
> Holding over four hundred provinces
> In the palm of his hand
> And entertaining at a tea party?
> It's His Highness [Taiko]
> So mighty, so impressive.

When Hideyoshi gave a tea party, he savored the quiet essence of the tea ceremony as created by tea masters such as Sen-no-Rikyu. On the other hand, he could go to the extremes to which his nature inclined. His passion for tea reached such a height that when he held a tea party for the public at the Kitano Shrine in October of 1587, he invited "even those from China" to attend. One had only to bring a mat to sit on and a tea bowl. Some five thousand people are said to have attended the "tea party."

On Hideyoshi's death, the emperor Go-Yozei in 1599 ordered that a Shinto shrine to Hideyoshi's spirit be constructed at the foot of Amida-ga-mine (Mount Amida) to the east of Higashi-oji-dori since in death Hideyoshi was seen as a god. The shrine became a gathering place for the people of Kyoto on the anniversary of Hideyoshi's death, a great festival being held before the shrine. The festival was captured in a painting done on a six-panel folding screen by Kano Naizen (owned by the shrine and on public view in its treasury) in the early 1600s, documenting the admiration of the people for Toyotomi Hideyoshi.

Such esteem for his predecessor concerned the new shogun, Tokugawa Ieyasu. As a result, through the years Ieyasu did all that was possible to erase Hideyoshi's name insofar as he could. Gradually the shrine and burial place of Hideyoshi were eliminated by Ieyasu.

With the end of the Tokugawa (Edo) era in 1868, however, the new Meiji government began the restoration of Hideyoshi's reputation together with the shrines connected with him. On April 9, 1875, the prefecture of Kyoto was sent an imperial order to rebuild the shrine to Hideyoshi. A ten-year reconstruction program gradually restored the Hokoku Shrine to its previous glory—but on a major portion of the grounds of the Hoko-ji instead of at its original site at the foot of Amida-ga-mine (Mount Amida) to the east of Higashi-oji-dori. Thus, the Hoko-ji was reduced drastically from its original size and importance, a result of the Meiji government's hostility to Buddhism and a policy of downgrading Buddhist temples. The former Kara-mon (Chinese-style gateway) which once had stood before Hideyoshi's Fushimi Castle, was brought to the Hokoku Shrine in 1876 from its previous location, depriving the Konchi-in Buddhist sub-temple of the Nanzen-ji of one of its treasures.

To create the appropriate space which Meiji grandeur demanded for the restored Shinto shrine to Hideyoshi, some of the buildings of the Hoko-ji were moved to the north, thereby restricting the temple to but a corner of its original site. By September 15, 1875, the shrine was in place, and, in a great ceremony, Hideyoshi's spirit was transferred to the inner shrine building. Hideyoshi's cynicism in the creation of the Hoko-ji with its great Buddha was now being equaled by that of the Meiji government in the recreation of this Shinto shrine in order to undo the disdain of Ieyasu for Hideyoshi—but its underlying motive was to show the new government's hatred of the Tokugawa shoguns and their 260 years of political rule of Japan.

The Hokoku Shrine consists of a number of buildings, and, as with most Shinto shrines, all but the Honden (Spirit Hall) and its enclosure are open to the public. A traditional torii stands at the entrance to the grounds, and beyond it a series of lanterns (in vermilion painted wood) are raised on posts leading to the Kara-mon. The Kara-mon faces west down Shomen-dori, and from it hangs the original tablet-name for the shrine, created by the emperor Go-Yozei in 1599. The cypress-bark-roofed Kara-mon is supported by six large, wooden pillars. Relief carvings of cranes on the transoms enhance the doors of this gateway as do the two finely carved cranes under the front gable. So realistic are the carvings of the cranes by the noted sixteenth-century sculptor Hidari Jingoro that it is said he left them without eyes so that they would not fly away. In keeping with the ostentatiousness of the Momoyama art of Hideyoshi's day, the ornaments of the restored gate were gold plated.

Beyond the Kara-mon is the Honden, the sacred building where the spirit of Hideyoshi is enshrined, ensconced behind a fence which separates the sacred from the secular realm. A statue of the seated Hideyoshi stands before the fenced inner area. To the north of the main pathway is a smaller Shinto shrine with a series of small vermilion torii before it.

To the southeast of the Honden is the treasure house which holds items connected with Hideyoshi and his times, including the folding screen mentioned above which commemorates the seventh anniversary of Hideyoshi's death. In addition, swords, armor, iron lanterns, and manuscripts of the sixteenth century, all associated with Hideyoshi, are on display.

In contrast to the late nineteenth-century attempt to glorify Hideyoshi at the Hokoku Shrine, a short walk to the northeast of the shrine brings one to a simpler and more attractive site. It is not too often that a visitor to Kyoto can see the interior of a traditional Japanese house, but the Kawai Kanjiro House offers just such an opportunity.

KAWAI KANJIRO HOUSE

On leaving the Hokoku Shrine, a right turn brings one onto Yamato-oji-dori. This street should be followed to the north for three streets. At the third cross-street, one should turn right and follow this new street to the east for two streets before turning left (north). One will thus arrive at the Kawai Kanjiro House midway down the east side of the street. The house is open from 10:00 a.m. to 4:30 p.m., except on Mondays. It is closed from August 10 to 20 and from December 24 to January 7. Entry fee.

Born in 1890, Kawai Kanjiro became noted as a twentieth-century potter and a master of ceramic craftsmanship. His growing interest in traditional pottery led him in time to become one of the founders of the Japan Folk Craft Museum in Tokyo and to bring attention to traditional Japanese folk crafts. Living in Kyoto, the center of traditional craftsmanship, he established a kiln at the rear of his house. In 1937 his home was destroyed in a storm that caused serious damage in Kyoto, and in rebuilding his residence and work area he was inspired by traditional rural Japanese house architecture. Both his home and his studio can be visited today.

The entrance to the house has a hall which would have been the area in which a farmer kept his animals. Here Kanjiro hung one of his wooden sculptures, an art form he took up in his later years. Beyond the entry hall is the reception room with a Korean-style wooden floor and an open hearth. A calligraphic inscription on the rear wall translates as "Folk Craft Study Collection," and display shelves, which can be viewed from either side, hold some of his treasured folk collections. Beyond the reception room is the family dining area with a large table which could seat up to ten people. Under the table is a *kotatsu,* the traditional brazier used to provide warmth to those sitting at the table. An image of the Buddha carved by a seventeenth-century priest/folk artist sits upon the table.

A traditional staircase with drawers beneath the steps leads to the upper sleeping quarter with its wooden floor and ceiling. Adjacent to this is a small room with a tokonoma, and on its wall is a calligraphic riddle whose answer is "tea." Here Kanjiro and his friends could enjoy tea in a relaxed manner rather than with the formality called for by the traditional tea ceremony. The walls of this room, as with some of the other rooms, are decorated with the wooden masks that the artist began to make in his seventies.

Behind the rooms on the first floor a gravel path set off by bamboo plants leads to Kanjiro's workshop and "Smoking Room" where pieces of his ceramic ware are on display. Here are the potter's twin kick-wheel and the stepped *noborigama* kilns. These kilns were used by Kanjiro from 1919 until his death in 1966, and they continued to be in use by some of his followers until 1971 when new antipollution laws forced the closing of all wood-fired kilns in Kyoto.

The Kawai Kanjiro House is a charming memorial to a famed potter, a house that illustrates the manner in which a prosperous artist tried to recapture the past in his daily life. It stands in sharp contrast to the golden images of the Sanjusangen-do or to the dreams of glory that Toyotomi Hideyoshi cherished.

On leaving the house, one can walk back (south) to the next street running east and west. A turn to the left (east) brings one to Higashi-oji-dori at the next corner. There a taxi or bus 18, 202, 206, or 207 can be taken for a return to the center of the city or to other destinations as desired.

TOUR
3

The Widow's Temple,
Memento Mori,
and the Gion Cart Temple

TO TRAVERSE the lanes between the temples and shrines of eastern Kyoto located near Gojo-dori and Shijo-dori is to stroll through the history of the city. The small Hokan-ji with its Yasaka Pagoda is one of the earliest temples in Kyoto, created even before Kyoto became the capital, a temple that retains the oldest extant pagoda in the city. The early middle ages in Kyoto are represented by the Choraku-ji, an insignificant and little-visited hillside temple, but one that is connected with the tragic and romanticized story of the Taira empress who alone survived the battle of Dan-no-ura in 1185 and who here took the tonsure and spent the rest of her days as a nun praying for her lost child and family.

The nearby Higashi Otani Cemetery with its tomb to the priest Shinran, who suffered from persecution for his faith, is a sacred spot to those millions who follow this great Buddhist religious reformer of the 1200s in the practice of the Jodo Shinshu faith. The close of the Japanese medieval period is also remembered by a site that again recalls the tempestuous relationship between Toyotomi Hideyoshi and Tokugawa Ieyasu, for it contains the Kodai-ji nunnery where Hideyoshi's widow Yodogimi spent her all-too-brief years following his death.

The modern age is not ignored, for the Ryozen Historical Museum is a monument to the heady days of the mid- to late nineteenth century when the Tokugawa shogunate was losing power and the new Meiji era and modern Japan were being born. An aspect of the unhappy consequences of the militaristic spirit of that period is also marked by the gigantic concrete Kannon image which arose after World War II in memory of and expiation for the millions who died in the two decades of Japan's Greater East Asia folly.

Then, in even more recent years, the new Daiun-in, with its unusual pagoda in the shape of a huge Gion cart adding a new element to the skyline at the foot of the Higashiyama hills, further enriches the city with examples of Buddhist murals from the Chinese caves of Dun Huang. There is also a lighter side to this area of Kyoto. Along with its many *ochaya* (teahouses), in the area along the narrow streets between Higashi-oji-dori and Kita-mon-mae-dori one may have the opportunity to savor the non-alcoholic delights of *amazake,* which was once the beverage of Buddhist nuns. There are also many restaurants in the area about Maruyama Park.

We begin this tour at the small Hokan-ji, best known for its Yasaka Pagoda.

THE YASAKA PAGODA AND HOKAN-JI

The Yasaka Pagoda is most easily reached from the bus stop at Higashi-oji-dori and Kiyomizu-michi, the same bus stop used in Tour 1. Buses 202, 203, 206, and 207 which run along Higashi-oji-dori serve the bus stop. After alighting from the bus, walk three streets north on Higashi-oji-dori and then turn right on to Yasaka-dori. A torii stands at the entrance to Yasaka-dori at Higashi-oji-dori, and that street, after a slight jog to the right and then the left, will lead one to the tall pagoda of the small Hokan-ji. The temple grounds are open between 9:00 a.m. and 4:00 p.m. Entry fee.

The Yasaka Pagoda and its few tiny buildings are all that remain of the Hokan-ji, one of the oldest temples in Kyoto. It is said to have been established by a family named Yasaka-no-Miyatsuko who had probably come to Japan from Korea and who settled in this region in the 500s, some two centuries before Kyoto was created as a city. Their religious life is claimed to have centered around the Hokan-ji which tradition says was created in 588 by Prince Shotoku, the founder of Buddhism in Japan. This claim is no doubt one of those pious but questionable traditions since the prince would only have been sixteen at that date. The temple was to become one of the principal Buddhist temples of Kyoto in the early centuries of the city.

Those who conquered the city were always anxious to display

their colors at the Yasaka Pagoda since it was historically regarded as the symbol of Kyoto. Time, however, has taken its toll of the original temple buildings, and the pagoda was replaced in 1192 by Minamoto-no-Yoritomo, founder of the Kamakura shogunate. The temple was later destroyed by fire, and of the rebuilding by Shogun Ashikaga-no-Yoshinori in 1440 only this five-story pagoda still remains, the oldest pagoda in Kyoto. It was restored in 1618 by the governor of Kyoto.

The Hokan-ji precincts are entered on its south side. Today the temple consists of the five-story pagoda of 1440 and a few small buildings to the north of the pagoda. Two of these units are memorial halls with flaming jewels atop their pyramidal roofs. The unit on the west (to the left when facing them) is the Taishi-do (Memorial Hall) to Prince Shotoku, the supposed founder of the temple. The Taishi-do contains an appealing image of the prince at the age of sixteen praying for his father, the emperor Yomei, who lay on his deathbed. This image is a favorite one which appears in many other temples.

The small building to the right of the Taishi-do is the Yakushi-do, known for its gilt image of the Buddha Yakushi, the Buddha of healing and medicine, bearing a staff in his left hand. To the right of the Yakushi-do is the small, modern treasure house, while to the east of the pagoda is a Shinto shrine.

The five-story Yasaka Pagoda is 126 feet tall, and the interior walls, ceiling, and columns on the base level are decorated with paintings, among which are images of bodhisattvas. The interior of many pagodas have been decorated in this manner, and this is one of those rare examples that are available for viewing. In the center of the base level, on each side of the main pillar which supports the pagoda, are images of the four Nyorai Buddha: Hojo on the south, Amida on the west, Ashuka on the east, and Shaka on the north. A large phoenix tops the spire of the pagoda, a symbol of the temple's rebirth after its destruction by fire.

To the east of the Yasaka Pagoda are three sites that a century ago ranked among the most important in the city: the Gokoku Shrine, a memorial to those who died in opposition to the Tokugawa shogunate which ended in 1868, and the Ryozen Rekishikan (Ryozen Historical Museum). (Today, they are seldom visited and are mentioned here more as curiosities.)

GOKOKU SHRINE

The Gokoku Shrine, also known as the Shinto Kyoto Shrine, is to the east of the Yasaka Pagoda at the top of Kodai-ji Minami Monzen-dori one street to the north of the street facing the entrance of the Yasaka Pagoda. Kodai-ji Minami Monzen-dori should be taken up the hill which the street ascends. At the top of the hill, on the left as the road turns to the south, is the Gokoku Shrine. The shrine is open during daylight hours without charge.

The Gokoku Shrine is an old shrine meant to serve as the protector of the city, and, as a shrine, it differs little from other Shinto shrines. The buildings are behind a vermilion fence on the left as one mounts the hillside street to the shrine entrance. Within the grounds, beyond the torii of the entryway, is the unpainted Heiden (Offertory), and beyond it is the Haiden (Oratory) and then the fenced Honden (Spirit Hall). As such, for the casual visitor it is of historical interest only. A century ago, when Shinto was being turned into a militaristic faith which served the military and the state, it held greater significance for the Japanese public than it now does.

To the south of the Gogoku Shrine, a monument/shrine of major importance was raised in the late nineteenth century, a site now almost forgotten. This monument was dedicated to the heroes of the movement, in the decade prior to 1868, who opposed the Tokugawa shogunate and who helped to bring about the Meiji Restoration and the modernization of Japan. Here are buried a number of the heroes of that era, including Kido Takayoshi (also known as Kido Koin, 1833–77), one of the leaders of Meiji times.

RYOZEN REKISHIKAN

The Ryozen Rekishikan (Ryozen Historical Museum) is the third formerly important site. It is located across the road from the Gokoku Shrine on Kodai-ji Minami Monzen-dori. It is open from 10:00 a.m. to 4:30 p.m., except on Mondays and the New Year holiday. Entry fee.

The Ryozen Rekishikan is a museum of the history of the period on either side of 1868, the year in which the Tokugawa shogunate passed into history and the modernization of Japan under the name of the Meiji emperor began. The displays consist of photographs, writings, armaments, and other articles which relate the epic period of change in Japanese political and cultural life. Special exhibitions on the Meiji era are also presented. In a sense, this museum replaces the memorial to the heroes of the Restoration, which is mentioned above, since time often effaces the public memory of men and events. As a specialized museum whose labels are in Japanese, few foreign visitors will be interested in or will patronize the museum, but it is mentioned for those interested in the period of drastic change which occurred in Japan from the 1860s on.

The Gokoku Shrine and the Ryozen Rekishikan represent the heady days of the 1870s when the new Meiji government came into power and Japanese nationalism began the flowering that would ultimately lead to disaster and the defeat of Japan in 1945. The Ryozen Kannon Temple, just a short distance from these two important nineteenth-century sites, marks the repentance most Japanese feel for the extremes to which nationalism took the nation.

RYOZEN KANNON

The route to the Ryozen Kannon temple heads back down Kodai-ji Minami Monzen-dori to Kita-mon-mae-dori, the first narrow street to the right. A turn on to this new street should bring into sight the towering image of the concrete Ryozen Kannon figure and then the entrance to the temple grounds. The temple is open from 9:00 a.m. to 5:00 p.m. Entry fee.

In 1955, a 79-foot-tall, seated Kannon image cast in concrete, a memento mori, was constructed by a transportation firm to honor the war dead of the Pacific War (World War II in the Pacific and Asia). It honors not only the Japanese soldiers who died in combat, but also the dead of the Allied forces who opposed Japan. After paying the entry fee, the visitor receives a lighted incense stick; this is to be placed in the large incense pot before the shrine where prayers may be said for the peaceful repose of the dead.

A modest gateway leading into the Ryozen Kannon grounds is guarded by a Nio (Deva King). Within the grounds, beyond the entryway, a reflecting pool is situated before a large, roofed incense pot where one places the lit incense stick received at the entry gate and where one can say a prayer for the dead. Behind the incense pot is the main shrine building, topped by the huge Kannon image. On the ground floor is an altar, under the base of the gigantic Kannon figure, and here an Eleven-faced Kannon, the deity of mercy, is the main image. In the northwest section of this level is an image of the recumbent Buddha as he appeared when he passed from this life on achieving nirvana. A five-foot-tall Buddha is in the southwest area. A staircase behind this portion of the building leads into the lower part of the huge Kannon image where various altars are decorated with the figures of the zodiacal year.

Behind this main structure is a memorial hall to the Japanese war dead with a file of the names of all those who died in the years of the Japanese wars of the 1930s and 1940s. To the north of the main temple building is an eight-foot-long memorial footprint of the Buddha, and west of that is a five-foot-tall gold sphere. Beyond, to the north, is a garden. To the south of the main Kannon structure is a memorial hall to the war dead of the Allied forces of the 1940–45 Pacific War. An altar (with English captions) and a file of the names of the Allied dead are maintained here. The altar contains soil from each of the military cemeteries in the Pacific as well. Just west of the Allied memorial, toward the entry gate, is a modern shrine of one thousand Buddhas with an image of a Buddha holding an infant in his arms. To the south of the Allied memorial is an open, domed structure with an outdoor altar where memorial services may be held.

This solemn and impressive contribution of a private citizen's firm to the memory of the war dead is a fitting representation of the sorrow felt by the Japanese for the errors and disasters brought upon so many by the Japanese military rulers of the 1930s and 1940s.

Adjacent to the Ryozen Kannon and to its north is the Kodai-ji, the retreat in which Toyotomi Hideyoshi's widow lived when she became a nun after her husband's death in 1598. It represents, in a sense, the conclusion to the story of the hatred of Shogun Tokugawa Ieyasu, Hideyoshi's successor, for Hideyoshi and his family.

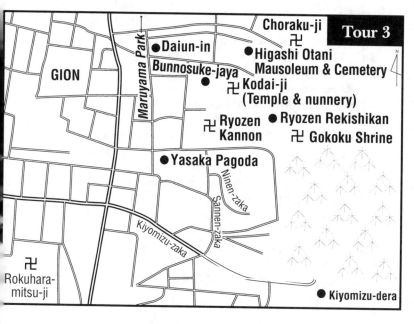

KODAI-JI: TEMPLE AND NUNNERY

When one leaves the Ryozen Kannon Temple, the entrance to the Kodai-ji nunnery is on the south side of the Kodai-ji grounds. This entry is adjacent to the open space which often serves as a parking lot for the Ryozen and Kodai-ji temples. If the nunnery is approached from Kita-mon-mae-dori, beyond the entrance to the Ryozen Kannon temple on that street, a path which turns to the right leads along the south side of the Kodai-ji to its entry gate. The Kodai-ji is a Zen temple of the Rinzai branch of Buddhism (Kennin-ji sect) and is open from 9:00 a.m. to 4:00 p.m. Entry fee.

The Kodai-ji is a nunnery which adds another interesting element to the Toyotomi Hideyoshi–Tokugawa Ieyasu relationship as illustrated in the descriptions of the Hoko-ji and the Hokoku Shrine of the second tour in this guidebook. The Kodai-ji was originally founded in 838, but its renaissance as a Buddhist nunnery began after Hideyoshi's death in 1598. In 1605, Shogun Tokugawa Ieyasu granted this temple to Hideyoshi's widow, Yodogimi, when she became an *ama* (nun) to pray for the soul of her husband, and here she lived until shortly before her death which occurred during the siege of Osaka Castle in 1615. The temple was designed by two architects under Ieyasu's orders, and by 1604 all of the temple structures had been erected. Sanko Joeki, former abbot of the Kennin-ji, was installed as its founding abbot. To further console Yodogimi, Ieyasu ordered that the So-mon gate to Hideyoshi's castle in Fushimi, with its carvings of foxes and dragons by Hidari Jingoro, be moved to the Kodai-ji in 1605, and this became the still-extant Omote-mon (Front Gate) to the nunnery. (The gate on the west side of the temple grounds is not open to the public; the front or main gate is on the southern side of the nunnery.) The Keisho-den was also moved from Fushimi to serve as Yodogimi's residence. This building was later turned into the Kohojo (Abbot's Small Quarters), but in 1847 it burned to the ground along with the Daihojo (Abbot's

Large Quarters), the Kara-mon (Chinese-style Gateway), and other buildings. The temple is said to have been one of the most attractive temples in the luxurious Momoyama style of the late sixteenth and early seventeenth centuries.

Yodogimi, who had taken the religious name of Kodai-in, spared no expense in the enhancement of the Kodai-ji. At best, Yodogimi spent tragic years here as a nun. The Hoko-ji and its Buddha were completed in 1612 in her husband's memory, and its great bell was dedicated in 1614. Ieyasu (as detailed under the entry on the Hoko-ji) interpreted the inscription on the bell as an offense against him. In November of 1614 Ieyasu led his army against Hideyoshi's son Hideyori at his Osaka Castle; a truce was arranged wherein the outer defensive walls were leveled and the moat was filled in. The following year, Ieyasu treacherously returned to the attack when he led 200,000 soldiers in a second battle against the castle (which Hideyori had inherited from his father). Hideyori's 100,000 men were overwhelmed, and the Toyotomi family was annihilated. Hideyori's son of seven was beheaded, his head being posted on a bridge over the Kamogawa river in Kyoto as were those of criminals or traitors. Hideyori's five-year-old daughter was sent to a nunnery in Kamakura for the rest of her life. (Alternative tales claim that Ieyasu permitted the Toyotomi family to escape by boat and that they were befriended loyally by one of the daimyo—a not too likely happenstance.)

Yodogimi died at the siege of Osaka Castle, reportedly by having one of her servants kill her so she would not fall into Ieyasu's hands. She died despite pleas made by Ono Harunage, who had rescued Ieyasu's granddaughter (left as a hostage with Yodogimi) from the flames. (Yodogimi is reportedly buried in the Daiyu-ji temple in Osaka.) After the siege of the castle and the death of its defenders, thousands of heads were placed on pikes to line the road from Fushimi to Kyoto as a warning to any prospective opponents of Ieyasu.

The Kodai-ji continued to exist as a Buddhist temple after the death of Yodogimi. Sanko Joeki, abbot of the Kennin-ji, had been appointed as founding priest at Yodogimi's nunnery, and the Kodai-ji has remained as one of the largest and most important sub-temples of the Kennin-ji since that time. The temple was damaged by a number of fires in 1789, and then, ironically, in 1863, as tension increased between the incumbent Tokugawa shogunate and those who wished to restore the emperor to power, the temple was damaged once more. The supporters of the imperial cause, suspecting that one of their Tokugawa opponents had taken refuge in the Kodai-ji, attacked the temple and set fire to some of the buildings. Thus today only six of the original seventeenth-century structures in the Kodai-ji still exist: the Omote-mon gateway (the So-mon) to the nunnery, the Kaisan-do (Founder's Hall), the Kangetsudai covered bridge and walkway, the Tamaya (Sanctuary), and the Kasa-tei and the Shigure-tei (two small teahouses). A new Hojo (Abbot's Quarters) was erected in 1913.

The Kodai-ji is entered through the Omote-mon gateway on its southern side, and the path leads one to the left to the ticket booth. From there one proceeds ahead and then to the right behind temple buildings toward the Kangetsudai and the Kaisan-do.

Kangetsudai   The Kangetsudai is a roofed corridor or bridge which leads over the stream between the Garyu Pond (Dragon's Pond) and the Engetsu Pond (Crescent Moon Pond) to the Kaisan-do (Founder's Hall). It has a small, four-pillared structure midway across, and in this center section, when the Kangetsudai was located at Hideyoshi's Fushimi Castle, Hideyoshi would sit to gaze at the moon. In the northern section of the ponds is an island in the shape of a turtle, while in the southern portion is a group of stones meant to resemble a crane, these two animals being the traditional symbols of longevity. Work on the pond and garden were begun by the famous landscape designer Kobori Enshu in the 1620s, but the design was not perfected for another sixty-five years.

Kaisan-do   A path leads alongside the garden to the front walkway to the Kaisan-do which was dedicated to the memory of Sanko Joeki, the founding priest of the Kodai-ji. To create a memorial hall befitting her temple, Yodogimi commissioned the decorating of the pillars, walls, and ceiling of the Kaisan-do by the leading artists from the Kano and Tosa schools of painting. The ceiling of the inner room boasts not only a dragon by Kano Eitoku (1543–90), but also the ceiling from Yodogimi's carriage. The ceiling of the front room contains a portion of the roof of the war junk created for use by Hideyoshi in his battles against Korea and China. The inner shrine contains an image of Sanko Joeki while the statues on either side of the steps are of Kinoshita Iesada and Unryo-in, Yodogimi's elder brother and younger sister. The four panels of the shrine in this hall are by the noted fifteenth-century artist Kano Motonobu.

Tamaya   The Kangetsudai, the roofed corridor with its moon-viewing pavilion, leads to the Kaisan-do from the west and is continued on the eastern side from the Kaisan-do to the Tamaya. The corridor is named the Garyoro (Reclining Dragon Corridor) from the resemblance of its sloping roof to the back of a reclining dragon, the roof tiles having been laid in a manner that resembles the scales on the back of a dragon. (Only a short length at its far end may be entered.)

If the Kaisan-do would appear to be overly decorated, it cannot match the Momoyama-period splendor of the Tamaya. A path leads from the central walkway of the Kaisan-do to the east and to the front gate of the Tamaya, a building enclosed behind white walls. Built to the east of the Kaisan-do in 1606, it is particularly noted for its *takamaki-e* (raised lacquer work), an early example of what has become known as the art of Kodai-ji-maki-e. Gold lacquer artistry reached a luxurious peak in the designs in this Spirit Hall, since the walls, furniture, cabinets, the altar, and the altar dishes are all decorated in the Kodai-ji-maki-e technique.

The altar is thus a masterpiece of lacquer craft. Its central image of worship is that of Kannon. Instead of having the usual bodhisattva images on either side of the main image, the Kannon in this memorial hall is flanked by two miniature shrines. The shrine on the left holds a wooden image of the seated Hideyoshi, the shrine case having designs in gold taken from Yodogimi's carriage. Hideyoshi's hat is the one sent to him by the emperor of China. On the opposite side of the altar on the right is a wooden image of Yodogimi as a nun. The building is further embellished with the classical painting of the "Thirty-six Poets" by Tosa Mitsunobu (1434–1525) and other works by artists of the Kano school.

Shigure-tei and Kasa-tei   East of the main buildings and further up the hillside are two small, thatch-roofed teahouses, also from the Fushimi Castle, which are connected by a thatch-roofed walkway. They bear the names of Shigure-tei (Shower of Rain) and Kasa-tei (Umbrella). The Shigure-tei was designed by Toyobo Sochin, a disciple of Sen-no-Rikyu, the great tea master and garden designer of the late 1500s. At the time of Hideyoshi's 1587 Tea Party at the Kitano Shrine, to which he invited everyone to be present, even "those from China," all the important tea masters designed teahouses which were exhibited at the tea party. Toyobo's teahouse eventually found a permanent home at the Kodai-ji. The Kasa-tei is so-named since, from the inside of the teahouse, the poles or struts supporting the thatched roof radiate from a central point at the conical peak of the roof—thereby resembling the struts of an opened umbrella from the underside. The real name of the teahouse is more romantic: Ankan-kutsu, "Place of Idleness."

Iho-an   Northwest of the Kangetsu-dai are two small buildings, one of which is the Iho-an (The Cottage of Lingering Fragrances). According to one account, it was the favorite tea ceremony house of a wealthy merchant and the courtesan Yoshinotayu, a famed dancer and beauty who later married the

merchant. Another account claims this to be an incense c___
emony building, supposedly of Hideyoshi's time. Nearby is the
Entoku-in, a sub-temple of the Kodai-ji which was once the
mansion of Kinoshita Toshifusa, a nephew of Yodogimi. The
1913-rebuilt Hojo (Abbot's Quarters) has a landscape painting
on its *fusuma* (sliding panel) which is thought to be by Tohaku
Hasegawa, while the garden of the Hojo lies to its north, a
Momoyama dry garden with magnificent rocks from Fushimi
Castle.

Among the treasures of the temple on display between November 1–10 each year are gold screens by Kano Motonobu (1476–
1559), Kano Koi, and Hasegawa Tohaku (1539–1610). Certain
relics of Hideyoshi and Yodogimi remain as well, notably his
writing box, her black lacquer "clothes horse," and a set of small
dining trays and covered bowls, all originally from the Fushimi
Castle of Hideyoshi.

BUNNOSUKE-JAYA

A lighter and less solemn aspect of a nun's life can be experienced across from the west side of the Kodai-ji on Kita-mon-mae-
dori at the Bunnosuke-jaya, one of the few remaining *amazake*
shops which once flourished in this area. *Ama* are nuns, and
Buddhist nuns are not supposed to consume alcohol. Thus the
lees of saké were used to make a sweet, non alcoholic beverage
(amazake), which was much favored by the nuns. One can share
the nuns' passion for *amazake* in this shop. Behind the building is
a small shrine to Daikoku-ten, the god of wealth, said to have
been brought to this spot by Yodogimi from Fushimi Castle since
Daikoku-ten was Hideyoshi's patron deity. Just north of this
teahouse is a garden (now in private ownership) which can be
seen from the teahouse property. Designed by Kobori Enshu, it is
a *karesansui* (dry garden) in which Kobori used stones taken from
Fushimi Castle after Ieyasu had it leveled in 1620, five years after
Ieyasu had eliminated the last of the Toyotomi family.

A brief digression into the narrow lanes to the west of the

Kodai-ji can be of interest. Between the Kodai-ji and Higashi-oji-dori is an area that once held the homes of Kyoto's well-to-do. The changes that occurred after the Second World War led to the abandonment of these villas by the merchants who could no longer afford to sustain them. Now the villas have become inns and teahouses. It is an interesting area to wander in, particularly in the evening when the inns and teahouses come to life.

Continuing to the north on Kita-mon-mae-dori from the Kodai-ji and Bunnosuke-jaya, one cannot help but be reminded that the Yasaka or Gion Shrine is not too far distant, for looming up ahead is what seems to be a gigantic Gion cart such as is pulled along the central streets of Kyoto every mid-July during the Gion Festival. The structure, however, is immense and is obviously a permanent "cart." What is seen is no cart; it is the huge and extraordinary pagoda of the Daiun-in temple.

DAIUN-IN

Kita-mon-mae-dori comes to an end as one walks to the north, and it is necessary to take a right turn and then a left turn at the next street on the left. This places one before the entrance to the Daiun-in. The temple is open from 9:00 a.m. to 4:30 p.m. Entry fee.

The Daiun-in temple buildings are an unusual twentieth century addition to the Kyoto scene. The temple precincts are entered through the administrative building with the large room to the right of the entry hall serving as a museum of the temple's treasures. At its focal point is a standing image of Amida with a seated monk to the right and the image of a medieval official to the left. The cases in the room display scrolls and other articles of a religious nature.

A path from the entry building leads along a garden to the entryway. At the base of the pagoda is an altar with a seated image of Amida, hands in the contemplative mudra. Behind the image, an aureole holds small raised Buddha figures which stand out from the traditional one thousand Buddha images impressed in the aureole. A series of stairways from the entry hall lead up to the two outer platforms at the top of the pagoda; the walls and ceilings along the way are covered with paintings depicting the Buddhist murals in the Dun Huang caves of western China. Explanations of the paintings are provided in both Japanese and English. The two outside platforms under the roof of the pagoda provide an excellent view over Kyoto on three sides with the Higashiyama mountain range on the fourth side to the east.

Leaving the Daiun-in and continuing north along the path, one comes to the beginning of Maruyama Park straight ahead and on the right. The rear portion of the Yasaka or Gion Shrine is on the left. But first, a digression is in order to a small temple at the beginning of the slope of Higashiyama mountain on the right, a temple associated with a romantic and tragic story much beloved by the Japanese.

CHORAKU-JI

A road runs eastward along the south side of Maruyama Park in the direction of the mountain. At the end of this roadway lies a long stone stairway which leads to the Choraku-ji. The temple is open from 9:00 a.m. to 5:00 p.m. Entry fee.

The Choraku-ji was built by Priest Saicho (Dengyo Daishi), one of the two major Buddhist priests at the time of the founding of Kyoto in the 790s. The temple was created by him sometime between 782–806 as a Tendai sect temple, but it was rebuilt in the fourteenth century by the priest Ippen who converted it to the Ji sect of Buddhism (see below). Successive emperors worshipped here; thus, the temple had a degree of prominence.

A minor temple today, the Choraku-ji is perhaps best known for the most noted individual associated with it: Taira-no-Tokuko, better known as the ex-empress Kenrei Mon'in. At the sea battle of Dan-no-ura between the Taira and Minamoto in 1185, she and her mother-in-law (who was holding Kenrei Mon'in's seven-year-old son, the emperor Antoku) jumped into the sea with the child to end their lives when the battle was lost. The empress was saved from drowning by being dragged from the water by her long hair. Sent back to Kyoto, she lived in a miserable hut belonging to a poor priest, and at twenty-nine she took the tonsure at the Choraku-ji. As an added catastrophe after the deaths of her family and her degradation, an earthquake destroyed the hut in which this former empress had taken refuge. She was moved to the Jakko-in temple in the Ohara region to a retreat house of ten square feet, and there she lived out her life in prayer for her dead family.

Up the long, stone stairway of this hillside site, the entrance to the temple leads to a further climb to the only early buildings remaining: the Hondo (Main Hall), the Shoro (Bell Tower), the Kuri (Priests' Quarters), and a modern treasure house which completes the complex. The small Hondo has a double roof and, within, a black lacquer altar bearing a noted image of Honen in its altar case, which is sometimes left closed. The Shoro is to the left (north) of the Hondo, and beyond it a little way further up the hillside is a charming dell. Here a small, roofed, open-sided unit holds two Jizo images. Beyond it, a small waterfall descends from the hillside. Across from the resulting rivulet is an equally small Shinto shrine dedicated to the deity of the temple land.

Adjacent to the shrine is the modern treasury. Within the treasury on the left wall is a picture of Kenrei Mon'in as a nun with Awa-no-Naishi, her faithful aide. The statues of seven priests once associated with this temple are ranged across the back of the building. In the row of priests, the end two are seated images while the third from the left is a monk seated in a Chinese-style chair. The middle image, carved by Kosho in 1420, is of Ippen (1239–89), founder of the Ji sect of Buddhism which was dedicated to the continuous repetition of the *nenbutsu* (*Namu Amida Butsu*—Praise to the Buddha Amida). (Ippen chose as his Buddhist name a word that means "for one and for all," indicative of how the *nenbutsu* usage was making Buddhism a universal religion in Japan rather than just an aristocratic religion as it had first been.)

The full-length statue of Priest Ippen chanting the *nenbutsu*, with the small Amida images issuing from his lips as he walks on a pilgrimage, is stiff and angular, and it is nowhere as successful in portraying a walking devotee of Amida as is the image of Kuya in the Rokuharamitsu-ji (see Tour 4). Its sharply carved cheeks are reminiscent of the style of carving employed in Noh masks.

HIGASHI OTANI MAUSOLEUM AND CEMETERY

Down the path from the Choraku-ji, on the left-hand side of the street is the entrance to the Higashi Otani Mausoleum and Cemetery. The grounds of the site are open from 9:00 a.m. to 5:00 p.m. without charge.

Established in 1671 as a mortuary chapel for the abbots of the Higashi Hongan-ji temple in central Kyoto, the Higashi Otani has become an important cemetery since a portion of the remains of Priest Shinran Shonin, the founder of the Jodo Shinshu sect of Buddhism, was reburied here in 1653. Followers of this sect often desire to have their cremated remains buried close to the ashes of the founder of their sect of Buddhism.

A handsome gateway decorated with carvings of chrysanthemums and other flora provides an entrance to the grounds, and then a sloping path turns to the right. Ahead on the right is the roofed purification basin with an extended bronze dragon from whose mouth the water issues. Directly beyond this structure is a long temple building with a hall for funeral services. Across from these units is the small Hondo with its altar figure of Amida sculpted in wood. A shrine on the right holds a portrait of Shinran and one of Prince Shotoku while on the left are portraits of past abbots of the Higashi Hongan-ji temple. Behind the Hondo are other temple buildings not open to the general public.

In front of the Hondo, a flight of steps to the east leads up to the forecourt of the massive mausoleum of Shinran. A small, roofed oratory stands before the richly ornamented Kara-mon gate to Shinran's tomb, while a lattice-fenced wall stretches to the right and left of the gateway. Behind the gate is a plain granite wall which encompasses the tomb of Shinran. Rectangular in shape, it is 30 feet high with a circumference of 102 feet. The wall is crowned in front with what is said to have been Shinran's favorite stone, the Tiger Stone, so-named from its supposed resemblance to the shape of a tiger.

Returning down the steps to the level of the Hondo, a short path to the left (south) passes the temple bell and goes through a gate. To the left, rising tier upon tier up the hillside, is the Higashi Hongan-ji cemetery, crowded with thousands of tombstones. Part way up the hillside is a memorial building. On August 15 each year, the twenty thousand graves are decorated with candles as a part of the service for the dead whose souls return briefly to this world and then return to the world of the dead at the end of the Obon festival period (July 13–15 in some places, August 13–15 in others). The candle-lighting ceremony begins at 6:00 p.m.

MARUYAMA PARK
From where the walk to the Choraku-ji began, a right-hand turn brings one to Maruyama Park bounded on the north by the grounds of the Chion-in temple, on the east by the mountains, and on the south by the Higashi Otani Mausoleum grounds and the Choraku-ji.

Maruyama Park is one of the larger public parks in Kyoto. In the past it was the site of several temples, but all have been destroyed by fires. Within the park is the site of the former Sorin-ji which was established by the great priest Dengyo Daishi (Saicho) in the latter part of the eighth century; its site is now marked only by the Yakushi-do shrine. The famed twelfth-century poet Saigyo lived here in a cell at the Sorin-ji at one time. In 1871 the government turned the area into a public park, one of the first such public pleasure parks in the city. With the wooded Higashiyama mountains as a background on the east and the shrine and temples on its three other sides, it is an oasis away from the traffic and noise of the city streets. Two ponds with a charming arched bridge over the stream between them, a water spout tossing a spray of water into the air, the maples, the willows, the cherry trees, and the shrubbery have made this a favorite area for Kyoto's residents. With restaurants about it, for over a century the park has been a place in which to enjoy quiet relaxation.

The center of the park is noted for its hundreds of cherry trees whose blossoms in early April provide an additional pleasure. In the past they were viewed in the evening by torchlight, and this tradition is still maintained, albeit modern illumination is now also provided.

A pleasant rest in the park or the enjoyment of refreshments can occur before returning to Higashi-oji-dori to the west of the park. Here at the intersection with Shijo-dori a number of bus lines or taxis are available for transport to the various sections of the city.

TOUR
4

The Realms of the Dead,
the Dancing Saint,
and Zen Beginnings

建仁寺　六波羅蜜寺　珍皇寺

THE CONTRAST of the secular and the religious has always permeated Kyoto life and history. The Kennin-ji, one of the earliest and most important of Kyoto's Zen monasteries, for example, is a next-door neighbor to the pleasure quarters which have made the name "Gion" synonymous with the pursuits of the "floating world" of Kabuki, of *ochaya* (teahouses) where men can be well fed while being entertained by geisha (if they can afford such luxurious pleasures and have the proper introduction to the proprietress), as well as of other delights both licit and illicit. This is the area to be explored on this and the next tour of Kyoto.

The Rokuhara district has its own major shrines beginning with the Ebisu Shrine whose festive occasions are thronged by businessmen and the general public—all who have hopes of increasing their wealth. The Wakamiya Shrine, just north of Gojo-dori (Fifth Street), presides over the district itself as well as the great pottery fairs held annually. Here, too, is the Rokuharamitsu-ji which enshrines the magnificent, realistic image of that saint of the marketplace, the priest Kuya, portrayed as though still walking the streets of the city, beating his drum and repeating the *nenbutsu* (*Namu Amida Butsu*–Praise to the Buddha Amida) which issues from the image's mouth in the form of tiny Amida figures.

The Rokuhara district where this tour begins was once the seat of the proud and powerful. Here, in the mid-1100s, the Taira clan and its followers had their mansions and governmental offices. Taira-no-Kiyomori made the mistake, after his forces had killed Minamoto-no-Yoshitomo, of permitting the Minamoto children to live on the condition that they would be placed in monasteries to become monks. In time they grew up and revolted against Taira rule, a revolt which in 1185 led not only to the burning of the palatial mansions of the Taira clan (and much of eastern Kyoto), but to the death of Kiyomori's family, his followers, and his imperial grandson. Here in the Rokuhara district, the Minamoto victors set up their Kyoto headquarters, and the area remained the locus of political power under the rule of the Minamoto shoguns of Kamakura between 1185 and 1333.

There is mystery in this sector as well, for portions of the Rokuhara district were once burial grounds for the common people, and here are supposed to be located the six avenues leading to the other world where the souls of the dead reside until called back by the bell of the Chinno-ji temple for the brief Obon period each mid-summer. The Yasui Konpira Shrine in the district, while not mysterious in itself, has its mystery in that Konpira, the deity worshipped at the shrine, has never been truly identified, and confusion reigns as to his true identity—which in no way discourages those who pray to him for safety in travel.

It was at the Kennin-ji temple that tea first became popular as a beverage that alerts but does not intoxicate. When the priest Eisai (1141–1251) established the Kennin-ji monastery, he reintroduced tea as a beverage from China, a refreshment that had previously not received the welcome that it was to engender from this time on. Tea moved eventually from the monastery into daily life, and special establishments were created for the enjoyment of the beverage. While the *ochaya* of the area serve a more potent beverage today, the origin of tea culture is still remembered not only in the formal tea ceremony which is celebrated for the general public at the Gion Corner and elsewhere in Kyoto, but in the historical procession made each spring to commemorate the bringing of the first, tender tea leaves to Kyoto from Uji each year for the benefit of the shogun—a procession still celebrated as a remembrance of times past.

CHINNO-JI AND THE SIX REALMS OF THE DEAD

Bus 206 or 207 travels north and south on Higashi-oji-dori, and it can be taken to the Kiyomizu-michi bus stop on Higashi-oji-dori (the same bus stop as in Tour 1). Then, starting from the intersection of Higashi-oji-dori and Kiyomizu-michi, take Matsubara-dori (the westward version of Kiyomizu-michi) to the west for one long block. A turn to the north brings one to the Chinno-ji which lies at the end of this side street.

The Chinno-ji buildings are only open occasionally; thus, it is best to inquire at the Tourist Information Center downtown as to times of admission.

The Rokudo-mairi, the Six Roads Pilgrimage, is the legendary road that links the world of the living with the world of the dead or the spirit world. An old belief held that if one were to stand in the middle of this road while beating a gong and calling out the name of a deceased family member, the voice and sound would guide the ancestral spirit back to this world for the annual visit to its former home.

The Rokudo-mairi is thought to be near the Chinno-ji which is also known as the Rokudo-san, the "Six Realms of the Dead Temple." The association of the temple with the road of legend can be attributed to the fact that the Toribeno Cemetery once extended from the Kiyomizu-dera and the adjacent Nishi Otani Mausoleum to the Rokuharamitsu-ji area which lies north of Gojo-dori and between Higashi-oji-dori and the Kamogawa river to the west. This area was known as "the land of the dead," a place where the bodies of those who died without family were often abandoned. A pilgrimage to Toribeno was a symbolic journey through Rokudo (the Six Realms of the Dead). The small Rokudo-no-Tsuji square in front of the Chinno-ji temple is said to stand at the beginning of the six avenues leading to the several levels of hell. This connection of the temple with the supposed avenue led to the custom among the poorer people of Kyoto of praying here for the souls of their deceased loved ones.

The Chinno-ji is a small, rather nondescript temple which lies north of Matsubara-dori. One walks from Matsubara-dori to the north into the brief street which leads to the small square formed by the Chinno-ji temple buildings on the east, north, and west sides. In the middle, before the Hondo (Main Hall) is a modern, stylized, five-part memorial stone sixteen feet tall, standing within a stone fence and with pine trees along its side. On the left (west) side of the square is a small shrine, and just beyond it to the north is a plastic-roofed area covering a large Jizo image with a stone lantern before it and a stone flower-holder on either side. Around this central unit are some two hundred smaller Jizo images and inscribed stones. (Images of Jizo are often placed in cemeteries or places associated with death since he is a protector of the dead.)

On the right side as one enters the square is a small *kura* (storage building) and then a building that houses those connected with the other world. This right side of the entrance to the square was a favorite place for the itinerant nuns *(bikuni)* who gathered here in the mid-summer Obon season when the souls of the dead return to this world for a brief stay. Here they would solicit alms by exhibiting picture screens of hell to the people who gathered to pray for the souls of the deceased. (The "floating" population of Japan in the period after the 1500s, despite the attempts to control the movement of the populace by the Tokugawa government, consisted of those who were pious monks and nuns and those who were artists involved in raising funds for their own benefit.)

The hall beyond the *kura* can be looked into from the outside even when it is not open. It is divided into two parts: the left section contains an image of Enma, the king of hell, with an attendant on either side; the second or right-hand section of the building holds a statue of Ono-no-Takamura, a noted poet of the first half of the 800s whose fame as a writer led many to believe that he was a messenger to and the secretary of the ruler of hell. He is accompanied by two emissaries from hell.

At the north end of the square is the Hondo which contains a statue of the Buddha Yakushi, a particularly important Buddha for this area since it is believed that he is able to rescue the suffering from hell.

Mukaegane   The temple bell, the Mukaegane (the Bell of Welcome) to the southeast of the Hondo, is rung during the Obon seasons of July and August, and it is thought that its sound can be heard in the other world, the world of the dead. The sound ostensibly leads the spirits of that region back to earth during the Obon period. When Priest Keishun, said to have had the bell created, left for a three-year visit to China to study Buddhism, he had the bell buried. Curiosity overcame the priest left behind in charge of the temple, who unearthed the bell and rang it in order to hear its pure sound. On his return to Japan, Keishun reproved the curious priest since, he claimed, he had heard the sound of the bell even in China.

If the Chinno-ji is connected with beliefs involving the dead, the nearby Rokuharamitsu-ji is associated with the pious priest Kuya who was concerned with saving the souls of individuals while they were still living and assuring them of a place in Amida's western paradise after death. He is remembered at the Rokuharamitsu-ji which he first established.

ROKUHARAMITSU-JI

The Rokuharamitsu-ji temple lies to the west and south of Matsubara-dori, the same street that must be traversed in order to reach the Chinno-ji. Coming from Higashi-oji-dori, a turn to the left at the fourth street on the left brings one to the Rokuharamitsu-ji. The temple is on the west side of this new street and is open from 8:00 a.m. to 4:30 p.m. There is an entry fee for the treasure house, but no fee for the temple itself.

The Rokuharamitsu-ji was established by the priest Kuya, the "Dancing Saint" or "Saint of the Marketplace," in 963. The continued existence of the temple is a testimony to the importance of this saint who so affected the lives of the common people of his own and later times.

Kuya (903–72), according to some accounts, was the son of the emperor Daigo (reigned 897–930)—a claim often made to give distinguished individuals of the common life a noble heritage. Whatever his lineage, noble or otherwise, he devoted his life to helping the common man, to traveling from village to village, to aiding and instructing the peasants in digging wells, to building and repairing bridges and roads, and to caring for the sick. A devotee of Amida, he spread belief and faith in Amida as he traveled from town to town, chanting and singing the *nenbutsu* to folk tunes while he danced and beat upon his wooden eating bowl. Clad in a thin deerskin, wearing a bell about his neck to draw attention to his mission and carrying an antler-headed staff in one hand, he danced the byways of villages and the streets of towns singing:

> One never fails
> To reach the Pure Land
> If one calls,
> Just once,
> The name of Amida.

(This chanting dance is still performed at the Todai-ji in Nara on May 2 in honor of the emperor Shomu and at the Kuya-do in Kyoto in mid-November in memory of Kuya.)

Kuya came to Kyoto in 938, making his home in the market-places where he begged for food, a standard practice of Buddhist monks since the giving of alms by the faithful to monks is considered a religious duty. He sang and danced the praises of Amida, but he also attended the sick and the poor, making a green tea from bamboo for them and offering them a little pickled plum with the tea while he intoned a Buddhist invocation. Many of the sick were healed under his care. The populace named him "The Saint of the Marketplace" or the "*Nenbutsu* Saint"—just as villages had named the wells he helped them dig "Amida Wells."

In 948 he arrived at the great monastic center of the Enryaku-ji on top of Mount Hiei to the northeast of Kyoto, and there he was received into the monastery for study and monastic discipline. He was given the name of Kosho by the noted priest Ensho of the Enryaku-ji. In 951 a plague settled upon Kyoto, and Kuya returned to the city. He carved a large image of the Eleven-faced Kannon which he pulled on a cart through the streets of Kyoto thereby, according to popular belief, helping to end the plague. Eventually, he built a temple, the Saiko-ji, on land given by the great Taira family (whose mansions lay in the district), and here he served as its head priest. Here too his image of Kannon was ensconced, and thus began the history of the Rokuharamitsu-ji. His temple was enlarged by his successors, but, though tradition states that the present main hall of the Rokuharamitsu-ji is the original Seiko-ji Hondo, the original building was destroyed in a fire. The present hall and its Kannon image date from 1463.

As with other legends concerning noted figures in early Japanese history, it was recorded that at his death Kuya washed and put on clean clothes, then lay down facing west with his eyes closed in meditation. Thus, he died, facing toward the Western Paradise where he would meet Amida. It is said that a heavenly perfume and music filled the air at the moment of his demise.

After Kuya's death, his disciples expanded the Rokuharamitsu-ji temple, and it became a center of Tendai Buddhism. During the period of the ascendency of the Taira clan (1140–83), the Taira and their followers had their mansions in this area, and the temple flourished under their patronage. At the fall of the Taira in 1183, when Minamoto Yoritomo attacked Kyoto and the Taira forces, the Taira set fire to all twenty of their mansions before fleeing the city. Some four thousand to five thousand houses of their retainers and of the general populace went up in flames, but the main hall of the temple was spared during the conflagration which destroyed much of this portion of eastern Kyoto. Fires have destroyed the Rokuharamitsu-ji buildings on numerous occasions since that time, and the Hondo of 1463 is the oldest unit of the temple still standing. When Hideyoshi built his Great Buddha at the Hoko-ji in the 1590s, he also generously repaired the Rokuharamitsu-ji as well. A further restoration was carried out in 1969.

Hondo   The one-story Hondo, of decorated vermilion posts and beams contrasting with white plaster walls and a dark-tiled roof, offers an attractive sight in the heart of a busy city district. Before the steps leading into the hall are a large incense pot and a perpetual flame. To the left of the steps is a box of stones from which the devout can build small stupas—in accordance with the belief that the souls of dead children wander at the border of the River Sai (similar to the River Styx in Western mythology) condemned to pursue salvation by building towers of stone which are kicked down by sadistic demons. Jizo, the guardian of children, drives away the demons; thus, the piling up of stones, such as at this temple, can help the souls of the children to Buddhist salvation.

Within the Hondo, the main image is an Eleven-faced Kannon with a Jizo (one of five standing Jizo images owned by the temple) on its left and a Yakushi Nyorai on its right. At the four corners of the altar, four images of the Shitenno (Deva Kings), carved by the great thirteenth-century sculptor Unkei, stand guard against the forces of evil.

Treasury   The main reason for visiting the Rokuharamitsu-ji is to see the statues preserved in its treasury. The treasury is a separate, small, fireproof and modern ferroconcrete building located to the southwest of the Hondo. It contains a number of notable statues of the twelfth to thirteenth centuries. A display of scrolls is placed on either side of the interior entry of the building while among other treasures the temple also holds the written will of the great priest Kobo Daishi (Kukai). Against the left wall in the treasury proper is a free-standing image of Enma, the unpleasant-looking king of hell, with a scribe and attendants on either side. Against the right wall is an image of Yakushi Nyorai, the deity of healing, holding a medicine pot in his left hand. He is flanked by life-sized Shitenno guardian images on his right and left.

The major treasures of the temple are lined up along the rear wall of the building (some labels are in English), and they include a number of the finest portrait statues of the Kamakura period (1185–1333). The seated images are approximately 3 feet tall, and, from left to right, the statues are:

1. A seated statue of the sculptor Tankei holding a rosary in his hand. This 1264 image is claimed to be a self-portrait. It is 2.5 feet tall and is of painted wood.

2. A twelfth-century, realistic, seated image of Jizo by Unkei. This Jizo was originally the main object of worship in the Jurin-in of the Bodai-ji temple near Hachijo-dori (Eighth Street), and it is thought that it was flanked by the figures of Unkei and Tankei—which still stand on either side of it today. As the Kei family temple, the Bodai-ji was created by Unkei near his Shichijo-dori (Seventh Street) workshop. The image, now darkened by time, was once painted in rich colors; traces of cut gold-leaf patterns can still be ascertained on parts of the robe. The image has the extended ear lobes of a Buddhist prince, pendant earrings, crystal eyes, and the third "eye" of knowledge in mid-forehead. A separately carved wooden necklace has been placed upon its chest. In its left hand, it holds the magic jewel associated with Jizo.

3. A seated, painted wooden image of the sculptor Unkei, 2.5 feet tall, also holding a rosary in his hands. It is thought that this too may be a self-portrait.

4. A thirteenth-century 2.7-foot-tall seated image of Taira-no-Kiyomori (1118–81) reading a sutra scroll is realistically represented—but as a monk, a role beyond his moral capabilities. The sutra scroll of sacred texts is held in both his hands as he peruses it; his sleeves flow in rich drapery from his arms.

5. A life-size, 5-foot-tall Jizo by the eleventh-century sculptor Jocho. The deity appears in the form of a young monk with long sleeves, holding a fly whisk of hair in his left hand. His empty right hand would once have held the mystic gem which Jizo normally holds. His eyes are of glass and a fretwork aureole of small Buddhas stands behind him.

6. The famed, 3.9-foot-tall painted wooden image of Kuya by

Kosho, the fourth of Unkei's sons (Kosho's name appears on the inside of the statue). Kuya is seen as the itinerant priest that he was in life, clothed in his short, shabby deerskin covering, his feet shod with straw sandals. A round gong hangs down his chest, supported by a harness worn around his neck. In his right hand he holds a T-shaped wooden hammer with which to beat the gong as he dances and sings the praises of Amida, and in his left hand he holds a wooden staff topped with antlers. From his mouth, on a wire, issue a row of six tiny Amida images, symbolizing his constant repetition of the *nenbutsu* in praise of Amida. These six images represent the six characters of the spoken *nenbutsu;* thus, Kosho has, in a sense, carved the voice of Kuya as he chants the *nenbutsu* while walking on a pilgrimage.

A realistic portrait down to the wrinkled and worn deerskin, the prominent Adam's apple of his neck, the veins in his arms and legs, and even the seams on the inside of his sleeves–all are portrayed in a lifelike manner. Here the "Saint of the People" is represented as he would have appeared to the people of his time. An innovative and original presentation of an active saint, it was created in a novel and successful manner, and it represents the climax of Kamakura-period realism in sculpture.

7. An image of a member of the Taira era wearing an *eboshi* (headgear worn by nobles in court dress), a formal representation of a governmental figure of the middle ages.

8. A figure of Kobo Daishi (Kukai), 2.25 feet tall, seated on a Chinese chair, his shoes beneath the chair. This realistic but restrained portrait was created, it is thought, by Chokai, a disciple of the master sculptor Kaikei, between 1249 and 1256. The signature of Chokai is within the image. In his right hand Kukai holds a rosary and in his left hand is a *vajra* (thunderbolt). This portrait-sculpture is modeled after the image in the To-ji as created by Kosho, but it is a stiffer representation of the great Buddhist priest. It was carved twenty years after the sculpture of Kukai in the To-ji.

The Rokuhara district we have been in is a portion of central

Kyoto which was developed as a commercial center through the years, and thus it is only appropriate that a shrine to Ebisu, the Shinto patron of success in business, should be enshrined here. Thus, we move from a saint who was concerned with helping people reach Amida's Western Paradise after death to a deity whose concern is wealth in this life.

EBISU SHRINE

The Ebisu Shrine is located west and then north of Matsubara-dori. After returning to Matsubara-dori, turn to the left and then to the right (north) on Yamato-oji-dori, the next through street. The Ebisu Shrine will be on the left-hand side just ahead. The shrine is open during daylight hours with no entry fee.

Ebisu is one of the Seven Gods of Good Luck and he is the patron of business and merchants, thereby making him a very popular deity. A chubby fellow, he appears with a fishing line and a *tai* (sea-bream) in his hand. His shrine in the Gion district is behind two torii decorated with the usual shrine stone lanterns

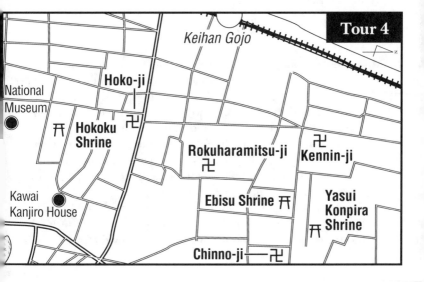

and protective *koma-inu* (Korean lion-dogs) before the second set of torii. Shrine buildings line the left (south) side of the precincts while a dragon fountain at the water purification basin is on the right. Straight ahead is the Haiden (Oratory), behind a wooden fence on which is a large drum. The Honden (Spirit Hall) enshrining the god spirit is behind the Haiden. To the left of the rear portion of the Honden is a life-size statue of a white horse; white horses are often found at Shinto shrines since they are said to be favorites of the gods. Beyond is a formal gateway to the street on the west.

The shrine is most noted for its ceremonies which occur throughout the year. Current festival dates can be ascertained at the Tourist Information Office.

The festival-loving Ebisu and his joyous ceremonies reflect one aspect of the Japanese temperament when it comes to religion: the acceptance of the life of this world and the pleasure that can be enjoyed while one is here. On the other hand, there is the contemplative aspect of the Japanese nature as well, and it can be realized just a short walk along Yamato-oji-dori to the north at the Kennin-ji Zen monastery.

KENNIN-JI

As an active monastery, the interior of the monastic buildings of the Kennin-ji temple and its sub-temples are generally not open to the public, but they may be visited in the morning if permission is obtained in advance in writing from the temple office. Generally, permission is granted for morning visits if one's purpose is of a serious nature. The temple Hondo, a few sub-temples, and the temple treasury are open to the public from November 1 to 10 from 9:00 a.m. to 4:00 p.m. The grounds are open to the public daily without charge.

Kennin-ji was the first Zen temple to be established in Japan and, as such, remained the head temple for Zen monasteries in Kyoto for many years. The temple was begun by the priest Eisai

(1141–1215) in 1202 at the request of the shogun, and it is here that he established the Rinzai sect of Zen Buddhism in Japan. When he was fourteen years old, Eisai went to the monastic community of Mt. Hiei on the mountaintop to the northeast of Kyoto to enter the religious life. Here he studied the Tendai version of Buddhism. In April 1168, after achieving the goal of many Japanese monks, he eventually journeyed to China, the source of Japanese Buddhism, to study at Tendai monasteries. He made a second trip in 1187, not returning to Japan until September 1191 when he settled at a temple in Kyushu where he began to teach the doctrines of Zen Buddhism.

With his belief that Zen would protect the state during the age of Mappo (The Age of the Disappearance of the Buddhist Law), his doctrines attracted the attention of Shogun Minamoto-no-Yoriie who invited him to Kyoto to head Kennin-ji and to establish the Rinzai sect of Buddhism there. In time, he was to establish Zen monasteries in Kamakura as well, the seat of the shogunal government. At his death, Eisai was buried at the Kennin-ji.

Eisai lived during the age of Mappo, a period which was thought to have begun about 1050, in which men would realize the inability of man to understand Buddhist doctrine or belief. In these degenerate days, it was believed that one could no longer depend on one's own mind or one's own efforts, nor could one call on Amida or on scripture or ceremonies for help.

What was needed, according to Eisai, was an intuitive method of spiritual training which would enable the believer to obtain a lofty transcendence over worldly care, a transcendence of and beyond the individual which would permit the seeker to reach the fundamental unity which pervades all existence and the universe. The mental discipline involved in this method would develop a mind receptive to the basic truths of the universe, a mind that was under control and free of the fear of physical danger from without or passion from within. A mind under such control was worthy of an abbot—or a soldier, as the military of the Kamakura shogunate (1185–1333) came to believe.

The encouragement of the growth of Zen monasteries was one aspect of shogunate policy, and, in the case of Kennin-ji, its physical size was so huge that it was made a national project, with its construction completed in 1205. Unfortunately, the growth of military government would in time lead to war and the fall of the Kamakura government. Burned in 1256, rebuilt in 1257–59, the monastery was enriched by the Minamoto, the Hojo, and the Ashikaga rulers in turn. At the height of its power, it had fifty-three sub-temples. The wars of the Sengoku Jidai (The Period of the Warring States) in the fifteenth and sixteenth centuries, particularly the Onin Wars of 1467–77, led to the virtual destruction of Kyoto as a city. Kennin-ji was spared during this time, but in 1556, in another outbreak of fighting, the temple was almost completely destroyed. Much of what can be seen of the temple today is thus of a later era than its founding.

Many of the present Kennin-ji buildings date from the eighteenth century or later. Only the Chokushi-mon (The Imperial Messenger's Gate)—also called the Yatate-mon (Arrow Gate) from the scars left upon it during the civil wars of the fifteenth and sixteenth centuries—remains from the early period of the temple's existence. This black gate at the southern edge of the temple precincts is said to have once been a portion of the nearby Rokuhara headquarters of the Taira clan.

Butsu-den In 1763 the restoration of the temple began in earnest both through new construction and by the transport of buildings that belonged to other temples to the Kennin-ji site. The Butsu-den (Buddha Hall), originally at the Tofuku-ji just south of the main portion of the city of Kyoto, was put in place in 1763 and was handsomely refurbished. What is now the abbot's apartment (Hojo) was originally a building from the Ankoku-ji in Hiroshima Prefecture. This structure, built by the first Ashikaga shogun, Ashikaga Takauji, in the fourteenth century, was moved to the Kennin-ji in the 1590s.

Marishiten Shrine Near the south gate of the temple grounds is the Marishiten Shrine, built in 1327 by Seisetsu, a Chinese priest. The image of Marishi (Queen of Heaven) with her white face and colorful clothes, seen here riding upon seven golden boars, is made from clay said to have been brought from China by Seisetsu. The shrine has always been a popular one among the geisha of the Gion district.

Among the most noted treasures of the monastery are the paintings of Kaiho Yusho (1533–1615). In the late 1590s, a few years before his death, the priest Ekei, the abbot of the Ankoku-ji in Hiroshima Prefecture, moved to the Kennin-ji and, with the financial help of Hideyoshi, began the restoration of the fire- and storm-damaged abbot's quarters. In 1598 he had his artist friend Kaiho Yusho create five sets of painted, sliding panels *(fusuma)* for the Hojo. Yusho is noted for the directness and vitality of the straight line which succeeds in simplifying technique—as would be expected in paintings done for Zen monasteries. He painted landscapes and dragons at the Kennin-ji, the temple that holds his largest body of work. In this century, in 1934, a typhoon did serious damage to the temple, and the paintings were remounted as fifty hanging scrolls. Done in the Chinese "impressionistic" style, these paintings present vistas of temple buildings with hints of trees and hills about the structures. The paintings have since been placed in various sub-temples of the complex.

Zenkyo-an Sub-temple The Zenkyo-an sub-temple on the grounds of Kennin-ji was also restored in 1599. Here, Yusho created a dozen panels of pine, bamboo, and plum trees painted with black ink on a gold-leaf ground, based on a theme in Chinese paintings. Other screens by Yusho are in the Kanzen-ji (another sub-temple) as is a pair of six-fold screens in the Reito-in. The subjects of the Reito-in screens are those of scholars talking or viewing the distant scene. Many of these paintings can be seen during the November showing of the temple treasures.

Perhaps the most noted aspect of the Kennin-ji is not only the Zen faith which was first brought here, but the monastery's connection with tea as well. Although Kobo Daishi (Kukai) introduced tea into Japan from China in the 800s, it did not become fashionable until it was reintroduced into Japan by Eisai. Eisai brought the plant and beverage to Japan for religious purposes since it helped to keep monks alert during long, nightly devotions. It could also serve as a mild medicine in certain illnesses. Eisai wrote a book about the value of tea, and a simple tea ceremony which began at the Kennin-ji was later to be developed into the highly formal and stylized approach of Sen-no-Rikyu and others in the late sixteenth century and thereafter. Legend holds that Eisai's devotion to tea was supported by the young shogun Minamoto-no-Sanetomo after Eisai weaned him from imbibing wine to drinking tea.

YASUI KONPIRA SHRINE

At the beginning of this tour, it was indicated that a mystery surrounded the Yasui Konpira-gu. Thus, perhaps, it is well to move from so serious an institution as the Kennin-ji Zen temple to a shrine that could insure one's well-being when traveling.

The Yasui Konpira-gu is between Higashi-oji-dori and the Kennin-ji temple to the west of the Yasaka Pagoda. The shrine can most easily be located by starting from the Higashiyama-yasui bus stop (the bus stop midway between the Kiyomizu-michi and the Shijo-dori stops) and then by walking to the west. Turning to the left at the first through street, the second street on the left (south) leads to the shrine. The shrine is open during daylight hours. Its museum (Konpira Emakan) of *ema* (votive tablets) is generally open from 10:00 a.m. to 4:00 p.m., but is closed on Mondays. It is advisable to check with the Tourist Information Office downtown as to whether the museum is currently open.

There is confusion about the identity of the deity Konpira. (Konpira originally was the Indian deity Kumbhira, the crocodile god of the Ganges.) Although some say he is one of the various Shinto deities, others claim that he is an early Japanese emperor. Nonetheless, he is a being who is worshiped and who is found to be efficacious in answering prayers from his believers despite his anonymous nature. A temple to Konpira was erected in Shikoku in the ninth century, perhaps by Kukai (Kobo Daishi). In time, a number of similar temples sprang up all over Japan. In 1872 the Meiji government made the Shikoku temple a Shinto shrine (as with other Konpira units) to Okuninushi-no-Mikoto, god of Izumo, but the identity of the resident deity still remains unclear. Be that as it may, Konpira is a very popular deity who is invoked by travelers and seamen in times of need or in gratitude for past favors.

Down the narrow street from Higashi-oji-dori, one arrives at a shrine that is not unlike similar Shinto shrines. The Heiden has racks to the north and south of its platform on which *ema* have been hung. (*Ema* are prayer boards on which one writes a prayer or a wish. They usually have a depiction of the deity or of a scene connected with the deity of the shrine.) Then beyond the Heiden to the west is the Honden with its *kara* (Chinese-style) roof. Additional buildings are on either side of the main shrine buildings, the museum of *ema* being to the east (in front of the Heiden). A curious stone with a hole in its center is to the left of the Heiden and is covered with *fuda*, the name-stickers pilgrims usually affix to the gates of Buddhist temples indicating to the deity that one has been reverential.

Back on Higashi-oji-dori, bus 5, 206, 207, or a taxi can be taken in either direction toward one's next destination.

TOUR
5

The Pleasure Quarters, the Floating World, and the Gion Shrine

T HE SECTION of Kyoto that is bounded by Sanjo-dori (Third Street) to Shijo-dori (Fourth Street) on both sides of the Kamogawa river can truly be called Kyoto's pleasure quarters. There are historic reasons for this, for the section of the city to the east of the Kamogawa river encompasses the Gion district which, since the late 1500s, has been the geisha and *ochaya* (teahouse) district, and here it was that Kabuki also had its start. Although the ranks of geisha have thinned out in these more modern times, the geisha and the *ochaya* still have their place here despite their dwindling numbers, and Kabuki continues to delight its followers on the stage of Minami-za (South Theater).

The area to the west of the Kamogawa river offers a different type of pleasure since the streets between Karasuma-dori on the west, the Kamogawa river on the east, Shijo-dori on the south, and Oike-dori on the north form a shoppers' paradise. Here department stores and specialty shops can please the most avid of consumers, be they connoisseurs of the finest of crafts, fashion, or the latest in tourist ephemera. Although modern commercialism abounds within this crowded enclave, traditional pleasures are not overlooked. Each year during July, this western sector enjoys the annual Gion Festival when the great Gion carts are pulled through the streets by men dressed in traditional garb in commemoration of the city's deliverance from a plague many centuries ago. That ceremony begins at the Yasaka or Gion Shrine to the east of the river, and it is in this area that the tour begins.

MAIN BUILDINGS AND MAJOR FESTIVALS OF THE YASAKA (GION

The Yasaka (or Gion) Shrine is situated
Shijo-dori and Higashi-oji-dori. It can be
206 or 207 to the Gion bus stop. The shri
No admission fee is charged.

The Yasaka (or Gion) Shrine is one of the most important Shinto shrines in Kyoto and is much beloved by its citizens. As the shrine to the spirit of the god who is honored at the great Gion Festival, it is the starting point for the festival procession that winds its way through the streets of Kyoto every July 17. It is, as well, a special center for worship on New Year's Day and on other traditional occasions.

Reputedly founded in 656, before the creation of Kyoto as a city, the shrine is dedicated to the Shinto deities Susa-no-o (the wayward brother of Amaterasu Omikami, the supposed progenitor of the emperor), his spouse Inadahime-no-Mikoto, and their five sons and three daughters. It became an important center of worship after Kyoto was established as the capital of Japan in the 790s since epidemics were often rampant, and Susa-no-o was regarded as the Shinto god of medicine. An epidemic in 869 led to the origin of the Gion Festival when thousands prayed to Susa-no-o for relief from the spread of the plague. The head priest of the shrine led a procession of citizens through the city as a supplication to the god. The plague ended and the event became a popular festival which has continued ever since.

Under the movement known as Ryobu (dual) Shinto, beginning in the 800s, an attempt was made by the Buddhist clergy to show that the Shinto deities (whom the mass of the people then still preferred to the Buddhist gods) were but temporary manifestations of the major Buddhas and bodhisattvas. Thus, an amalgamation of the two faiths developed, and most Shinto shrines came under the control of Buddhist monks. Even the architecture of many shrines (the Yasaka Shrine for example) took on the style of Buddhist religious buildings. With the restoration of imperial rule in 1868, Buddhism was forced to separate from Shintoism, and Shinto shrines reverted to a non-Buddhist form—albeit certain practices and architectural styles Buddhism were retained. Thus, the Yasaka Shrine became a Shinto shrine once more.

Ro-mon The approach to the shrine from Shijo-dori is by means of a brief set of steps which lead to the Ro-mon, the main two-story gateway built in the style of the Muromachi period (1338–1573) with vermilion posts and white walls. A Shinto guardian in each bay on both sides of the entryway stands guard against any evil influences which may impinge upon these sacred grounds. Once beyond the entry gateway, an additional brief set of steps, guarded by stone *koma-inu* (Korean lion-dogs), leads to a torii and the main area of the shrine.

Haiden Within the shrine grounds, there are a number of buildings both large and small dedicated to various Shinto gods. The main portion of the shrine has a roofed water basin for purification ahead on the right, and to its left in the center of the precinct is the roofed Haiden (Offertory), while the important Honden (Spirit Hall) is further to the left. Beyond the Haiden, to the right, is a roofed ceremonial stage for religious perfor-mances. On the northern edge of the precincts are the storage buildings for the Gion Festival *mikoshi* (portable shrines). Most of the shrine buildings date from a 1654 reconstruction, and some of the *mikoshi* storage units are enhanced with paintings commis-sioned by worshipers of the shrine deities.

Honden The Honden (Spirit Hall), the most important unit, is a single-story building with a half-hipped and half-gabled roof covered with thick wooden shingles. This main structure is painted the vermilion of Shinto buildings and is sixty-nine feet long by fifty-seven feet deep. Three long ropes are suspended from the front overhanging roof with a metal pan-shaped bell at the top of the ropes. These ropes are pulled by worshipers to sound the bell so as to attract the attention of the god of the shrine. They then face the altar within and bow with their hands held in prayer fashion.

On the south side of the grounds, a second entrance to the

shrine is through a thirty-foot-tall stone torii dating from 1646, one of the largest such Shinto stone gateways in Japan. Beyond it, matted casks of saké are found at the side of a large vermilion gate with archers on either side of the entryway.

The shrine is much frequented by citizens of Kyoto, some in modern dress, some in traditional kimono. One of the most charming sights to see is newborn infants being brought to the shrine (often held by proud grandmothers in formal, traditional attire) for registration—or children in formal kimono or *hakama* (formal over-trousers) brought to the shrine in November at the time of the Shichi-go-san (Seven, Five, and Three Year Olds') Festival for blessings given by shrine attendants.

Festivals and Ceremonies   Although there are frequent fair days at the Yasaka Shrine, a number of festivals are outstanding: the New Year Festival (Okera-mairi) at the beginning of January and the Gion Festival in July in particular. On New Year's Eve, a herb called *okera* is burned in the lanterns at the Yasaka Shrine from 8:00 p.m. through to the dawn of New Year's Day. It has been customary in the past to come to the shrine with a thin rope to be lit from the lanterns, or to obtain a few embers from the fires. The flame would then be taken home to be used to light the cooking fire of the New Year. If one's cooking fire were lit from the sacred shrine fire and *zoni* (rice cakes boiled with vegetables) were made over this fire on New Year's Day, health and happiness were bound to ensue throughout the new year.

Hopes for a good year can be further insured by praying at the shrine on New Year's Day. On this occasion, traditional garb is often worn by women, and the *maiko* (apprentice geisha) attend in black kimonos patterned in white. The *maiko* also place ears of rice in their hair to mark this festive occasion.

On February 3 and 4, Setsubun (the beginning of the spring season) celebrations mark the traditional end of the coldest part of winter. Roasted beans are scattered in temples and shrines to drive out demons and to bring in good luck for the new season. The ceremony is celebrated at many temples, and at the Yasaka Shrine an evening bonfire brings the festivities to a close.

Another festival, this one held on May 2, is the Ochatsubo Dochu (Traveling Tea Canisters) ceremony. Each spring, prior to 1868, the shogun required the tea dealers of Uji to present the first tea leaves of the year to his provisioners. The leaves were packed in large ceramic jars. In remembrance of this event, large tea jars are paraded from the Kennin-ji along Yamato-oji-dori to Shijo-dori and thus to the Yasaka Shrine by bearers wearing costumes of the past.

The Gion Festival is the most spectacular of the shrine events. The first ceremony to mark the festival begins on July 2 when the shrine *mikoshi* are taken from their storage sheds and blessed for the coming Gion Festival. On July 10 the most important shrine *mikoshi* is carried to the Kamogawa river for a ceremonial cleansing and purification by the chief priest of the shrine. Afterwards, the *mikoshi* is carried back to the shrine on the shoulders of the young men who took it to the river. On the same day, celebrants in traditional garb welcome three *mikoshi* of the Yasaka Shrine as the Gion Festival season starts. With lanterns on long poles, they accompany the *mikoshi* to City Hall at the intersection of Oike-dori and Kawaramachi-dori. Three dance groups perform in front of the City Hall building. Thereafter, the procession returns to the Yasaka Shrine.

From July 15 to 17, the main events of the Gion Festival occur. This great festival is celebrated by the people of Kyoto and by thousands of visitors who come to the city particularly for this occasion. On July 15 and 16, the festival carts are stationed along Shijo-dori west of the Kamogawa river where they may be viewed closeup. Music and festivities occur each night. On the morning of July 17, the festival parade of the many large and small floats takes place along Kawaramachi-dori and Oike-dori; concession stands along Oike-dori provide seats which may be reserved in advance. This summer festival provides a colorful and intriguing time both for its participants and for those who observe the carts and the costumes of other centuries.

Other festivals and ceremonies occur at the Yasaka Shrine throughout the year. These are listed in the monthly calendar distributed by the hotels and by the Kyoto Tourist Office.

Leaving the Yasaka Shrine from the main entrance at Higashi-oji-dori, Shijo-dori lies straight ahead. This street will be the main route for the next portion of this tour, some diversions to its north or south occurring along the way. The geisha districts of Gion lie to the south of this street while the geisha districts of Shinbashi lie to the north.

THE PLEASURE QUARTERS

Beginning in the late 1500s, with the revival of Kyoto life at the end of a century or more of wars, the original pleasure districts of Kyoto developed on either side of the Kamogawa river just below and above Shijo-dori. Today the geisha quarters, *ochaya*, restaurants, and theaters are still located in these districts.

The pleasure quarters of Kyoto, in particular the Pontocho, Gion, and Shinbashi areas, present aspects of Japanese life that deserve an adequate description. Since the activities of portions of these quarters are by their nature only quasi-public (language, expense, and proper introduction barring most foreigners from the *ochaya* and the world of the geisha), or since the theater performances that offer a sampling of geisha talents and an introduction to tea ceremony are restricted to certain months or seasons of the year, an introduction to the pleasure quarters follows.

Traditionally, the areas on either side of the Kamogawa river at Shijo-dori (as well as the dry areas of the riverbed) became the center of the pleasure quarters of Kyoto from the late 1500s. With the prosperity that began under Hideyoshi in the 1580s and that continued under the Tokugawa shoguns, a new merchant class developed in Kyoto. Although the merchant class was the lowest unit of society, as far as official policy was concerned, the merchants were prosperous and had money to spend. Thus, the shogunate permitted them some leeway in behavior, other than was normally prescribed for their class, in the licensed quarters where they could find entertainment and pleasure.

Four elements composed the *divertissement* of the pleasure quarters. There were the restaurants or teahouses on either side of the river—as well as on the dry riverbed in the summer where dining could take place—and many of these continue to serve the public today along the narrow, stone-paved pathway of Pontocho and on the west bank of the Kamogawa river. There were the *ochaya* in which the geisha and *maiko* (apprentice geisha) entertained the wealthier of Kyoto's pleasure seekers. There were (and are), as well, theaters for Kabuki, Bunraku, and other such forms of entertainment. Lastly, there was the illicit trade of prostitutes (both female and male) of which the puritanical shogunate did not approve but which it condoned in

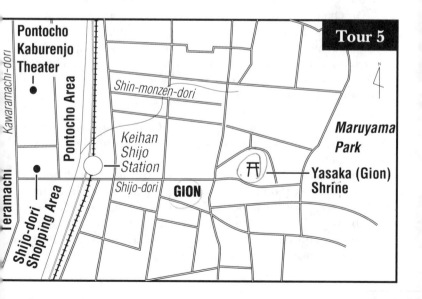

recognition that certain activities could never be fully controlled by either Confucian precepts or governmental decrees.

KABUKI

Kabuki had its beginnings here in the late 1590s when a young woman in the service of the great Shinto shrine of Izumo on the Japan Sea appeared in Kyoto. A performer of sacred Shinto dances, Izumo-no-Okuni began to offer such dances in 1596 in an improvised "theater" on the dry bed of the Kamogawa river in the Shijo-dori district. (A plaque on the west wall of the Minami-za theater at Shijo-dori on the east side of the Kamogawa river commemorates Okuni's performances at this riverbed location.) Okuni and her small group of female dancers performed the *Nenbutsu Odori,* a religious dance which had its roots in the religious "dances" as practiced by Kuya (see Tour 4) many years before. This religious observance had developed into a type of folk dance which, although it had its roots in religious practice, had become a form of popular entertainment as well. (The Obon dances in many communities still follow this tradition.)

In Okuni's hands, the *Nenbutsu Odori* was able to blend folk, Shinto, and Buddhist dance forms into a popular format which was soon imitated by other female performers. The popularity of her dances can be ascertained by the fact that Toyotomi Hideyoshi is said not only to have viewed these performances with pleasure, but that he rewarded Okuni with a coral necklace. From these religious dances, Okuni and her group soon branched out into a type of primitive theater of a farcical nature which came to be known as Kabuki. Many of her skits (for they weren't really plays in an artistic sense) were of an erotic nature concerning the relationship of young men and prostitutes in bath houses and teahouses. (Some of her cohorts were well-suited by inclination and experience to portray aspects of the seamier side of life with great realism.) These farcical skits eventually came to the attention and displeasure of the authorities, and by 1629 the shogunate banned such female performances.

Another form of Kabuki, therefore, developed with young men (many of them very attractive late adolescents) as the actors. Much given to acrobatics and mock sword play, these young actors soon developed a following of their own—particularly among the samurai and Buddhist priests who vied for the young men's charms. These two social classes were not supposed to attend functions that were primarily licensed for the merchant class—the lowest form of society in Tokugawa times. At any rate, attend they did, and many of these attractive youths aroused a homosexual passion among their viewers (homosexuality being accepted by many samurai and priests) and, in the fights that broke out among the members of the audience for the favor of particular actors, there was a breakdown of decorum which the shogunate could not permit. Thus, in 1652 "young men's Kabuki" was banned—but not until after the death of Shogun Tokugawa Iemitsu (1604–51), who reputedly had a certain fondness for youthful actors.

Thereafter, Kabuki was permitted to continue if the performers were adult males—and ostensibly less physically or emotionally attractive to the audience. Women's roles were also taken by males *(onnagata)*, a tradition that continues to this day. By the Genroku period (1658–1710), a full-fledged Kabuki drama had developed with plays being written by capable authors, such as Chikamatsu Monzaemon (1653–1724), and with stage craft that was innovative and spectacular in its use of revolving stages, trapdoors, and other theatrical devices.

THE WORLD OF THE GEISHA

Women did continue to have a part to play in the pleasure quarters (aside from the activities of prostitutes whom society neither recognized nor condoned but who continued to flourish). A group of entertainers known as geisha developed, women of talent who could dance, sing, play traditional instruments, and who could carry on witty conversations—and above all could please the male patrons of the *ochaya* in which they practiced their arts. The role of the geisha was an honorable one, the word itself implying a trained artist. (They were not prostitutes, as is supposed in the West, although they often became the lovers of well-to-do patrons who supported them, the cost of their costumes and general upkeep being exceedingly expensive.)

Two areas became the center of the *ochaya* in which geisha entertained those who could afford an evening of their professional services of song and dance—as well as the delights of the palate as catered to by the *ochaya* owners. These *ochaya* developed both north and south of Shijo-dori—along Hanamikoji-dori on either side of Shijo-dori and along the Shirakawa river to the north of Shijo-dori. This latter came to be known as the Shinbashi (New Bridge) district from the name of the bridge crossing the narrow river. Both the Kamogawa and Shirakawa rivers were much given to flooding; by 1670 an attempt had been made to control the overflowing of these two rivers, and they were both contained within walls. This led to an increase in the land available for development (once the flood plain was narrowed), and an improved and expanded pleasure district resulted on the east side of the Kamogawa river. Teahouses and theaters flourished, and from 1712 the *ochaya* of Gion were licensed for geisha performances by the government.

ICHIRIKI OCHAYA

The areas of Shinbashi (along the Shirakawa river to the north of Shijo-dori) and Gion (south of Shijo-dori) are still the heart of the geisha quarter of Kyoto. While many of the two-story teahouses in these two districts appear to be very old, most of them were built since the great fire of 1864 devastated this area of Kyoto. *Ochaya* are generally wooden two-story, architecturally traditional buildings with protruding, rust-colored, latticed windows *(bengara goshi)* on the first floor and reed screens *(sudare)* for privacy flapping in the breeze on the second floor. *Noren* (a short curtain over the entryway with the name of the establishment upon it) and *inu yarai* ("dog screens," slatted, curved, bamboo barriers which keep dogs and people at a proper distance from the first-floor windows and walls of the building) provide a distinctive and traditional ambiance to the scene.

Several entire streets in the Shirakawa and the Gion areas preserve these traditional buildings, thereby supplying an idea of what Kyoto looked like in days gone by. Today, it is claimed that some one hundred and nineteen *ochaya* exist in Gion where an evening can be spent at a dinner with entertainment by geisha and *maiko*. In 1974 the city of Kyoto placed the Gion and Shinbashi districts under special protection and the areas were made into a preserved district the following year. In 1976, architectural guidelines were set for seven distinct *ochaya* façades, and city-subsidized grants have assisted in the maintenance of the façades of the buildings in these two preserved districts.

Of all these *ochaya*, the three-hundred-year-old Ichiriki on the corner of Shijo-dori and Hanamikoji-dori is perhaps the most noted. It is known not only for its traditional architecture and ambiance, but as a locale where historic events have taken place. Here Oishi Yoshio (1659–1703) led a life of planned dissoluteness, giving himself over to the frivolous life of the pleasure quarters, seemingly drinking to excess—all to disguise his real intentions and thereby mislead the shogunal spies who were observing him.

Oishi was a *ronin*, a masterless samurai who no longer had a lord (daimyo) to report to since his lord had fallen into disgrace and had been forced to commit *seppuku* (ceremonial suicide). Determined to avenge the unfair treatment of his master, Oishi divorced his wife and entered into a life of debauchery to disguise his revengeful intentions. Eventually, Oishi and forty-six other *ronin* had a rendezvous in Edo (Tokyo), killed their master's opponent, and were eventually forced by the shogunate to commit ceremonial suicide. All are buried with their master at Sengaku-ji in Tokyo. (Their story, *The Forty-Seven Ronin*, has become a classic in Japanese literature and a Kabuki play as well.)

Some one hundred and fifty years later, the Ichiriki again

became the center of intrigue. In the mid-nineteenth century, in the latter days of the Tokugawa shogunate, some of the opponents of the Tokugawa government would gather at the Ichiriki under the pretense of a few friends having an enjoyable evening at a geisha party. Their real goal, however, was the overthrow of Tokugawa rule. Their plotting, and that of others of like mind, came to fruition in 1868 when the last shogun signed papers at Nijo Castle in Kyoto dissolving the shogunate and ostensibly returning the emperor to power.

Today the Ichiriki plays host to Japanese power-figures of the business world rather than the political world, but its attraction as one of the prime geisha houses in Kyoto remains. Perhaps Hanamikoji-dori, the street on which the Ichiriki is located to the south of Shijo-dori, is one of the best preserved of the old Gion streets of the *ochaya* and the traditional pleasure quarter of Kyoto. Thus, it is a delightful area architecturally as well as historically. Many of the geisha live along Hanamikoji-dori to the south of the Ichiriki, and in the evening at about 7:30 the *maiko* and geisha begin their walk to the *ochaya* that have requested their services for the evening. Their fine kimono and high coiffure make a delightful sight.

PONTOCHO AREA

The area on both sides of the Kamogawa river thus became the center of entertainment in Kyoto, particularly after legal authorization for geisha entertainment was granted by the shogunate. Today, restaurants (as well as *ochaya*) can be found not only in the Gion/Shinbashi area on the east side of the Kamogawa river but also along Pontocho, a very narrow pedestrian street on the west side of the river. The Pontocho pleasure quarter, once the red-light district of Kyoto, lies between Sanjo-dori and Shijo-dori and is a particularly intriguing section due to its highly colorful illuminated signs. (Prostitution was abolished by law in 1958, but the area has its recent modern "love hotel," as the type has been so aptly nicknamed, where rooms can be rented by the hour.)

The Pontocho area consists of two narrow streets. One is a pedestrian walkway rather than a normal street, a home to many expensive restaurants and bars and the modern replacement for traditional geisha entertainment: hostess clubs. Pontocho is the street closest to and parallel to the Kamogawa river, and many of the restaurants in the old buildings along this stone-paved passageway overlook the river. Some of these establishments have *yuka,* wooden platforms by the river's edge on which one can dine and enjoy the cool breezes. At night in summer, the illuminated signs hanging from each restaurant or bar on Pontocho provide a colorful and striking visual enrichment. Pontocho's parallel companion street to the west is Kiyamachi-dori with its more modern buildings situated along the Takasegawa, the Takase Canal. At night, the canal's dark waters provide an interesting contrast to the colorful, and sometimes garish, illuminated signs of Kiyamachi-dori reflected in the water.

Toward the Sanjo-dori end of Pontocho is the Pontocho Kaburenjo Theater. Each spring (April–May) and autumn (October–November), the theater offers the Kamogawa Odori (Kamogawa River Dances). This theatrical spectacle, which had its beginning in 1872, offers Kyo-mai (Kyoto or Capital Dances) as performed in the traditional geisha manner. Demonstrations of tea ceremony are also provided.

Upon returning to the eastern side of the Kamogawa river, one finds three theaters that offer traditional entertainment. The Minami-za is the oldest theater in Kyoto and in Japan, having first opened its doors in the seventeenth century–although the present building dates from 1925 and was modernized in 1990. The home of traditional Kabuki drama, the highlight of its Kabuki season comes every December at its Kaomise (Face Showing) performances. During this month, the most important stars of Kabuki appear in scenes in which they can demonstrate their prowess as performers.

(A stone monument on the west side of the Minami-za marks the area where Izumo-no-Okuni first perf nascent form of Kabuki, this area once having been a part of the riverbed before the river was walled for protection against flooding and before the area of dry land was extended.)

About 165 feet east of the Minami-za theater on Shijo-dori is the Meyami Jizo Shrine (also known as Chugen-ji) with its front gate and red lanterns. It is believed that the Jizo of this shrine can cure eye disease.

On a side street south of Shijo-dori between Hanami-koji-dori and Higashi-oji-dori are the Gion Kaburenjo Theater and Gion Corner. Each April and May, the Miyako Odori (the Cherry Blossom Dance—Miyako is the old name for Kyoto, so this is really the Capital Dance) is presented by geisha and *maiko*. In the adjacent Gion Corner is the Yasaka Kaikan, a small hall attached to the Gion Kaburenjo which seats some 250 people. From March 1 through November 29, twice each evening, a sample of traditional Japanese arts is performed for visitors to the city. Created by the Kyoto Visitors' Club in 1962, these twice-daily demonstrations of geisha dancing, ancient court music, Bunraku, flower arrangement, and tea ceremony are presented. An English-language commentary is provided. In addition, at the Gion Kaikan hall north of Shijo-dori on Higashi-oji-dori, the Gion Odori performances by geisha and *maiko* take place in October and December.

SHIJO-DORI SHOPPING AREA

The streets from the Kamogawa river west to Karasuma-dori between Shijo-dori and Oike-dori embrace the consumer center of Kyoto. ̄ ̄ ̄ ̄ ̄-dori are a number of the great department

ialty shops which are always thronged with purchasers. Covered arcades on Kyogoku-

-dori between Shijo-dori and Sanjo-dori etween Shijo-dori and Oike-dori provide purchase anything from fine old prints of cheap souvenirs. Movie houses and umber offer further *divertissement,* and the area is always crowded with tourist groups from the provinces, with hundreds of students on school tours, as well as with local citizens.

TERAMACHI

This area of Kyoto became a commercial center fairly late in the city's history. At the time of Hideyoshi (late 1500s), a protective wall was built along the eastern edge of the city—where Kawaramachi-dori now runs. Teramachi (Temple District), the name of this area, is so-called since after 1583, as Toyotomi Hideyoshi rebuilt Kyoto as "his" capital, he had many of the temples that were favored by the people relocated into two areas along Teramachi-dori in the center of Kyoto and Teranouchi-dori in the north central part of the city. Those along Teramachi were primarily of the Jodo sect of Buddhism, while the ones along Teranouchi were of the Nichiren persuasion. Time and fires have seen to the dispersal of many of these temples, but some still remain in this area.

Among the temples in the Teramachi area, perhaps the most famous is that of the Honno-ji because of its associations with Oda Nobunaga. Nobunaga was Hideyoshi's predecessor who ended virtually all the internecine wars of the 1500s. It was at the Honno-ji that Nobunaga was trapped by a traitor and was forced to kill himself and his family, a deed that Hideyoshi avenged. Today it is an association in name only—since the original Honno-ji was located a few streets to the south and west (south of Rokkaku-dori and east of Abura-no-koji-dori) before it burned down, and thus the present temple complex is from post-Nobunaga times.

In the post-Meiji era (after 1868), Kawaramachi-dori was opened as a street as was the Shinkyogoku-dori (New Capital Boundary Avenue). Kawaramachi-dori was to become a street of shops between Oike-dori and Shijo-dori. In addition, Kyogoku-dori and Shinkyogoku-dori were created after 1871 and became known as "Theater Street" by foreigners who came to Kyoto. It is still an entertainment area although small shops, many specializing in tourist souvenirs of an ephemeral nature, and restaurants rather than theaters predominate. It is a thriving and often crowded area and is still popular with Kyoto residents as well as Japanese school tour groups.

One of the interesting byways of central Kyoto is Nishiki-koji-dori which houses the Nishiki-koji Market (Brocade Alley Market). It is one street north of Shijo-dori, and it runs from Shinkyogoku-dori (a torii gate stands at the entry to the street before the small Nishiki Tenman-gu [Nishiki Tenman Shrine]) to Takakura-dori near the Daimaru Department Store. Since the middle ages, there has been a public market in central Kyoto. Virtually all of the city was destroyed in the Onin Wars of 1467 to 1477; thus, the market was reestablished in the late 1500s when Hideyoshi replanned the city. There are about 150 dealers in food along this 492-foot-long, stone-paved street. Most of the shops remain open until early evening, and the street presents a fascinating aspect of everyday life. (Most shops close on Wednesday; fish stores are closed on Sundays.)

THE TOKAIDO ROAD

This walk will eventually become a complete circle, returning to the Yasaka Shrine, and thus it next leads east on Sanjo-dori (Third Street) which runs through the arcaded streets mentioned above (and is itself arcaded for a short while) as it heads eastward toward the Kamogawa river and the Sanjo Bridge. The Sanjo Bridge over the Kamogawa river was originally built at the order of Toyotomi Hideyoshi in 1589, and after 1600 it marked the beginning of the Tokaido Road (Eastern Highway), the 320-mile route with fifty-three relay stations between the emperor's capital in Kyoto and the shogun's headquarters in Edo (Tokyo). This link became a major route of commerce between 1603 and 1868 as travel on Sanjo-dori headed east to the valley between Kyoto, Lake Biwa, and the Tokaido Road. Its importance as a major highway diminished in the late nineteenth century with the coming of the railroad, and its eclipse was virtually completed when the new expressway to Kyoto entered the prefecture to the south of the city in the middle of the twentieth century. The very first milestone of the route, from which all distances were measured, stood at the eastern end of the bridge, today a memento of a vanished era.

Later times have, of course, necessitated the replacement of Hideyoshi's bridge by a structure that can carry the heavy traffic of a mechanized age. Only the *giboshi,* the bronze ornaments atop the posts of the railings, go back to the sixteenth century, all gifts of the leading daimyo of those days. Some of the stone pillars at each end of the bridge are original as well, the other stones having been used for stepping stones in the pond in the garden of the Heian Shrine when it was created at the end of the nineteenth century.

At the southeast corner of the Sanjo Bridge, amidst the confusion of the overhead electrical wires, the tracks of the Keihan rail line to Otsu, the terminal for the many buses, and the underground railway station, is a statue of a samurai bowing toward the northwest. The statue commemorates Takayama Masayuke (1747–93), also known as Takayama Hikokuro, who came to Kyoto when he was eighteen and there began to delve into the history of the nation. He was astonished to discover that the shogunate had usurped the power of the emperor and had controlled the country. (He did not realize how powerless the emperor had been through most of the centuries of the existence of the imperial line.) He therefore traveled through the various provinces in an attempt to revive the prestige of the imperial house.

On his return to Kyoto, he fell upon his knees at the Sanjo Bridge to bow toward the emperor in his palace to the northwest in order to manifest the esteem due the imperial house, as he is still bowing in this monument. Eventually, he offered himself as a symbolic sacrifice to the imperial cause by committing *seppuku* (ceremonial suicide) for the sake of imperial rule—one of the first overt acts of challenge to the shogun's supremacy. In honor of the memory of this exemplar of fidelity to imperial rule, the statue was erected at the corner of the Sanjo Bridge after the Meiji Restoration of 1868.

STREETS OF ANTIQUES

Although antique and curio shops abound in various areas of Kyoto, three streets in the Gion/Shinbashi district are noted for the proliferation of such stores. Nawate-dori is one such street, running north and south one street east of the Kamogawa river and south from the transportation hub at Sanjo-dori. Parallel to it is Hanami-koji-dori to the east, and then two other streets which run from Nawate-dori to Higashi-oji-dori. These two streets are Furomonzen-dori and Shinmonzen-dori, also a center for major antique shops. Furomonzen-dori is the second street from the transport square, while Shinmonzen-dori is the next street south. The latter street has the greatest concentration of such specialty shops.

In the shops of these three streets, the variety and splendor of Japanese arts and crafts can be obtained for a goodly price— since such antiquities are in great demand by connoisseurs of Japanese art. Among the treasures found here are screens *(byobu)*, woodblock prints, chests *(tansu)*, Imari ware, Kutani ware, pearls, porcelains, scrolls, wood carvings, netsuke, Noh masks, fans, obi, kimono, brocades, silk textiles, lacquerware, jade, silk embroideries, damascene ware, and Buddhist religious art.

The merchants of the area issue a brochure describing the stores of the district, a brochure that is available at hotels, at the Tourist Information Center downtown, as well as at member shops.

Moving further south on Nawate-dori beyond Furomonzen-dori and Shinmonzen-dori, the fourth street on the left when coming from the Sanjo-dori area, is Shirakawa-minami-dori which runs parallel to the narrow, canalized Shirakawa river. With its willow trees and old houses with their rolled-down blinds on the second floor, a remnant of the other traditional teahouse area remains. As a center of the geisha quarters, it was loved by the poet Isamu Yoshii (1886–1960), and one of his poems has been inscribed on a stone in this area:

> No matter what they say,
> I love Gion.
> Even in my sleep
> The sound of water
> Flows beneath my pillow.

Thus on November 8 at eleven in the morning, geisha and *maiko* perform a tea ceremony at the stone monument which records his affection for the pleasure quarters and its traditional delights, delights the geisha continue to maintain.

Continuing south to Shijo-dori, a turn to the left leads back to the Yasaka Shrine at Higashi-oji-dori where a bus or a taxi can be obtained at the conclusion of this tour.

TOUR
6

Awata Palace,
Fine Arts and Crafts,
and the Martial Arts

平安神宮　岡崎公園　青蓮院

J INGU-MICHI, which is central to this tour, provides everything from museums to a zoo to a concert hall to a center for the martial arts. It also has a shrine and a temple, both of which once served as palaces. One would think that a temple was a temple while a palace was a palace, but this was not always true in Kyoto. The imperial palace had a periodic propensity for being destroyed by fire, and, from time to time, the emperor and his court had to find temporary refuge while the palace was rebuilt. Such refuge could be found in a temple which was temporarily sequestered by the court and, on more than one occasion, the Shoren-in temple was so honored. As a result, the temple has enjoyed not only imperial favor, but has been modified to suit imperial tastes, and it still preserves some of the splendor with which the court endowed it.

That portion of Jingu-michi on which the Shoren-in (or Awata Palace as it is also known) is located leads to the north to the cultural center which has developed in Okazaki Park over the past one hundred years. At the north end of this street, beyond a gigantic torii which crosses the road, lies another palace, this one being a memorial to the imperial palace of early Kyoto rather than a residence for royalty. The imperial palace of the late 700s has long since been destroyed by fire, and its original location was abandoned by the court centuries ago.

At the end of the 1800s, on the occasion of the 1,100th anniversary of the founding of the capital at Kyoto, a portion of the original palace was reconstructed in two-thirds scale as a shrine to the emperor Kammu who had established Kyoto as Japan's capital and who had the first imperial palace built in the city. Thus the Heian Shrine, located at the end of Jingu-michi, provides an idea of what the early palace looked like and also serves as a shrine to the spirit of the first and last emperors to reside in Kyoto when it was the capital of the nation. More noteworthy than the building, however, is the lovely garden behind it and to its side.

Between the temple/palace of the Shoren-in and the partially reconstructed palace of Heian times (794–1185) lies the Okazaki cultural center. Here one can find museums of contemporary art, of traditional arts and crafts, and of general art, as well as one of the first public libraries in Japan. A cultural hall for musical events and additional private museums border the area as does the Hall of Martial Arts, a unit that once was a part of the early palace and today continues the tradition of the martial arts still enjoyed by many Japanese. The Kyoto Zoo can be found in Okazaki Park and the firemen's display of skill and derring-do is also held here at the beginning of each year.

SHOREN-IN (AWATA PALACE)

The Shoren-in (Awata Palace) is on Jingu-michi, the street that runs south from the Heian Shrine to Maruyama Park. Buses 11, 12, 18, 202, 203, 206, or 207 take one to the Chion-in-mae bus stop from which one walks east to Jingu-michi (in front of the Chion-in) and then turns left (north) to the Shoren-in. Alternatively, one can take bus 5 to the Jingu-michi bus stop and then walk south on Jingu-michi to the temple. The Shoren-in is open from 9:00 a.m. to 5:00 p.m., closed on October 4. Entry fee.

An exquisite former palace of the *monzeki* princes (sons of the imperial family who became abbots), as well as the sometime residence of the imperial ruler when the imperial palace burned, the Shoren-in has a lovely Muromachi-period (1334–1568) garden surrounding a pond. The site has been a Tendai sect temple for centuries and has served as an imperial palace as well.

The Shoren-in had its beginnings as a Kyoto residence for Buddhist priests of the Tendai sect from the great Tendai monastery of Enryaku-ji on Mt. Hiei. Priests from the Enryaku-ji often came to Kyoto in the 800s and later to lecture, to teach, to hold memorial services for the dead, or to pray for the prosperity of individual aristocratic families as requested by members of the nobility. Thus, a need for housing for such priests on these occasions became a necessity, and, as a result, the Juraku-in was created at the site of the future Shoren-in to house the priests from the mountain monastery.

In 879 the emperor Seiwa retired, built a detached palace, the Awata Palace, on the grounds of the Juraku-in, and became a priest in the temple, a practice that was to become a normal procedure for retired emperors in the future. The present Shoren-in was founded in 1144, and in 1153 the emperor Toba ordered that new buildings be constructed. Two years later the emperor's seventh son, Prince Kakukai (1134–81), became the head priest and second abbot of the Shoren-in. Thus began a tradition of the temple being a *monzeki* temple; that is, a temple whose abbot was a member of the imperial family. This heritage lasted until 1868 when the *monzeki* tradition was broken by the new Meiji government as part of its anti-Buddhist program. In 1868, the princes returned to secular life, and the tie to the imperial family ended.

After paying the entry fee at the booth, one walks to the entrance to the right where shoes are removed. One then proceeds along the corridors to the two main buildings or to the garden viewing room which also serves as a tea room. A roofed corridor to the left of the entryway leads to a second corridor on the right and to the Kogosho (Small Palace), a lovely little building with a veranda on three of its sides. The corridor leading ahead from the entry brings one to the Shinden, the main palace structure.

Shinden   The original Shinden, the main palace structure, was built at an early time as a copy in miniature of an imperial residence, even to the cherry tree on the left and the wild orange tree to the right in front of the building. Originally, the forecourt, which holds these two ceremonial trees, was composed of white sand, but the shade from the huge camphor tree within the grounds has led to the sand being covered with cedar moss. Destroyed in the Onin War of the late 1400s, the Shinden was quickly reconstructed. Then, in the seventeenth century, the daughter of Hidetada, the second Tokugawa shogun, became a consort of the emperor Go-Mizuno-o (reigned 1611–29), and a palatial mansion was built for her at the imperial palace. When the structure was no longer used, portions of it were given to various temples, and the unit which came to the Shoren-in replaced the Shinden. It became an imperial palace in actuality in 1788 when the empress Go-Sakuramachi moved here temporarily after the imperial palace burned in the great Tenmei fire of that year. A subsequent fire in 1893 destroyed the building, and two years later the present structure was erected.

The present Shinden is enriched with the earlier art of Tosa Mitsunobo (1434–1525) and Kano Eitoku (1543–90), among others. Mitsunobo painted the *fusuma* (sliding panels) in the main entrance while Eitoku is represented in the Royal Messenger Room, both on the west side of the building. The three main rooms of the Shinden face south and have corridors on all sides, the north corridor being an internal one while the other three are on the periphery of the building. Today one enters the Shinden by means of the wooden-floored corridor which runs along the east side of the Shinden from the rear of the building to the front.

The interior rooms are tatami-matted, and the first room one comes to (the southeast room) is known as the Ao Fudo (Blue Fudo) Room. It has *chigaidana* (staggered shelving) on the left one-third of the rear wall, while the other two-thirds consist of a large tokonoma which has the painting of the Ao Fudo who protects against evil spirits. The most impressive Heian-period portrait of Fudo, the original painting (now in the Kyoto National Museum) is from the second half of the eleventh century and is in color on silk. It is 6.6 feet high by 4.8 feet wide. The Ao Fudo has a blue body with a contrasting orange garment; red flames rise behind his blue body instead of from the normal *mandorla* (aureole). His left hand holds a sword while his right hand grasps a rope. Before him are his two *doji* attendants, a boy and an old man, Seitaka and Kongara.

Kinkaku-ji.

Ginkaku-ji.

The dry garden at the Zenrin-ji.

Dragon fountain at the Kiyomizu-dera.

Kiyomizu-dera.

Bronze statue of
Toyotomi Hideyoshi,
Hokoku Shrine.

Hokoku Shrine.

Shinsen-en.

Nanzen-ji garden.

Deva King at the Ninna-ji.

Jizo statues at Joju-in.

Boy's Day offerings.

A street in Gion.

Hozugawa river, Arashiyama.

The middle room is the altar room, the rear section having *ihai* (mortuary tablets) on either side of an Amida image in memory of the prince/abbots of the temple. The third room is called the Pine Beach Room from the painting by Sumiyoshi Gukei of a beach and a pine tree on a gold ground. The cedar doors outside this room have quaint paintings of the Gion Festival floats, also by the same artist. Behind these three rooms is the internal north corridor previously mentioned and then a ten-mat room with a *kago* (a large, closed palanquin with the imperial chrysanthemum crest) in it. This heavy vehicle stands out against the background of the white *fusuma* on three sides of the room with their paintings of storks among pine and cherry trees. A Kara-mon (Chinese-style gateway) to the Shinden is on this west side of the building. It marks the end of a path from the large Kara-mon in the external wall to the grounds, obviously a onetime entrance to the Shinden for its imperial occupants and royal messengers.

Kogosho   The Kogosho was originally a portion of the imperial palace, and the present tatami-matted building was moved to this site beside the Ryushin Pond (Dragon's Heart Pond) at the request of Empress Go-Sakuramachi (1762–70) when the temple became her temporary imperial palace. After her departure, the Kogosho served as the living quarters for the imperial abbots.

The Kogosho is separated into three tatami-matted rooms by its *fusuma*. These are approached by way of a wooden-floored veranda/corridor which can be separated from the three rooms by movable shoji panels. The audience room at the east end, nearest the pond, has a raised platform in its inner area on which the empress or the prince/abbots would be seated. Behind it is a decorative alcove or tokonoma whose rear wall is decorated with flowers on a gold background. To the right of the tokonoma are *chigaidana* shelves with a painted tree as a background while birds are painted on the cupboard doors at the bottom of the *chigaidana*, the paintings being by Kano Motonobu (1476–1559). Two *fusuma* and two cedar doors separate this inner area of the audience room from the main portion of the tatami-matted building. These two *fusuma* are decorated with a domestic scene of women with children while the two wooden doors display a painting of a cart with a bouquet (the left side) and a loom (on the right).

The middle of the three rooms has a painting of a waterfall and a pine tree by Kano Motonobu while the third room has two cedar doors painted with birds and trees closing off the rear area. The entire interior of the Kogosho can be closed off from its wooden-floored verandas and corridors by shoji.

Shijoko-do   The Shijoko-do is a small, square building, situated behind the Kogosho, with Zen-style cusped (bell-shaped) windows and a pyramidal, tiled roof topped with the large flaming jewel such as is found on memorial buildings. This building is the heart of the temple since it holds an image of the Shijoko Buddha. Here prayers were said for the welfare of the imperial house and the nation.

Gardens of the Shoren-in   The roofed corridor which connects the main entrance with the Kogosho and the Shinden leads at its east and north end to a large room from which one can view the Kogosho and the gardens. Tea may be obtained here, and a small counter sells guidebooks to the temple as well as small religious articles. The gardens of the Shoren-in are credited to Soami (1472–1525) and Kobori Enshu (1579–1647). Thought to have been created between 1443 and 1489, probably by Soami, the Ryushin Pond (Pond of the Dragon's Heart) and Senshin Waterfall (a three-level stone waterfall which faces the boat landing stone) were meant to be viewed from the Kogosho. A thirteen-tiered stone pagoda stands just beyond the pond while a small bridge crosses one end of the water. The gardens were damaged in the 1893 fire and reconstituted in 1909 by Ogawa Jihei.

The slope of the hill behind the pond is planted with Kirishima azaleas from the mountain of that name. A path leads through the garden, around the lake, and up the hillside, passing en route the Kobun-tei, a small building to the north of the Ryushin Pond. Created as a study for the abbot between 1764 and 1771, it has an altar as well as three places in which tea can be made. In the late eighteenth century, when the empress Go-Sakuramachi was in residence at the temple, she used the building as a study. It also has been used as a teahouse. The garden and pond are lovely at all times, but they are particularly attractive in early April when the cherry blossoms cover the trees and again in autumn when the maples brighten the hillside with their gold and red leaves.

While they are not part of the garden, the five, huge, old camphor trees of the Shoren-in are noted. Four of these giant trees are just outside the temple walls, while one is next to the Shinden. One of the four "outside" trees is at the entry gate—a gate that was formerly the kitchen gate but which now serves as the main entrance to the temple grounds. The long, roofed gate to the right of the present entry, above the wide, stone steps, was the original entrance to the temple.

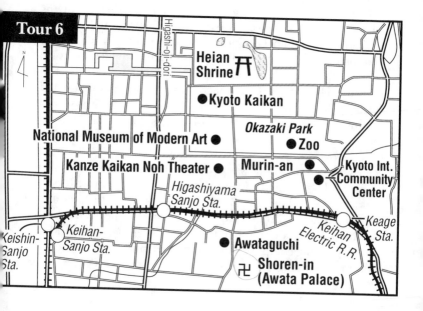

AWATAGUCHI

Leaving the Shoren-in and walking north on Jingu-michi, the next cross-street marks the Awataguchi area which has long been an entryway to Kyoto from the east. Here along Sanjo-dori lay the old Tokaido highway with its flow of traffic to Edo under the Tokugawa shoguns. Until the end of the last century, much of this portion of Kyoto lay beyond the built-up part of the city, and the area was more noted for its temples to the east, north, and south, or for the famous swordsmiths who followed their craft in the vicinity.

In the 1870s, with the Meiji Restoration, the government levied its restrictive laws against Buddhist temples and monasteries, and much temple land in this district was alienated and became available for private or civic development. Many estates of wealthy or noble individuals came into being and, by the turn of the century, the area to the north of Sanjo-dori also had its beginning as a cultural center. The Kyoto Municipal Public Library, one of the first public libraries in Japan, was begun in 1872 and found a home along what was to become Jingu-michi. The anniversary of Kyoto's 1,100th year as a city (all but twenty-five of which had been spent as the imperial capital) was further commemorated in 1894 when Okazaki Park was laid out north of Sanjo-dori in conjunction with the construction of the Heian Shrine. The partial reconstruction of the original Daigoku-den (Great Hall of State of the imperial palace) served also as a shrine to the first emperor to reside in Kyoto as the capital. Nine years later, a portion of the adjacent area became the home of the first municipal zoo.

By 1933 a new note was added to the park and to the shrine surroundings when the Kyoto Municipal Art Museum was opened, and two years later the Butoku-den center for the traditional martial arts was brought to the west side of the Heian Shrine grounds. An exhibition hall had been developed as an addition to the growing complex, a multipurpose unit, and as with all such multiuse buildings, its acoustics were not satisfactory for musical presentations. In 1960 a proper theater for musical and other related events found a new home in the Kyoto Kaikan (Kyoto Hall). By 1963 a Museum of Modern Art was added to the complex, joined in 1976 by the Traditional Industry Museum and the Nishijin Design Center. The area was further enriched by the positioning of the Kanze School of Noh in the Kanze Kaikan (Kanze Hall) on Niomon-dori, a school whose beginnings go back to the 1300s. The Fujii Art Museum settled here as well. In 1989 the Kyoto International Community Center made its appearance not too far from this cultural agglomeration, providing for diversified cultural offerings.

Before heading into the cultural center of Okazaki Park, it is worth turning to the east at Niomon-dori, one street to the north of Sanjo-dori, to visit one of the estates that came into being after 1868 when temple lands were confiscated by the Meiji government or when temples had to sell portions of their property so as to support themselves. Industrialists and government officials were able to obtain land in this area into which Kyoto was spreading as a city. One of these fortunate officials was Duke Aritomo Yamagata who created the Murin-an villa.

MURIN-AN VILLA AND GARDEN

The Murin-an is north of Sanjo-dori and south of Niomon-dori just before Shirakawa-dori. Walk two streets east on Niomon-dori from its intersection with Jingu-michi and then turn to the right. The entrance to the Murin-an garden is down the side street on the right, and it is open from 9:00 a.m. to noon and 1:00 p.m. to 4:00 p.m., closed on Mondays and during the New Year holiday period. Entry fee.

In the late 1800s, the Nanzen-ji sold off some of its land, a result of economic necessity under the punitive attitude toward Buddhist temples taken by the Meiji government. Some of the land was purchased by Duke Aritomo Yamagata (1838–1922), a Meiji statesman and sometime prime minister. The Murin-an villa was begun in 1894 by Yamagata, but its construction was interrupted by Yamagata's absence from Kyoto during the Sino-Japanese War. On his return, the villa was completed in 1896.

The garden, finished in 1898, was designed by Yamagata and created with the assistance of Ogawa Jihei. It is a comparatively modern garden which varies from traditional garden planning guidelines by including unusual plants and an open lawn. The garden is in the shape of an elongated triangle about three-fourths of an acre in size, but it seems larger than it is since it uses the device of borrowed scenery from the adjacent Higashiyama mountains. A stream runs through the gardens, its water coming from the nearby Biwako-sosui canal. Laid out on a slight slope, the water runs in three cascades into a pond and thence into the garden stream. A large rock—so large that it had to be dragged into place by twenty oxen—is one of the important elements of the garden.

The villa is composed of three buildings, a traditional two-story main house and a two-story Western-style building; in the garden there is a teahouse modeled after an example of the Yabunouchi School of Tea.

As a minister of state, Yamagata was involved not only in the Sino-Japanese War, but in the Russo-Japanese War of 1905 as well. Just before that latter conflict, the Murin-an Conference was held on the second floor of the building on the western side of the villa. It was here that an aggressive Japanese foreign policy was determined upon by Prime Minister Taro Katsura; Foreign Minister Jutaro Komura; Hirobumi Ito, who led the Seikyu-kai political party; and Marshal Aritomo Yamagata, who was a military man as well as a prime minister.

Yamagata died in 1922, and in 1941 the Murin-an was given to the city of Kyoto which maintains it as a cultural asset for the public. The teahouse is available, for a fee, for private or public use as are the Japanese-style rooms of the main house.

A short walk from the Murin-an brings one to the Kyoto International Community Center (Kyoto Kokusai Koryu Kaikan) where programs of interest are available.

KYOTO INTERNATIONAL COMMUNITY CENTER

The Kyoto International Community Center is located at the eastern edge of Kyoto between Niomon-dori and Sanjo-dori. A walk east on Niomon-dori to Shirakawa-dori and then a turn south brings one to the Center. Activities and their schedules are listed in the English-language tourist publications available in Kyoto.

In September 1989, the large International Community Center was opened by the city of Kyoto in the eastern portion of the city. As its name implies, it is meant to serve the growing international community in Kyoto and to provide educational and cultural activities on Japanese and international topics. A varied program is offered, and schedules of events may be obtained from the center. The building houses a library, meeting rooms, computer and video terminals, and an intimate stage for dramatic productions, poetry readings, lectures, recitals, and other educational or cultural activities.

Returning along Sanjo-dori or Niomon-dori to Jingu-michi, a turn to the right on Jingu-michi brings one to the Okazaki Park cultural center.

OKAZAKI PARK AND ITS MUSEUMS

Performances or exhibitions at the museums or halls below are listed in the English-language newspapers and in the listing of events distributed by the Tourist Information Center and the City Tourist Office, available at most hotels and at the Information Centers. Bus 5 or 32 will leave one at the Kyoto Kaikan Bijutsukan-mae bus stop.

Okazaki Park   Okazaki Park (Okazaki Koen) was opened in 1904 and consists of twenty-one acres along the Biwako-sosui canal which brings water to Kyoto from Lake Biwa on the other side of the Higashiyama mountain range. In springtime, the cherry blossoms and, in the fall, the maple leaves of the trees in the park and in the zoo make the area a colorful and delightful place.

Fujii Museum   The Fujii Museum (Yurinkan) is off Niomon-dori on the south side of the street before the entrance to Okazaki Park; the entry to the building is at the rear. The museum is open from noon to 3:00 p.m. on the first and third Sunday of each month, but is closed in January and August. The museum will be opened upon a written request submitted a week in advance of the requested visit. No entry fee is charged, but a contribution is welcomed. The Fujii Museum is a private museum dedicated to Chinese art. Its holdings range from early bronzes through ceramics, paintings, jade, porcelains, furniture, costumes, and other aspects of the art of China. Its paintings are primarily from the Ming and Ching eras. Some bronzes from India and early mirrors of Japanese provenance are held as well. For the better protection of the collections, the museum may be closed during inclement weather.

Kanze Kaikan Noh Theater   The Kanze Hall, on the south side of Niomon-dori and west of Jingu-michi, is a center for performances of traditional Noh and Kyogen. The Kanze School of Noh, begun by Kan'ami (1333–84) and then developed by his son Zeami (1363–1443) is one of five schools of Noh drama.

Kyoto Municipal Art Museum   The Municipal Art Museum (Kyoto-shi Bijutsukan), opened in 1933, lies on the eastern side of Jingu-michi, the north-south street in the middle of the Okazaki cultural area. It is the first building on the right (the east side) of Jingu-michi after Niomon-dori. The museum is open from 9:30 a.m. to 5:00 p.m., except on Mondays and from December 25 to January 3. The museum is open on Mondays when that day is a national holiday, but then closed the next day. Admission ranges from free to a charge of varying levels depending on the exhibition being shown.

The museum's holdings are primarily in nineteenth- (post-1868) and twentieth-century Japanese and Western paintings, sculpture, and handicrafts. Aside from showing portions of its own collections, the halls are used for traveling or loan exhibitions as well as the work of local artists.

Kyoto Prefectural Public Library   The Kyoto Prefectural Public Library, opposite the Municipal Art Museum, was first opened in 1872 and is one of the oldest such institutions in Japan. The monument to an Occidental in front of the library is that of Gottfried Wagner, a German who was brought to Kyoto in 1878 to help introduce new techniques in ceramic making and in the dyeing of fabrics.

Kyoto National Museum of Modern Art   Established in 1963 and rebuilt in 1986, the four-story museum designed by Fumihiko Maki is on the west side of Jingu-michi just north of Niomon-dori. It is open from 9:30 a.m. to 4:30 p.m. (until 7:30 p.m. on Fridays), except for Monday and the New Year holiday. Open on Monday if that day is a national holiday, but then closed the next day. Entry fee.

The museum (Kyoto Kokuritsu Kindai Bijutsukan) has an extensive collection of contemporary Japanese prints, paintings, sculpture, ceramics, lacquer work, and other crafts. It is particularly rich in the ceramic artistry of Kawai Kanjiro as well as the works of Hamada Shoji. In addition, the museum collects modern art from throughout the world, and its photographic collection, based on the Arnold Gilbert collection of Chicago from the late nineteenth century, is noted. The large and spacious halls of this modern building are used to mount major exhibitions from Japan and abroad.

Public Exhibition Hall   The Public Exhibition Hall (Kangyo Kaikan) on Nijo-dori to the west of Jingu-dori holds exhibitions of a commercial, educational, or cultural nature.

Kyoto Museum of Traditional Industry and Nishijin Design Center The Museum of Traditional Industry which opened in 1976 is in Okazaki Park at Nijo-dori. The museum is open from 9:00 a.m. to 5:00 p.m., closed on Mondays, except on national holidays, and from December 28 through January 3. Admission free.

The Museum of Traditional Industry exhibits and offers demonstrations of the making of those traditional crafts for which Kyoto has been noted. These include silk, bamboo, lacquer, paper, ceramics, damascene ware, dolls, cabinetry, and Nishijin weaving on Jacquard looms. The crafts are available for purchase as well. A replica of an "eel house" or "bedrooms for eels," the traditional, narrow, Kyoto house, has been built on the lower level of the museum. The museum building is a striking modern architectural unit with a curved lower level and a square upper part. The Nishijin Design Center on the third floor of the Museum of Traditional Industry offers special exhibitions.

Kyoto Kaikan The Kyoto Kaikan is a multipurpose building used for national and international meetings, for exhibitions, and as a concert hall and a theater. Built in 1960 by architect Maekawa Kunio, a pupil of Le Corbusier, it contains two concert chambers and a conference hall large enough for 2,500 people. It is a center for musical performances for the city.

Kyoto Municipal Zoo The municipal zoo, which was created in 1903, lies behind the Kyoto Municipal Art Museum to the east of Jingu-michi in Okazaki Park. It is open from 9:00 a.m. to 4:00 p.m., but closed on Mondays. Its cherry trees in the spring and its maples in the autumn provide a colorful backdrop. Entry fee.

Martial Virtue Hall Built in 1935, the Martial Virtue Hall (Butoku-den) is located in the northwest corner of the Okazaki cultural complex to the west of the Heian Shrine. The Butoku-den serves as a school for fencing, jujitsu, and archery every day except Sundays and holidays. The annual competition in these skills is held here from May 4 each year.

HEIAN SHRINE

The Heian Shrine is in the northern portion of the Okazaki cultural area. Take bus 5 or 32 to the Kyoto Kaikan Bijutsu-kan-mae bus stop. The shrine entrance is at the head of Jingu-michi, beyond the huge red torii that towers over the street. The shrine is open from 8:30 a.m. to 5:00 p.m. from April through October and from 8:30 a.m. to 4:30 p.m. from November through March. Entry to the main part of the grounds is without charge, but there is an entry fee for the gardens.

Kyoto had been the imperial capital of Japan from 794 to 1868 until the capital was moved to Tokyo on the demise of the Tokugawa shogunate and the beginning of the Meiji Restoration. The loss of the seat of government was a shock to citizens of Kyoto since the city had been the imperial and cultural center of the nation for over one thousand years. The combination of the court and the great temples had enlivened and enriched the life of the city; now only the temples remained and were under attack from a new government which was oriented to the Shinto faith and was anti-Buddhist.

The court may have disappeared, but Kyoto's heritage was a fact that could not be ignored. In 1892 it was determined that the 1,100th anniversary of the founding of the city needed to be celebrated, and thus it was decided to re-erect a scaled-down version of the Daigoku-den, the Palace of the Hall of State, of the original capital of 794. Consideration was given to creating the replica on the site of the initial palace in the north-central area of the city (north of the Nijo Castle), but finally the decision was reached to place the project in the Okazaki area.

The rebuilt, smaller edition of the Hall of State was dedicated to the memory of the emperor Kammu (737–806) who had created the city of Heiankyo (Kyoto) in 794. In 1940, under wartime nationalism, the emperor Komei (reigned 1846–67), the father of the emperor Meiji and the last emperor to reside permanently in Kyoto as the capital, was enshrined here also. Thus, the spirits of these two emperors are in the Heian Shrine. The rebuilt Daigoku-den burned in 1976 and was reconstructed three years later.

The creation of a portion of the palace of Heiankyo in 1895 was accomplished on a two-thirds scale of the original structure. The Daigoku-den, the East and West Main Halls, the Ote-mon (Main Gate), the corridors connecting the Ote-mon and the Daigoku-den, and the Soryu and Byakko towers of the corridors were rebuilt. A purification water basin lies to the left front of the Ote-mon gate outside of the grounds proper.

In 1929, a huge concrete torii bearing the imperial sixteen-petal chrysanthemum in gold was constructed a good distance from Heian Shrine on Jingu-michi. The torii stands 80 feet high and the top rail is 111 feet long.

The shrine (and this is a Shinto shrine with a worship area at the innermost portion of the grounds) is entered through the Ote-mon, a two-story gate which is a replica of the main gate of the original palace grounds. This vermilion-painted structure with a blue tile roof has corridors extending to the east and west and thence to the north toward the Daigoku-den. The East and West Main Halls stand before the north-south corridors just beyond the Ote-mon. The ground of the forecourt between the corridors, the gate, and the Daigoku-den to the north is covered with white sand. At the end of the north-south corridors are two towers in the Chinese style, the Soryu-ro (Blue Dragon) on the east (right) and the Byakko-ro (White Tiger) on the west. In front of the Ote-mon to the west is the roofed purification basin.

Daigoku-den   At the far end of the courtyard is the Daigoku-den which was the main government hall where the emperor held official business of state. When the Daigoku-den burned in 1177, it was never replaced—until this scaled-down version was created. The present building is 110 feet long, 40 feet wide, and 55 feet high. As with the Ote-mon, the structure is vermilion with a blue tile roof. To the east side of the front steps is a cherry tree, while to the west is a citrus tree, two traditional plantings as existed in the early days of the palace.

Honden   The Honden (Spirit Hall) which holds the spirits of the two emperors is behind the Daigoku-den. Its innermost sector is an unpainted structure of *hinoki* (cypress) wood 27 feet by 28 feet which is not open to the public and is surrounded by a wooden fence. The Honden was constructed in traditional Shinto style with vermilion posts and beams, white plaster, green barred windows, and a tiled roof. Before the Honden in the Daigoku-den is the Haiden (Oratory) where people facing the Honden can pray.

Heian Garden   The entry to the gardens (admission fee) is to the left when facing the Daigoku-den. The garden was designed by a modern landscape gardener, Ogawa Jihei, who attempted to keep to the spirit of Heian gardens. Thus, the 322,928-square-foot garden is centered on a large pond, the Seiho Pond, as would have been true one thousand years ago. The first part of the garden is a stroll garden with many cherry trees and eventually a small pond. The path then leads on to the Seiho Pond, which is connected with the Soryu-ike (Pond of the Green Dragon) by the Garyu-kyo (Dragon Stepping Stones) which provide a "path" across the water. (These stones once formed the base to the Sanjo-dori Bridge from Hideyoshi's time [1589] and became available when the bridge was modernized at the end of the nineteenth century.) A roofed bridge built about 1910 in the Chinese style, the Taihei-kaku (Bridge of Peace), crosses the lake. It is topped by a phoenix, and it bears a resemblance in style to both the Gold and Silver Pavilions. Divided into four sections (east, west, north, and south), the garden is lovely in all seasons: in the spring when the weeping cherry trees of the south garden and the azaleas are in bloom, in the summer when the iris and the water lilies provide a visual delight, in the autumn with the color of the maple trees enriching the gardens, and in the winter when snow blankets the buildings and the garden.

Transportation by bus 5 or 32 from the Kyoto Kaikan Bijutsukan-mae bus stop or buses on Higashi-oji-dori can be taken to various sectors of the city from the Okazaki Park complex.

TOUR
7

The Silver Pavilion
and
the Philosopher's Path

銀閣寺　哲学の道　法然院　安楽寺

THE SHISHIGATANI area along the foot of the Higashiyama mountains in eastern Kyoto is one of the more delightful sections of the city with its private garden of a traditional artist, its artistic retreat of a medieval shogun, and its quiet and charming hillside temples. With the exception of the Silver Pavilion, it is a section the tourist agencies usually overlook since it is not conducive to the easy herding of groups of tourists, yet this portion of the city is a favorite one for the citizens of Kyoto and for knowledgeable visitors who have long enjoyed the Tetsugaku-no-michi (Philosopher's Path) which borders a canal.

One can walk the path in either direction, north or south, but many prefer to start at its northern end with the Silver Pavilion and then to explore the quiet Honen-in and Anraku-ji temples located along bypaths leading from the canal. If one is energetic, the walk can be continued to the Nanzen-ji and its noted Zen gardens. The Silver Pavilion at the beginning of this walk was a shogun's toy, a palatial villa where he could ignore the vicissitudes of war, starvation, and famine which were rampant in Kyoto in his day. Here in the northeast part of Kyoto, beyond the city itself, he and his friends could turn life into an art and create and enjoy new aesthetic pleasures despite the horrors around them.

The era was one of important cultural advances despite the dreadful conditions in Kyoto for the mass of people. It was a period that set the standards for Japanese taste and which saw the creation of those elements which are often regarded as purely Japanese, from the use of shoji and tatami to the development of the tea ceremony, Noh theater, and other cultural elements. Influenced by the Chinese culture that Japanese Zen monks brought to Japan and to the court, the well-to-do created their paradise here on earth while the majority of the people only had a hope of a paradise in the future through their devotions to Amida. Thus, it is somewhat ironic that the Philosopher's Path moves from the earthly glories of the Silver Pavilion to the humble temples of the Honen-in and the Anraku-ji where the worship of Amida brought hope for the future at a time when life on earth was so bitter for those caught in the midst of famine, disease, and war with all of its destruction.

Just outside the Silver Pavilion or along the canal of the Philosopher's Path are small restaurants where one can enjoy a simple lunch while strolling from site to site or where one can sit on a bench alongside the canal to enjoy a box lunch purchased in advance. On the eastern side of the canal are the lovely Honen-in and the Anraku-ji temples, both with thatch-roofed gateways which lead to the main hall where Amida is reverenced. Other temples, shrines, and tombs enrich the walk, but it is the path itself and its environs, (one of the lovelier corners of a fascinating city), which make the visit to the sites worthy of a full day's enjoyment.

We begin our walk at a handsome private garden.

HAKUSASON-SO VILLA AND GARDEN

At the far eastern end of Imadegawa-dori, just before the pathway to the Ginkaku-ji (Silver Pavilion) is the Hakusason-so villa. Take buses 5, 203, or 204 to the Ginkaku-ji-michi bus stop and walk to the east from Shirakawa-dori along the extension of Imadegawa-dori. The villa and its gardens are on the right-hand side of the street and are open from 10:00 a.m. to 5:00 p.m. Entry fee.

The painter Kansetsu Hashimoto (1883–1945) was one of those happy individuals whose artistic abilities were recognized in his day and who was able to create his own form of an earthly paradise near the pleasure palace of a onetime shogun. The Hakusason-so, built in 1916, was his private villa, and here he not only had his residence, but his studio as well. Kansetsu painted in the traditional style, and a small gallery behind the villa exhibits selections of his work on a rotating basis as well as pieces of Greek and Persian pottery, Chinese clay figures, Indian miniatures, Chinese and Japanese paintings, and calligraphy, all of which he collected.

The villa is noted for the garden created around a pond and a stream. A thatch-roofed gateway leads to the attractive garden and to the path along a meandering brook which empties into the pond. The main villa lies across the water. This building was Hashimoto's atelier. The pond and the path are encompassed by azaleas along with pine trees and various types of shrubbery. Ferns and mosses cover much of the ground while large carp of varied colors enliven the pond and stream. A stone-slab bridge over the pond outlet, with large, ornamental pine trees, stone lanterns, and five-tier memorial stones, leads to a second portion of the pond which is in front of a small viewing hut that has a large "moon window." Across this second and smaller pond is a teahouse, the object of the view from the hut opposite it. The garden, which makes use of the "borrowed scenery" of Mount Daimonji, is at its best in the springtime with its cherry blossoms and then again in the fall with the many-colored hues of its maples.

Hashimoto was fascinated by ancient Japanese stone carvings, and thus various small stone images can be found in a bamboo grove behind the villa. These stone mourners for the Buddha were obtained from throughout Japan, and in the springtime they peer out from among flowering irises. A small seven-story stone pagoda and a small Hokyo-in pagoda in the Indian style further enhance the grounds.

For a small fee, one can enjoy powdered green tea *(matcha)* and a traditional tea cake in a tatami room in the main villa which has a view across the pond.

JODO-JI

On leaving the Hakusason-so villa, a turn to the right along the extension of Imadegawa-dori directs one toward the small Jodo-ji which lies in front of and to the left of the Silver Pavilion along with the previously mentioned restaurants on the right. Primarily meant for local worship and not a tourist attraction, the Jodo-ji (Paradise Temple) is today an insignificant temple whose history, however, goes back to the early years of the Heian period (794–

1185). This temple was once a large establishment situated in a village outside of Kyoto called Jodo-ji-mura. As was the case with many temples, in the eighth century it burned to the ground. The next morning, a blaze of light on the nearby hillside led the curious to the source of the brilliant glow, and there on the hillside they found the Amida image of the temple, charred but intact. It had ostensibly fled to safety on the hillside during the conflagration.

Legend has a way of involving great men with individual temples or events, and in this case it is Kobo Daishi (Kukai) who is so honored. It is claimed that one of the plagues to which Kyoto was susceptible was decimating the city in the early 800s. Therefore, Kukai built a large *dai* ideogram 大 (*dai* means "great"—in this case in reference to the law of the Buddha) on the hillside where the Amida image of the Jodo-ji had taken sanctuary and the great plague came to an end. From that time on, whenever plague or famine or other evil ensued, a great *dai* would be raised on the hillside and burned. So began the ceremony, still observed today, wherein a huge *dai* is set on fire on nearby Nyoigatake hill each mid-August at the end of the Obon Festival to light the spirits of the deceased back to the other world.

The Jodo-ji still exists as a temple, despite a later fire in 1449 and the seizure of much of its lands by Shogun Ashikaga Yoshimasa when he built his Silver Pavilion pleasure palace on the temple grounds. In the rebuilt Jodo-ji main hall, a large image of Kobo Daishi and the charred Amida image still have a place of honor. The Jodo-ji, however, is but a curious footnote to history, for the important site lies to the right of the small temple where the path from Imadegawa-dori ends at the entrance to the Silver Pavilion.

MAIN BUILDINGS AND SIGHTS OF THE SILVER PAVILION (GINKAKU-JI)

The Silver Pavilion today belongs to the Shokoku School of the Rinzai Zen sect of Buddhism, and, while it is one of the more important tourist sites in Kyoto, it also serves as a temple. It is open from 8:30 a.m. to 5:00 p.m. from March 15 to November 30 and from 9:00 a.m. to 4:30 p.m. from December 1 to March 14. Entry fee.

Just prior to the start of the Onin War (1467–77) in which Kyoto would be laid waste by a senseless conflict in which the city itself was the battleground between opposing forces, Shogun Ashikaga Yoshimasa (1436–90) turned his back on the capital. In the northeast area of the plain on which Kyoto sits, beyond the confines of the city and Yoshida hill and just below the Nyoigatake mountain, he built a pleasure palace of a simple and refined nature where he could enjoy the garden, tea, incense, and the more esoteric pleasures of this world. Symbolically, it faced to the east away from the realities of the miseries the people of Kyoto suffered during the decade of internecine fighting. That a temple, the Jodo-ji, stood in the way of his plans was of little concern. The temple was removed, leaving but a relic of the former religious center.

Work on the villa, dedicated to the pleasures of the aesthetic senses, began in 1460 but was interrupted by the Onin War only to be resumed once more after Yoshimasa's retirement on June 27, 1480. Three years later, Yoshimasa took up residence at the Silver Pavilion, and construction continued until his death at the age of fifty-six in January 1490 by which time there were some twelve buildings and an exquisite garden in the complex. Upon his death, the palace became a Zen temple. (The temple was named the Jisho-ji after Yoshimasa's posthumous name.)

The villa was so huge, some thirty times its present extent, that it was called Higashiyama-dono (Eastern Hills Palace) rather than a villa. In time, fires destroyed all but two buildings: the Silver Pavilion itself (Ginkaku-ji) and the Togu-do (East Request Hall). Although restored in the seventeenth century, by the 1860s the complex had fallen into ruin once more, and, as an 1890s guidebook reported: "The palace is so dilapidated as to be scarcely worth looking at, except from an antiquarian point of view." Fortunately, in this century it has been restored to its quiet but elegant beauty once more.

In Yoshimasa's time, the villa and its gardens were the cultural and aesthetic center of the nation. It was the nursery of the arts; noted painters enjoyed the support of the shogun, and here the art of the tea ceremony was brought to new heights. Banquets, moon viewing, incense parties, tea ceremony, flower viewing, and poetry appreciation all became high arts again as they had been in Heian Kyoto (794–1185). Yoshimasa himself summed up his feelings for the villa:

> I love
> My hut
> At the foot of the Moon-awaiting Mountain
> And the reflection
> Of the sinking sky.

(The mountain behind the villa to the east is Tsukimachiyama, "Moon-awaiting Mountain.")

A stone path rising gently through a row of pine, cedar, and maple trees leads from the city street and the small restaurants to the simple, tile-roofed So-mon main gate of the Silver Pavilion. Within the gateway, one turns to the right to proceed along a pathway bordered by camellia trees and other bushes edged by a low stone wall above which rises the unique, tightly made bamboo fence of a rustic nature known as the Ginkaku-ji-gaki style of fencing. At the end of this sand-covered pathway, another ninety-degree turn to the left leads one to the ticket booth and the simple one-story, tile-roofed gateway to the inner grounds of the temple. This tree-lined and fenced entrance corridor is but preliminary to the beauty that lies beyond the second gateway and the Kuri, the priests' large, tile-roofed, private living quarters.

A diamond-shaped stone pathway set in sand, with raked sand and azalea bushes on either side, leads to the imposing, heavily gabled, curved-roof Kara-mon (Chinese-style gateway) of the first half of the seventeenth century. Beyond the gateway, a Zen-style arched (cusped) window offers a preview of the main Ginshaden garden which lies ahead. The entry to the Ginshaden sand garden is through a small doorway in the garden wall to the right. This doorway opens onto the Ginshaden garden with the Silver Pavilion on the right and the Hondo (Spirit Hall) on the left. The path continues, leading one toward the Hondo (not open to the public) from which the sand garden can be viewed, a garden that is described after the Hondo and Togu-do are viewed.

Hondo The original Hondo was destroyed by fire, and the present structure with its cedar-bark roof dates from the second quarter of the seventeenth century. The building has four rooms

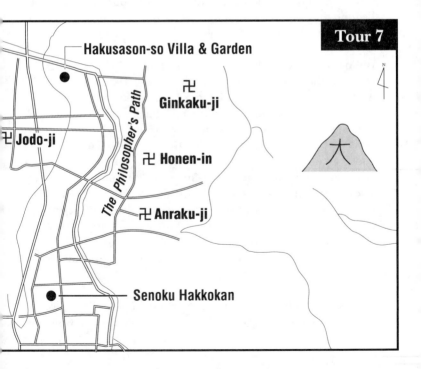

Tour 7

Hakusason-so Villa & Garden

卍 Ginkaku-ji

卍 Jodo-ji

卍 Honen-in

The Philosopher's Path

卍 Anraku-ji

Senoku Hakkokan

of eight to ten mats. A small altar at the rear of the tatami-matted central Buddha Room has an image of Sakyamuni (Shaka) on display as the object of veneration. In the front of the room is a cushioned seat and drums for use in worship.

Togu-do   Between the Hondo and the adjacent Togu-do is a small garden with a stone water basin of the so-called Peasant or Priest's Robe style, as well as a granite lantern of the Uzumasa type. Built in 1487, the four-room, thatch-roofed Togu-do is one of the two original buildings still standing from Yoshimasa's day. It is claimed that Yoshimasa used the front room of the Togu-do, the *butsuma* (Buddha Room) of eight mats and thus the largest of the rooms, as his residence. A wooden statue of Yoshimasa in a monk's robe is housed in this room, a statue which replaced the two noted images of the Buddha and the one of a Kannon. Legend has it that Yoshimasa himself carved this blackened image and adorned it with crystal eyes.

Dojin-sai   Perhaps the most famous unit of the Togu-do is the room in the northeast of the building, the Dojin-sai (Friendly Abstinence), a small four-and-one-half-mat room which Yoshimasa used for tea ceremony. In a sense, it is the prototype of what has become the traditional tea hut or tea room. (The tea room is preceded by a four-mat room in the southeast corner where guests awaited permission to enter the tea room.) The Dojin-sai has a tatami-matted floor, a board ceiling, a built-out writing alcove, a tokonoma (an alcove in which a flower or perhaps a scroll is displayed), *chigaidana* (staggered shelves), and a fire box which is sunk into the center of the floor. Its outer walls are divided at waist level into sliding wooden panels below shoji. It is an intimate room meant for seating no more than four to five people at a time.

Rosei-tei   A two-room building to the north of the Togu-do, the Rosei-tei was constructed for Yoshimasa as a pavilion in which he could enjoy the pleasure of incense. The building disappeared over time, but in 1895 an exact reconstruction of the original Rosei-tei was re-created.

The gardens of the Ginkaku-ji were planned by Soami (1455–1525), the most noted landscape designer of medieval times. He was responsible for the design of the buildings as well as of the gardens. Divided into two sections, one part of the garden is typical of the *karesansui* (dry garden) of sand while the other is a classical Japanese garden with a lake, a stream, and plants.

Ginshaden   The first section of the garden, a *karesansui* garden, is encountered when one passes through the gateway from the Kuri (Priests' Quarters) garden into the Hondo area. This garden of 1.75 acres is the Ginshaden, the Sea of Silver Sand, composed of a two-foot-high plateau of sand raked in a pattern suggestive of a sea in motion. The Ginshaden is so placed that when the moon appears over Tsukimachiyama (Moon-awaiting Mountain) to the east, the sand sea seems to ripple in the gleam of the silvery moonlight. This sand sea is often referred to as Seiko (West Lake) to draw a parallel between it and the famed West Lake located near Hangchow, China, after whose shape it was designed.

Kogetsudai   Adjacent to the sand sea there rises the Kogetsudai, the Moon-viewing Platform. A large, truncated cone of sand, this shaped hill has been described as a miniature Mount Fuji, as a moon-viewing platform, or as a cone of sand designed to reflect and heighten the effect of moonlight on the sand sea. From the upper floor of the Silver Pavilion, it is said that the cone appears to be a silvery full moon reflected on the bosom of a silver lake. Ginshaden and Kogetsudai are also seen as a combination of the sea and the mountains. Kogetsudai is six feet high by sixteen feet in diameter and is reputed to be where Yoshimasa sat to gaze at the moon. (It is interesting, however, that these two sand units which are so striking were not mentioned before the Edo period

[1603–1868]—and it is also known that they presently occupy the site of buildings that burned to the ground.) Mounds of sand originally existed in dry gardens so that the paths and designs could be replenished as needed. Here such a mound has become an aesthetic attraction in itself.

The second part of the garden is of the classical Japanese type which employs water, rocks, and plants. The rocks and stones come from all over Japan, tribute or duty to the shogun from his feudal lords. Each stone has a name and a recorded history. In a sense, this is a stroll garden, for one needs to walk its paths to savor and enjoy the changing views of water, trees, stones, and plants. Azaleas and moss complement the water and the rocks placed in the shade of large trees.

Kinkyo-chi Central to this garden and adjacent to the Silver Pavilion is its pond Kinkyo-chi (Brocade Mirror Pond) with the Crane and Turtle Islands named for the two symbols of longevity. (Real turtles nap in the sun on the islands.) The scene is enhanced by the Sengetsu-sei (Moon-watching Fountain), a tiny waterfall whose ripples in the water into which it falls are meant to "wash away" moonlight on the surface of the pond. Every stone, as mentioned previously, has a name; one stone in the midst of the pond is known as the "Stone of Ecstatic Contemplation," while a small stone bridge (one of seven over the waterways) is the "Bridge of the Pillar of the Immortals." Each vista is meant to bring to mind a reference to one of the Chinese or Japanese literary classics.

A path leads past the Togu-do and Rosei-tei up the hillside to the spring whose sparkling waters served as the basis for the shogun's early tea ceremony. The spring remains as the source of water for the stream and pond in the garden. Naturally, each temple needs its Shinto shrine to appease the spirit of the land it occupies. There are two such small shrines on the ground of Ginkaku-ji, the smaller in the northeast corner of the grounds and the larger one next to the Silver Pavilion.

The Silver Pavilion   The Silver Pavilion building, which despite its name was never given the intended coating of silver leaf, was Yoshimasa's attempt to create as perfect a retreat as his grandfather, Shogun Ashikaga Yoshimitsu, had created at the Gold Pavilion (Kinkaku-ji). A surprisingly small and simple building, it was designed to a different aesthetic than was to be observed by later, more ostentatious, military rulers of Japan. A rather plain, wooden building of two stories, its lower floor is divided by *fusuma* (sliding panels) to provide for rooms of varying sizes as desired. The first floor is twenty-two feet by eighteen feet and has sliding waist-high wooden doors with shoji above the lower wooden portion. Its interior has a flat board ceiling.

The upper floor has three arched or cusped (bell-shaped) windows in front and back while the two sides have two such windows and a pair of paneled doors between them. This upper level is surrounded by a railing running along its narrow exterior "porch." The roof which flares upward at its four corners is surmounted by a gilt bronze phoenix.

The lower floor is named Shinkudan (Empty Heart Hall) and has an enshrined image of Jizo, protector of children, on display along with one thousand small Jizo images. The upper floor, called Cho-onkaku (Roaring Wave Hall), has a gilt Kannon image reputed to have been created by Unkei (thirteenth century). The interior is varnished with black lacquer against which the gilt image is resplendent. Because of the Kannon image, the building has also been known as the Kannon-den (Kannon Hall).

THE PHILOSOPHER'S PATH

After one has viewed the Silver Pavilion building (unfortunately, only from the outside), the path leads around the pavilion toward the exit from the grounds. Back on the extension of Imadegawa-dori from which one entered the Silver Pavilion grounds, one should walk to the canal which passes below the street. The Philosopher's Path, which runs along the far (western) side of the canal, should then be taken to the left (south).

Away from the bustle of the city streets, one can follow the narrow canal past interesting homes, shops, and an occasional small restaurant. Quiet hillside temples offer separate attractions of a pleasant nature, one of the most interesting being that of the Honen-in temple.

The Philosopher's Path is so-named since it was once the locale of the daily walk in Kyoto of Kitaro Nishida, a Japanese philosopher (1870–1945). The path runs along a canal from near the Silver Pavilion for 1.3 miles south toward the Zenrin-ji/Eikan-do and thereafter along a city street to the Nanzen-ji. The canal and its adjacent path are embowered with cherry blossoms in early spring, while in autumn, the brilliant reds and vibrant yellows of the leaves of its various trees turn the area into a palette richer than that of an artist.

At the tenth small bridge over the waterway, one should leave the canal temporarily and turn to the hillside and the Honen-in.

HONEN-IN

The Honen-in temple is on the beginning slope of the hillside running along a north-south path through the woods. Having crossed the bridge over the canal, one walks to the north-south path beyond the canal, turns to the north (left), and eventually enters the grounds of the Honen-in. The temple grounds are open from 6:00 a.m. to 6:00 p.m. without charge. The temple's Hondo is only open for visitors from April 1–7 and November 1–7 since its primary purpose is to serve as a training center for monks. Entry fee.

The Honen-in temple is dedicated to the memory of Priest Honen (1133–1212) who had entered the Enryaku-ji monastery on Mount Hiei to the northeast of Kyoto at the age of fifteen where he astonished the monks with his religious precocity. Moving to the site of the future Kurodani temple in Kyoto, in his solitary studies he encountered the Jodo (Pure Land) doctrines in the *Ojo Yoshu* (The Essentials for Salvation) written by Priest

Genshin. Embracing these new doctrines, he rejected the Tendai teachings of the Enryaku-ji and became the popularizer of the repetition of the *nenbutsu* (*Namu Amida Butsu*–Praise to the Buddha Amida) as the only means for eventual entrance into Amida's Pure Land. It is said that he would repeat the *nenbutsu* as many as sixty thousand times a day.

In time, Honen and two disciples (Anraku and Juren) erected an image of Amida at the foot of the Nyoigatake mountain (the site of the present Honen-in) in order to perform services before this outdoor image three times a day as well as at night. For many years, the worship site consisted only of a roofed, open-air Amida image, a sculpture which has been attributed to Genshin (942–1017). Not too long after Honen's death in 1212, the roof over the Amida was destroyed by the monks of the Enryaku-ji temples of Mount Hiei, the enemies of Honen and his Jodo sect.

It was not until the Tokugawa shoguns came to power in the early seventeenth century (and after the Enryaku-ji temples and their monks had been eliminated by Oda Nobunaga in the mid-1500s) that the present main hall was built. Under Shogun Tokugawa Ietsuna, rooms from Toyotomi Hideyoshi's Fushimi Castle were granted to the temple, and these were then attached to the new Hondo.

It has been the tradition of the temple for the monks to place twenty-five flowers on the floor before the Amida image in the Hondo every morning. These flowers symbolize the twenty-five bodhisattvas who accompany Amida when he descends from his Western Paradise to receive the souls of the newly deceased. When the 4:00 a.m. bell is rung for morning services, fresh cut flowers are placed before the altar. (The bell is rung again at 4:00 p.m. for services.)

A great deal of the charm of the Honen-in comes from its location in the woods at the foot of Nyoigatake mountain. It offers a quiet retreat away from the city's clamor, for the walkway to the temple grounds is lined with cedars, great camellia trees, and bamboo. A simple gateway with a thatched roof and a gate of inset bamboo rods, reminiscent of a small Japanese country farmhouse, lies at the end of the path.

Beyond the gateway, one descends eight broad stone steps into the grounds of the temple itself. On either side of the path, just within the compound, lie two long, rectangular sand mounds. Periodically, the monks rake the surface of the sand to create a new design on each mound, generally with patterns symbolizing the seasons on the left. On the right side, abstractions of a religious nature are made, often in a water pattern which symbolizes the Buddhist theme of impermanence. Toward the hillside beyond the sand mounds is a small building with cusped windows. It is said that this building served as a bath house at one time and it is still used periodically for special exhibitions. Further up the hillside, above the entry gate, is the temple Shoro (Bell Tower).

Kura Just beyond the sand mounds, a stone bridge crosses a stream which leads from a small pond. On the left is a small *kura* (a fireproof storage building) whose interior is open to view. The temple sutras are arranged on shelves along three of its walls. In the center of the *kura* is a shrine with an image of Amida at the top and a case holding one thousand tiny Amida images below it. To the right of the main Amida image is a figure of Bishamon-ten, the protector against evil which always flows from the northeast. The figure holds a pagoda in one hand and a staff in the other. A companion figure on the other side of Amida has its hands clasped in prayer. Both images are colorfully dressed in Chinese-style clothes. Beyond and slightly to the southwest of the *kura* is a thirteen-tiered stone pagoda.

Hondo The main path leading from the entry gate crosses the aforementioned stone bridge which is composed of flat stone slabs and a low stone balustrade. At the north end of this path is the Hondo of the temple. The path diverges to the right and left when it reaches the Hondo, the left-hand path leading to the entry of the building. The right-hand path makes a ninety-degree turn to the north at the eastern end of the Hondo before ending at a wall. At the turn is a twelve-foot-high, five-tier memorial stone. At the end of the path, set into the hillside to the right, is a shrine to Jizo. A *bussoseki*, a stone with the imprinted footstep of the Buddha, is adjacent.

Naijin　When the Hondo is open to the public, a corridor to the right of the entry to the building leads to the inner sanctuary *(naijin)* of the Hondo. Here is the altar with its image of Amida, said to be by Genshin, posed in a contemplative mudra. At his side are the two bodhisattvas who accompany him, Seishi on the right and Kannon on the left. Additional images stand at the side of the two attendants. Twenty-five flowers representing Amida's followers are reverently placed on the polished floor before Amida each morning. The *naijin* is a one-hundred-tatami-matted hall with numerous "crab-shaped" drums for use during worship services.

The Hondo building has a double roof, bell-shaped windows, and an arched ceiling in the main hall. Internal courtyards flank both sides of the Hondo, the one on the north being noted for its seven-color camellia tree. These courtyards separate and connect the Hondo with the other rooms of the complex.

Fushimi Apartments　On walking down the interior corridor on the north side of the Hondo, one comes to the six rooms in the northeastern portion of the complex which came from the apartments of Hideyoshi's Fushimi Castle. These rooms formerly were part of Hideyoshi's audience hall, granted to the temple by Shogun Tokugawa Ietsuna shortly after the Hondo was re-erected in 1680. Outside, wooden verandas encircle the building. There is a private garden on the east of the apartments, separated from the public grounds by a wall of stone, earth, and hedges. In the private garden is a pond in the shape of a reversed C with a stone bridge crossing over one segment of the water. A stone lantern, a stone basin, and a Shinto shrine complement the bushes and moss which form the greenery of the garden as it is situated before the woods of the forested hillside beyond.

The four small rooms at the southern end of these apartments each have *fusuma* (sliding panels) painted with modern, abstract drawings in vivid colors. Two of these rooms (one each on the east and on the west side) are respectively six- and eight-mat tatami rooms. The two most important rooms of this complex are the two ten-matted rooms at the northern end of the apartments, rooms that are usually thrown together into one large room through the removal of the intervening *fusuma*. These rooms are preceded by a tatami-matted corridor on their east and west sides. The *fusuma* panels of the rooms have pine and willow trees, flowers, and birds painted by Kano Mitsunobu (1561–1608) on a gold ground. The north end of the second room has a tokonoma with large white flowers on a gold ground painted on its rear wall, while the adjacent *chigaidana* (staggered shelves) have painted scenes. The cedar doors at the end of the inner, tatami-matted corridor have a painting of a pine tree. The four smaller rooms to the south of these ten-mat rooms, as noted above, complete the Fushimi apartments.

On leaving the Fushimi apartments, the wooden corridor leads toward the west, past a number of rooms of which three should be noted. One room is a fifteen-mat room with a black-and-white dragon filling the *fusuma* on three sides of the room. The second room is a thirty-mat room with a tokonoma and a large *chigaidana* on its north wall, a room that runs the length of the building (east to west). During the April and November period when these apartments are open to visitors, large screens from the temple's treasures are on view in this room. The third room is a fifteen-mat room. At the end of the corridor on the east side of these rooms is a four-and-one-half-mat tea room with a tokonoma and a view of the previously mentioned inner garden and pond. The ceiling of the room is quite low which forces one to bend (to bow or humble oneself) on entering the room.

The monks' large dining hall (Jiki-do) with an image of Monju is where temple treasures are shown during the period when the temple is open to the public. A turn to the right leads to a two-story building whose upper floor of two small rooms has a view of Kyoto.

On leaving the Honen-in grounds through its thatched-roof gateway, one should follow the path to the south. Along the way on the left the temple graveyard is passed in which the novelist Tanizaki Jun'ichiro (1886–1965) is buried.

Mention has been made of Honen's two disciples who worshipped at the open-air shrine to Amida in the early days before the Honen-in existed as a formal set of buildings. These two men were to suffer the enmity engendered by Honen's enemies, and they are remembered at the Anraku-ji temple which lies to the south of the Honen-in along a continuation of the path on the east side of the canal.

ANRAKU-JI

The grounds of the Anraku-ji temple are open from 9:30 a.m. to 4:00 p.m. on Saturdays, Sundays, and national holidays in April and May, and during the second week of June, October, and November. Entry fee.

When, in the late twelfth century, Honen began to preach his doctrine that reliance on the *nenbutsu* was all that was needed for salvation, he was confronted with many opponents among the monks at Mount Hiei as well as many among the six Buddhist sects in Nara, and many within the court.

Two of his disciples, Anraku (?–1207) and Juren (1169?–1207), were most effective proselytizers of Honen's version of Buddhism. Unable to preach in the city without interference from their clerical enemies, they preached in the countryside at the foot of the Higashiyama mountains at Shishigatani where they created a small temple. Two noble ladies, Matsumushi (Pine Beetle) and Suzumushi (Bell Cricket) of the emperor Go-Toba's court (said perhaps to have been his concubines, although sources differ on their relationship to the emperor), became enamored of the new teachings as preached by Anraku and Juren—or with the conveyors of the teachings, depending on which account one believes—and became nuns.

The Emperor Go-Toba (1180–1239), furious at this seduction (real or imagined) of two of his court ladies, had Anraku and Juren seized. Another interpretation of the events states that the court had become convinced by Honen's enemies (primarily at Mount Hiei) that the new doctrines preached by Anraku and Juren of equal salvation for all people were incompatible with the safety and security of the state. Thus, persecution of the new belief and its followers was ordered on the pretext that two court ladies had been led astray by the two priests and had entered the new faith without imperial approval.

Given an opportunity to recant their belief in the Jodo tenets and in the *nenbutsu*, which they refused to do, the two priests were beheaded in the place of execution for criminals in the bed of the Kamogawa river at Rokujokawara. Anraku asked permission to say the *nenbutsu* before his death, telling his executioners that after this recitation, on his tenth repetition of the name of Amida, they could execute him. He repeated the *nenbutsu* several hundred times and then Amida's name ten times. At that decisive moment of the tenth calling of Amida's name, and as the executioner acted, great purple clouds gathered in the west, the direction of Amida's Western Paradise to which Anraku was being welcomed by Amida and his bodhisattvas.

The court ladies are reputed to have committed suicide. Honen himself was defrocked by order of the emperor and exiled to Tosa for his teaching of the *nenbutsu* as the only way to salvation—an action which evidenced the power of Honen's monastic enemies within the court. For Honen, exile provided an opportunity to spread his truth in new realms. Evidently, time took its toll on the emperor's conscience, for when unpleasant dreams plagued various individuals and these dreams were reported to the court, they were interpreted as being caused by the emperor's actions against Honen. After four years of exile, Honen was permitted to settle in Osaka. An oracle's interpretation in the year 1211 of additional dreams led the emperor to permit Honen to return to Kyoto, where the aged priest settled in Otani (at what was later to become the Chion-in temple) in a small hermitage. It is said that on his return from exile in 1212, Honen created the temple of Anraku-ji in honor of his slain disciples and their two converts at the place where the priests had preached on a portion of the grounds of the Jodo-ji.

The small temple of Anraku-ji in the verdant foothills of the Higashiyama mountains is a branch of the Nishiyama Zenrin-ji School of Jodo Buddhism. Its Hondo was erected about 1581, the original hall having been destroyed by fire. Stone steps lead to a simple thatched gateway at the entry to the temple grounds. Within the temple precincts, a narrow path bordered by azaleas, camellia trees, maples, pines, and moss leads to the hillside where the main building of the temple is hidden away in the greenery to the left. A life-sized image of Jizo stands to the west of the Hondo while a thirteen-tiered stone pagoda rises on an azalea-covered hillock.

Near the center of the temple grounds, a path on the right diverges from the main path. Following the right arm of the path at the crossing, one comes to the graves of Anraku and Juren surrounded by a low stone fence dating from a 1904 restoration. Straight ahead on the main path to the east, toward the mountainside and up two flights of steps, lie the graves of the two court ladies, Suzumushi and Matsumushi. Their graves were marked with a low stone fence when they were restored in 1897. (Other graves lie within the temple compound.)

Hondo   The Hondo lies at the end of the left arm of the transverse path. As can be expected, the central image in the rear section of the Hondo is of Amida with Seishi and Kannon to his left and right. It is claimed that these images, which predate the temple, are the tenth-century work of Priest Genshin (942–1017). An ancient Jizo image, together with two very large gilt hangings above the images, complete the altar figures. A shrine on the left has images of Honen and his noted disciple Shinran together with a Kannon figure. The Honen image (said to have been carved by Honen himself) stands in a small shrine built in the shape of a temple and covered with hundreds of *nenbutsu* inscriptions on paper. In a shrine to the right, framed with a colorful brocade, are images of Matsumushi (left) and Suzumushi (right) with Anraku and Juren behind and above them on the left and right respectively.

Shoin To the east of the Hondo, and connected to it by a covered walkway, is a tatami-matted Shoin (study) of two rooms (often joined into one room) designated for special use. Additional temple buildings for the staff of the temple are adjacent. Two small Shinto shrines near the Hondo offer the protection of the local god.

DAIMONJI BONFIRE

Leaving the Anraku-ji and crossing the first bridge over the canal, a return to the Philosopher's Path along the west bank of the canal continues the pleasant walk south along the waterway. The Nyoigatake hillside lies to the east; here on its top the Daimonji fire celebration takes place each August. We have already met with the legend of the apparition of Amida surrounded by a blaze of light which was seen on this mountain in the 800s. The bonfire which Kukai lit in the 800s as a protection against the plague finds a counterpart today on each August 16 when a huge *dai* ideogram 大 composed of large bundles of pine branches is created on a clearing 1,529 feet up on Nyoigatake (or Daimonjiyama as it is also known) above the Zenrin-ji/Eikan-do.

The horizontal stroke of the gigantic *dai* is 230 feet long. The left vertical is 510 feet in length, while the right stroke is 408 feet long. At 8:00 p.m. the ideogram is set on fire, and four other fires are lit on hills across the valley. The others include the Myoho (Supreme Law of the Buddha), the Funagata (Boat-Shaped), the Torii-gata (Gate-Shaped), and the Hidari-Daimonji (Left-handed Daimonji) ideograms. Since five mountains are involved, the festival is also known as the Daimonji Gosan Okuribi Festival (Five Mountains' Fires Which Return the Souls of the Deceased). This brings to a close the Obon Festival when the spirits of the dead, who have returned to their homes on August 12 for a brief visit, are now ready to return to the other world. This great flaming illumination is intended to guide the spirits back to that other world at the end of the festival.

Continuing south on the path which runs before the Anraku-ji, one crosses a bridge on the right over the canal, back to the Philosopher's Path on the west side of the canal. This path can be taken to the next major cross-street to the west (right). One street to the west and then to the north, the Senoku Hakkokan (Senoku Museum) will be reached. The museum is open from 10:00 a.m. to 4:00 p.m., but is closed on Sundays, Mondays, and national holidays as well as during July and August and from December through February. Entry fee.

SENOKU HAKKOKAN

The Senoku Hakkokan (Senoku Museum) consists of two modern buildings, one for its permanent collections and one for its changing exhibitions. The latter are generally shown from March 1 to June 30 and then from September 1 to November 30. The permanent collection is composed of items from the Sumitomo Collection (the Sumitomo family land is opposite the museum). The collection was begun by Kichizaemon Sumitomo who collected ancient Chinese bronzes for over thirty years until his death in 1926. In recent years, the Sumitomo family created the museum and a foundation for its continued support so that the public could view the collection and in order that the art world could benefit from scientific research supported by the foundation. Aside from the bronzes of the Chinese Shang and Zhou periods (1600–221 B.C.), Chinese paintings, musical instruments, and calligraphy are included in the museum holdings. The bronzes include mirrors, bells, Buddhist images, and vessels for wine and food. Approximately six hundred bronzes are shown at any one time in the four exhibition rooms of the permanent collections building. An English-language brochure is available in the museum.

On leaving the museum, one can either continue southward to the Zenrin-ji/Eikan-do and the Nanzen-ji (see Tour 8) by following the north-south street just to the east of the museum, or one can take the street in front of the museum to the west to Shirakawa-dori. Here buses 5, 203, 204, or a taxi can be obtained.

TOUR
8

Mikaeri-no-Amida
and the Tiger and Cubs
Zen Garden

TWO TEMPLES and a private museum may seem a scant number of sites to be described in a single tour, but these three can be seen by themselves or they can be combined with the temples and shrines along the Philosopher's Path in Tour 7.

Of the three places, the Nomura Museum is a highly specialized collection primarily of Japanese objets d'art placed together with choice selections of Chinese art. The major site, however, is the Nanzen-ji Zen temple and its sub-temples. The Nanzen-ji is particularly noted for its San-mon gateway, for its Shohojo (Abbot's Small Quarters) with its painted *fusuma*, and for its Zen-style "tiger and cubs" garden as well as for the gardens of some of its sub-temples. A few of the Nanzen-ji sub-temples serve vegetarian fare *(shojin)* or tofu, and these can be delightful places for lunch if one can speak Japanese or is with a Japanese-speaking companion.

The Zenrin-ji/Eikan-do is primarily known for its "Backward-Looking Amida" and the lovely story that accompanies it. As a temple with a number of buildings, the complex offers a variety of rooms with interesting *fusuma* and, above all, the Kannon mentioned above.

Should the sites in this chapter be visited as an extension of the Philosopher's Path, the Zenrin-ji/Eikan-do comes after the Senoku Hakkokan Museum. The Nomura Museum follows, and finally, one arrives at the Nanzen-ji. Thereafter, this leaves one at the crossing of Shirakawa-dori and Sanjo-dori where the Keihan Electric Railway surface train can be taken back to the Keihan terminus at Sanjo-dori and the Kamogawa river (for various buses to the center of Kyoto). Alternatively, one can find restaurants along Sanjo-dori or in the Miyako Hotel.

ZENRIN-JI/EIKAN-DO

The Zenrin-ji/Eikan-do temple is located south of the Anraku-ji temple and the Senoku Hakkokan Museum (see Tour 7), and is approximately due east of Okazaki Park. To get there directly, take bus 5 to the Eikan-do-mae bus stop and walk to the east to the temple which is open from 9:00 a.m. to 5:00 p.m. Entry fee. The temple treasures are on view from November 1 to 30 from 9:00 a.m. to 4:00 p.m.

The Zenrin-ji/Eikan-do was founded in 856 by Shinjo, a disciple of the great eighth-century priest Kobo Daishi (Kukai). The site was originally the villa of Fujiwara-no-Kanyu, but Shinjo was able to obtain the villa as a gift from the emperor and to turn it into a temple. In 983 the temple was rebuilt on a new and larger scale by the monk Eikan for whom the temple was later renamed in honor of his charitable and religious activities.

Eikan built a hospital (the Tonan-in) for the poor and homeless on the temple grounds in addition to rebuilding the temple. The hospital grounds extended from Awataguchi (Sanjo-dori) to Shishigatani, an extensive range of land. In order to create medicine for the poor, Eikan planted a plum orchard, called the Hidenbai, whose fruit could be used as the basis for medicines. Largely destroyed in the Onin War of 1467–77, the temple was rebuilt, and by the end of the 1500s most of the buildings had been restored. In the 1880s the Zenrin-ji/Eikan-do underwent a restoration under the monk Shugyoku who also recreated the hospital, reopened the Hino-oka Mountain Pass, and even made plans for a canal which would carry the waters of Lake Biwa to Kyoto.

Set on the peaceful hillside at the base of the Higashiyama mountains, the Zenrin-ji/Eikan-do is located amidst pines and maples. A small pond, the Hojo-no-ike (Abbot's Pond), in the forepart of the temple grounds is crossed by a graceful stone bridge; the temple is entered through the Chu-mon (Central Gateway). Another gateway, the seldom-used Chokushi-mon (Imperial Messenger's Gate), was built in the *kara* (Chinese) style with a heavy, arch-gabled roof. The priests rake designs on the surface of the long, raised rectangle of sand located just inside this gate. One removes one's shoes at the ticket booth and then proceeds along a planned pathway (pleasantly carpeted, which is a boon for walking in stocking feet in colder weather) through the wooden corridors and up the eventual stairs to the upper level of the temple precincts. The corridor "Dragon Path," with its many turns as it connects the various buildings of the temple, was built without nails. The temple's complex of buildings is based about two small courtyards with a split staircase leading to the upper levels of the hillside structures.

Kakujudai   The first building one passes on the left is the Kakujudai, a large tatami-matted room (as are all the rooms hereafter) with cusped windows. This building on the west and the next three units on the north, east, and south side form an enclosed courtyard around a garden which has a stream running through it. (This first building is one of the large display areas for the temple treasures shown annually in November.)

Kohojo   The second building on the north side of this first courtyard garden is the Kohojo (Abbot's Small Quarters) of five rooms. Some of the rooms of this and the other buildings which lie ahead have *fusuma* (sliding panels) which are worthy of mention. Most of these *fusuma* are covered with plain gold leaf while some have a gold ground with scenes of nature painted upon them. The fourth room of the Kohojo varies from the other three rooms since it has a tokonoma and a statue of a monk seated before a scroll.

Juisi-den   The Juisi-den on the east side of the courtyard also has five rooms. The first room holds the image of a monk (formerly gilded) seated on a Chinese chair with a scroll behind him. The *fusuma* of the second room have a hint of waves upon them, a Buddhist symbol of the impermanence of life. The third or middle room is an altar room. An image of Amida is seated on a lotus blossom while a Fudo image adorned with a *mandorla* (aureole) with flaming edges stands on a lotus blossom behind

Amida. The fourth room has white *fusuma* with abstract drawings symbolizing ocean waves, while the last room contains an image of a seated monk with a scroll depicting the temple layout hanging behind him.

Daihojo   The last building on the south side of this first courtyard is the Daihojo (Abbot's Large Quarters). The west side of the Daihojo faces the Chokushi-mon gateway with its raised sand garden and raked decorations, while the center room on the west side of the building has an altar with images of Amida, Seishi, and Kannon. The second room on the third (or south) side of the Daihojo (which faces onto the second courtyard) is a study for the abbot and has a set of *chigaidana* (staggered shelves) and a tokonoma. A portion of the south wall contains a writing shelf (desk) with shoji. A raised platform holds a Chinese chair without legs (the abbot's chair). The rear *fusuma* are decorated with paintings of trees, clouds, and Chinese figures against a gold ground, while the *fusuma* of the left wall depict mountains with a young man in Chinese garb in the center, a boat to the left, and trees to the right.

A standing screen three feet tall depicts the famous Amida Raigo (The Descent of Amida). In the painting, a golden Amida adorned with a huge halo is appearing over a hill. Seishi and Kannon, also in gold, are standing on white clouds beside Amida. At the bottom corners are small figures of the Guardians of the Four Directions, and in the center bottom are Bon-ten and Taishaku-ten. The picture is supposed to represent a vision which Eshin Sozu had on Mount Hiei, and it is a type of Amida Raigo painting which was particularly popular during the Kamakura period (1185–1336). It was not unusual for a dying person to grasp such cords as those which extend from the hands of Amida in such a picture (as was the case of the dying Fujiwara-no-Michinaga, court official of the Heian period, 794–1185), so as to be certain to arrive in Amida's Western Paradise immediately upon death. This particular portrayal of the descent of Amida is considered one of the finest of its kind.

Daiden   The corridor continues along the north side of this second courtyard, the east side of the corridor having a bell and public toilets behind it. The south side of the corridor runs along the north portion of the Daiden (Great Hall), a large hall with six cusped windows. The front third of the Daiden is for worshipers; the rear portion encompasses the altar area. Two Shitenno (Deva Kings) at the extreme rear on the right and left protect the closed cases holding the Daiden's main Amida image, and the large altar is enriched by the gold hanging baldachins *(tengai)* before it. At the right front is an image of Binzuru, a disciple of Buddha who fell from grace but who continued to follow the Buddha and to observe his teachings. (A physician in his lifetime, it is reputed to be efficacious if one touches the image and then touches the afflicted part of one's body.)

Mikaeri-no-Amida   The corridor leads around three sides of the Daiden, and at the rear of the building it splits into two directions, both mounting a series of steps. Taking the right-hand steps, one passes the Ihai-do with its memorial tablets and then at the top of some steps is the Amida-do (Amida Hall). The Amida-do holds the statue of the famous Mikaeri-no-Amida, the Backward-Looking Amida of legendary account. It is recorded that at 4:00 p.m. on February 15, 1081, when Eikan was reciting the *nenbutsu* (*Namu Amida Butsu*—Praise to the Buddha Amida) while walking around the image (the walking or dancing *nenbutsu* prayer), Amida came down from the altar to pray with him and to join him in the walking prayer. When Eikan stopped in amazement, Amida turned his head and over his shoulder said, *"Eikan, ososhi."* ("Eikan, you are slow!") To share this experience with others, Eikan had a three-foot-tall Amida image carved with its head half-turned to the right. The story and the image have become famous in Buddhist lore in Japan. Later, a statue of Eikan was placed behind and to the right of the Amida image.

The Amida-do has a colorful painted flower in each square of the coffered ceiling; its columns have been covered with gold leaf (now tarnished), and painted decorations (faded) enhance the upper parts of the columns and the ceiling beams while *apsaras* (flying angels) decorate the ceiling. The Amida-do has a number of other wooden figures of Buddhist deities or noted monks in place, but the small Backward-looking Amida is the major image in the Amida-do.

Returning to the point at which the corridor splits into a right and left wing, each with separate staircases, the steps can be taken to the north to the Kaisan-do (Founder's Hall) where the three founders of the temple are each seated on a Chinese-style chair. Beyond the Kaisan-do, the roofed corridor ends, and one puts on slippers in order to continue up the hill on the many steep steps leading to the Tahoto pagoda (closed). From this point, a limited view can be had of the whole of northern Kyoto across to the mountains in Arashiyama-Sagano.

From the Zenrin-ji/Eikan-do, one can continue to the Nomura Museum and then to the Nanzen-ji Zen temple.

NOMURA MUSEUM

From the Zenrin-ji/Eikan-do, one walks south along the main road in front of the temple until one comes to a high school. To the right, across from the school, is the Nomura Museum. The museum is open from 10:00 a.m. to 4:00 p.m. for the spring and autumn exhibitions. It is closed on Mondays and from June 10 to September 10 and from December 5 to March 10. Entry fee.

The Nomura Museum is a post-World War II museum which exhibits the private collection of Tokushichi Nomura, a financier who was responsible for the Daiwa Bank and Nomura Securities Company, among other enterprises. The collection of Japanese art includes paintings and hanging scrolls, lacquerware, pottery, Noh masks, costumes, calligraphy, and items concerned with the tea ceremony. The museum also holds Chinese ceramics. Only a limited number of objects are shown at any time, and these are changed each month.

NANZEN-JI

The Nanzen-ji is the next unit on this walk. Since one may wish to come to it directly, directions are given both from the Nomura Museum or the Zenrin-ji/Eikan-do temple as well as for the buses taken from the heart of the city.

The Nanzen-ji is located at the foothills of the Higashiyama chain of mountains at the eastern end of the extension of Niomon-dori, the street that runs along the southern perimeter of the Okazaki cultural area. Take bus 39 or 103 to the Keage bus stop and then walk .40 kilometers north and east to the temple, or take bus 5 to the Eikan-do-mae bus stop and then walk east to the road to the Zenrin-ji/Eikan-do and then south to the Nanzen-ji. If coming from the Zenrin-ji/Eikan-do or the Nomura Mu-

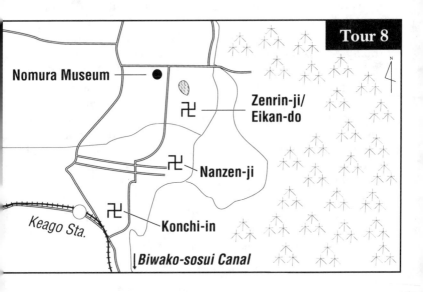

seum, one simply continues to the south on the street which runs in front of these units. The Nanzen-ji temple grounds are always open while the hours of the various buildings are 8:00 a.m. to 5:00 p.m. from May through October and from 8:30 a.m. to 4:00 p.m. from November to April. An entry fee is charged to the San-mon gateway and to the Hojo as well as to the sub-temples mentioned below.

The Nanzen-ji (South Temple of Enlightenment) belongs to the Rinzai school of Zen Buddhism and is located in a pine forest just below the Higashiyama mountains. As one of the major Zen temples in Kyoto, it will here be described in some depth since it is the only important Zen temple open to the public which is covered in its entirety in this volume. Aside from its major buildings, the Nanzen-ji has twelve sub-temples. At one time a very large compound, it is now reduced to some twenty-seven acres after having been forced to sell off much of its land during the Meiji era. A number of the sub-temples have notable gardens, but only a few of these are open to the public except through special permission. Fortunately, the three most important gardens are available for visitation with two of the sub-temples serving vegetarian lunches.

The temple was originally a villa for a retired emperor rather than a religious site. The emperor Kameyama, unhappy with his relationship with the Kamakura shogunate, abdicated in 1274 at the age of twenty-six and built a retirement retreat, the Zenrin-ji-den at the eastern edge of the city. Beautiful gardens were laid out, and two palaces were created, the Kami-no-miya or Natsu-no-miya (Upper or Summer) retirement palace and the Shimo-no-miya or Fuyu-no-miya (Lower or Winter Palace). Problems plagued the villa on a continuing basis; thus, in 1290 the emperor invited Priest Fumon of the Tofuku-ji to rid the palace of a ghost that was said to be plaguing it. Fumon accomplished the task simply through *zazen* (seated meditation) without the intoning of any sutra. The emperor was so impressed by this demonstration of the efficacy of Zen meditation that he rewarded Fumon by giving him a portion of the villa lands (the Shimo-no-miya) on which to create a temple.

The emperor continued to live at the upper palace (Kami-no-miya) studying Zen doctrines under Fumon, granting himself the title of Ho-o (Great Priest). Eventually, Fumon requested the second palace for his temple as well. His request was granted and Fumon began the creation of the Nanzen-in (now a sub-temple of the Nanzen-ji). The construction of the Nanzen-in was aided by the former emperor who personally helped to carry some of the dirt needed for its foundations. The Nanzen-in today contains a statue of the emperor as a priest; he took the tonsure in 1289. Thus was the Nanzen-in temple founded, the first unit of the Nanzen-ji complex which was to become the headquarters of the Zenshu branch of the Rinzai school of Zen Buddhism.

In 1297 the Butsu-den (Buddha Hall) of the Nanzen-ji was begun, and Zen flourished here to the envy of the ever-militant and parochial Tendai monks of Mount Hiei. Thus, on September 28, 1393, they raided the temple and put it to the torch. Fire again destroyed the rebuilt complex on February 16, 1447, and the reconstructed temple was leveled once more on September 16, 1467, during the Onin War. Toyotomi Hideyoshi rebuilt the temple in 1597, provided it with a new Butsu-den, and in 1611 the emperor Go-Yozei gave it the Seiryo-den of the imperial palace (which became the Daihojo, the Abbot's Large Quarters). Shogun Tokugawa Ieyasu granted it a building from Hideyoshi's Fushimi Castle for the Shohojo or Kohojo (Abbot's Small Quarters). Another gift was the Chokushi-mon gate which originally was the Nikka Gate of the imperial palace. The temple grounds were expanded in the Edo era (1616–1868) as the Nanzen-ji enjoyed shogunal favor, and it boasted sixty-two sub-temples on grounds covering 114,819 *tsubo*. (A *tsubo* equals approximately six square feet.) Unhappily, the anti-Buddhist mood of the new Meiji government after 1868 reduced its grounds to 33,966 *tsubo*, leaving it with but nine sub-temples. (Today the complex is back to twelve sub-temples.)

The esteem granted the Nanzen-ji can in part be credited to the fact that the most capable Rinzai Zen master has always been selected as its abbot. The temple continues to serve in the training of Zen practices, and monks come from throughout Japan to practice *zazen* (seated meditation) at the Nanzen-ji.

San-mon/Tenkanoryu-mon The huge, two-story San-mon or Tenkanoryu-mon (Mountain Gate or Dragon Gate) provides an impressive entry to the Nanzen-ji. One of the three largest gateways in Japan, it was first built in 1296 but destroyed by fire in 1447. In 1626, Todo Takatora, one of Shogun Ieyasu's most trusted generals, had the San-mon rebuilt as a memorial to the warriors of both sides who died a decade earlier in the battle in which Ieyasu's forces annihilated those of Toyotomi Hideyori (Toyotomi Hideyoshi's son) at Osaka Castle.

The gate, with its five openings between its six huge, upright columns, has a small building with bell-shaped (cusped) windows in the Zen style on either side and the entrances to the steep stairways leading to the upper level of the gate. A railing runs around the narrow platform outside the second story of the gateway from which a view of the city can be obtained. The gate is surmounted by a large roof with slightly turned-up corners and, as with many temple gateways, the sides of the openings of the gate are plastered with *senja fuda,* stickers with the names of the devout who have pasted them there. The higher the sticker is placed, the more likely is it to be noticed by the gods. As a result, an expandable/retractable walking stick and sticker-pasting rod was devised for use by pilgrims whose physical reach never satisfied their spiritual aspirations for divine notice.

The upper floor of the gateway is named Gohoro (Five Phoenixes) and contains a Buddha image, two bodhisattvas, and sixteen *arhats* (Buddhist hermits or holy men), as well as images of Tokugawa Ieyasu and Todo Takatora. The painted ceiling is the work of Kano Tanyu and Tosa Tokuetsu who decorated it with phoenixes and heavenly maidens. The San-mon gate has made its mark in literary history as well since there is a famous Kabuki drama with a scene from the life of Ishikawa Goemon who hid out in the upper level of the gateway to hide from the authorities. As a thief, he had killed in the course of his first theft and so became an outlaw. When he was thirty-seven, according to one story, he tried, unsuccessfully, to steal a Sung-dynasty celadon incense burner, the "Plover Incense Burner," from Fushimi Castle. (This incense burner of Hideyoshi's was claimed to have had the power of attracting plovers when its incense was burned.) Pursued and apprehended in 1585, he and his young son Ichiro were condemned to be boiled in oil in an iron kettle on the riverbed of the Kamogawa river. Ishikawa held his young son above his head during this ordeal before finally collapsing into the boiling oil with the child.

Hatto/Butsu-den The Hatto or Butsu-den (Lecture Hall or Buddha Hall) dates from 1918 since it replaces one which burned in 1895. It has a Shaka image accompanied by Fugen and Monju on a very high altar with *ihai* (mortuary tablets) before the main image. The ceiling is decorated with the painting of a dragon by Imao Keinen.

Daihojo The Abbots' Quarters consist of two joined buildings, the Daihojo and the Shohojo. The larger unit, the Daihojo, is the one that serves as the entry to these quarters. The Daihojo was originally the Seiryo-den of the imperial palace, built for the then reigning emperor by Toyotomi Hideyoshi in the 1590s. When Ieyasu came to power as the shogun, one of his strongest intentions was to erase Hideyoshi's name from the annals of history; thus, he gave the emperor a new palace in 1611 to replace the one commissioned by Hideyoshi. As a result, the Daihojo, as a former palace building, is constructed in the traditional palace manner with a hipped and gabled roof covered with cypress bark instead of the usual tiled roof of Buddhist temple buildings.

The entry hall has the ticket booth on the left where the fee for visiting the Daihojo and Shohojo is paid; the room on the right has a view of a small waterfall in the garden. From the entry hall, a passageway at the rear of the hall leads north past a series of four small rooms on the right. The paintings on the *fusuma* in these rooms of the Daihojo are by the artists of the Kano school of painting and were once part of the imperial palace. The first room has a *sozu* in the garden beyond it (a bamboo pipe that collects water until it becomes top heavy and then dumps the water with a thud—originally used to scare animals away from the garden crops or flowers).

The second room consists of the public toilets, while the third room has plain *fusuma*. The fourth room has waves painted on the *fusuma* on the left (all these rooms have plain shoji for their exterior wall), and the last room has a *chigaidana,* a tokonoma, and a writing-desk bay, the right wall having a painting of a dragon. At the end of the passageway, one turns to the left to the Shohojo which originally was part of Hideyoshi's Fushimi Castle, south of Kyoto.

Shohojo   The Shohojo is the more noted of the two buildings because of its dry garden and its painted *fusuma.* The outside corridor on the south side of the Shohojo opens onto four rooms noted for having Chinese figures or scenes of nature painted on a gold ground. The first room facing the garden is the Willow Room. This is followed by the Musk Room with paintings by Kano Motonobu (1476–1559). The room behind the Musk Room is the Naritaki-no-ma (Sound of the Waterfall Room), a small, six-mat room with a tokonoma and *chigaidana.* An ornate painting of a large waterfall with Chinese beauties in an idealized landscape hangs in the tokonoma. The emperor Go-Yozei (early 1600s) resided in this room when it was still part of the imperial palace.

Next to these two rooms is the Midday Room with Kano Eitoku's (1543–90) paintings of the Nijushiko, the "Twenty-four Examples of Filial Piety." This central room on the south side of the building facing the garden has a small altar room behind it, with a Heian-period Kannon image as the object of reverence. The West Room is the last of the four rooms on this side. The beams in the Shohojo were carved by the noted wood master Hidari Jingoro (1594–1634).

The Zen *karesansui* (dry garden) of the Shohojo is said to be the work of Kobori Enshu (1579–1647) and is among the more noted of such carefully designed Japanese Zen gardens. Here, sand, bushes, trees, and a few rocks constitute what is known as the Tiger and Cubs Zen Garden. There are many interpretations of its symbolism: does it represent a tiger and her cubs crossing a river, or does it represent the crane and tortoise, traditional symbols of longevity?

A teahouse by Kobori Enshu in the garden has paintings within by Hasegawa Tohaku (1539–1610). The building is not open to the public.

On turning the corner from the south side of the Shohojo to the west side, the first room is the Crane Room where the *fusuma* exhibit the artistry of Kano Eitoku.

The three rooms on the west side, also from Fushimi Castle, are famous for their paintings of tigers in a bamboo grove, the Tora-no-ma (Tiger Rooms). Altogether, there are thirty-nine murals showing tigers painted by Kano Tanyu (1602–74) on *fusuma* which were first covered with gold leaf. The rooms of this side of the Shohojo look out on a separate dry garden. The covered corridor turns from a northern direction to the east (a *kura* [fireproof storage building] is in the garden to the east) and then the corridor continues to the north; a dry garden is to the right, while a pond, two teahouses, and then a newer building for use by the priests is on the left.

Retracing one's steps along this corridor back to the northern side of the Shohojo, one passes a series of small rooms each having multipanel painted screens *(byobu)* on display. At the end of the corridor a *kago* is suspended from the ceiling. A *kago* is a traveling palanquin for the upper classes, a carriage that was carried on the shoulders of porters. As one turns the corner of the corridor, a larger room has a tokonoma and *chigaidana*. Scenes of a waterfall and of people in Chinese garb are painted on the *fusuma*. One last room has Chinese-style furniture on display.

Twelve sub-temples are in the Nanzen-ji complex, only a few of which are open to the general public on a continuing basis. These include the Nanzen-in, the Chosho-in, the Tenjuan, and the Konchi-in.

Nanzen-in   The Nanzen-in is located to the south of the Daihojo and the Hatto (Lecture Hall) and past the brick aqueduct coming from the Biwako-sosui canal which bears water from Lake Biwa. The Nanzen-in is open from 8:30 a.m. to 4:30 p.m. Entry fee.

The Nanzen-in was the first unit of the Nanzen-ji built on the site of Emperor Kameyama's Kami-no-miya or Natsu-no-miya (Upper or Summer) retirement palace. The original temple building was the one the emperor helped to create by carrying dirt for fill when its construction began. The deeply religious mother of Shogun Tsunayoshi had the Nanzen-in rebuilt (1703) along its original lines since it had been destroyed in the Onin War.

The grounds of the Nanzen-in temple are entered (entrance fee) through the western side of the precincts, and the path leads along this side of the Hondo toward the front of the building. The Hondo consists of a large tatami-matted main room with a shrine in the rear of the hall. A small memorial building sits within the temple grounds inside a walled area; a flaming jewel tops the Chinese-style roof. (A portion of Emperor Kameyama's remains have been interred in the Nanzen-in, and a statue of Emperor Kameyama, clothed in priestly garb, is held here also.)

The landscape garden, initially laid out in the 1300s, was the noteworthy element of the Nanzen-in, purportedly designed by Muso Soseki (1275–1351). The garden has been altered so often, most recently in Edo times (1603–1868), that little of its original design remains other than remnants of its large pond and stroll garden. It is, nonetheless, an attractive garden with moss and with cedar and maple trees about it. Tiny islands exist in the pond, one in the design of the ideogram for *shin* (heart). A hill rises sharply behind the pond and garden; a waterfall on the hill feeds the pond. Above, on top of the hill just alongside the top of the brick aqueduct, is the temple Shoro (Bell Tower).

Chosho-in   The Chosho-in is a small sub-temple (also called the Marishiten) north of the main gateway which has an image of Marishiten (Queen of Heaven in Chinese and Japanese Buddhism) brought from China by Priest Seisetsu. The garden is at its loveliest when the azaleas are in bloom. The Okutan restaurant within the Chosho-in serves fresh tofu to the public at lunch time; some three hundred years of serving vegetarian fare have perfected this culinary form.

Tenjuan   The Tenjuan sub-temple of the Nanzen-ji is to the south of the San-mon gateway and across the path which leads to the Daihojo. It is only open in the spring and autumn from 9:00 a.m. to 5:00 p.m. Entry fee.

The Tenjuan sub-temple was established in the mid- to late 1300s by Priest Kokan Shiren, a monk of the Rinzai sect and fifteenth chief priest of the Nanzen-ji, in honor of Priest Fumon, the founder of the Nanzen-ji. Destroyed in the Onin War of 1467–77, along with the other buildings of the Nanzen-ji, it was not re-established for one hundred and thirty years until Hosokawa Yusai rebuilt the Tenjuan's Main Gate, Hondo, and Shoin (study) in 1602. All three of these buildings are still standing.

The roof of the Hondo is wood-shingled, and in its principle room is a life-sized wooden statue of Fumon, while in one corner are the memorial tablets of the Hosokawa family. The year the building was erected, Hasegawa Tohaku painted the thirty-two *fusuma* of the main hall, some of which feature a nobleman riding a donkey; Daruma, the priest who began Zen Buddhism in China; landscapes with pines and cranes, etc. The temple holds a self-portrait of Fumon as well as portraits of Hosokawa Yusai and his wife.

The gardens of the temple were originally created at the time the Tenjuan was built. The front garden of the Hondo has a geometrically designed footpath in white sand and moss while its main sector is a raked-gravel and rock garden enriched with moss and trees. The southern garden near the Shoin has two ponds separated by a peninsula reaching from the Shoin and joined by another peninsula from the far side of the lake. A waterfall before the trees in the background provides a backdrop to the pond. The garden was remodeled in 1605 by Priest Kozan Kyose at the time of the reconstruction of the temple, and it was again remodeled in the late nineteenth century; an island with a bridge connecting it to the shore is a Meiji-period (post-1868) addition. A cemetery in the temple grounds includes the graves of Hosokawa Yusai (1534–1610) and his family as well as those of other noted individuals of the Meiji era and later.

Konchi-in   The Konchi-in sub-temple is located to the south and east of the Nanzen-ji main gate. It is open from 8:30 a.m. to 5:00 p.m. Entry fee.

Originally an independent temple at Takagamine in north-west Kyoto, the Konchi-in was moved to its present site in the late fourteenth or early fifteenth century and became affiliated with the Nanzen-ji. Shogun Ashikaga Yoshimochi was the person behind the establishment of the Konchi-in at the Nanzen-ji in 1400; he appointed Priest Daigo as its head priest. Damaged in the Onin War of the 1460s, it was restored in 1600 by Ishin Suden. The Hojo (see below) was moved here from Fushimi Castle. At one time, the Konchi-in had a Kara-mon (Chinese-style) gate from Fushimi as well, but in the late nineteenth century this was moved to the rebuilt Hokoku Shrine in honor of Hideyoshi, an action taken, no doubt, as a spiteful removal since the new Meiji government did not approve of the favor which the Tokugawa shoguns had shown to the Nanzen-ji.

Hojo The Hojo (Superior's Quarters) is a middle-sized Shoin built in the Momoyama style with a hipped and gabled cypress roof. It has six rooms in a U-shaped layout with *fusuma* featuring paintings of the Kano school. The center room is the altar room; it features a large black-lacquered altar and shrine. To the right of the altar room are two rooms; the inner room is the Chrysanthemum Room, while the room before it is the Crane Room. To the left of the altar or center room are two other rooms; the rear one has an elevated section *chigaidana* and a tokonoma decorated with a painting of a pine tree.

In front of the Hojo is a *karesansui* (dry garden) which has been documented as being created by Kobori Enshu (1579–1647). It was commissioned by Ishin Suden, the priest who acted as the Tokugawa government's representative on aid to temples and who was responsible for the restoration of the Konchi-in in the early 1600s; he used it as his administrative headquarters. Enshu was given the commission to design new gardens for the temple, including the one located in front of the Hojo. The background of this garden has an embankment planted with bushes and trees. Two groupings of rocks, one vertically laid out (to the right) and one created on the horizontal plane (to the left) represent the traditional crane and tortoise motif. The garden in front of the plantings changes from large stones to fine gravel to moss, with a contorted tree adding interest to the overall layout. The west end of the garden is closed by a memorial building in honor of Suden.

East of the Hojo is a garden built about a lotus pond with a crane-and-tortoise island, a two-slab stone bridge, and a small Shinto shrine sitting across from the pond. A path around the pond leads to a large ceremonial gateway standing before a path lined with lanterns leading to a torii. A walled enclosure is entered through an inner Kara-mon gate. Within the walls is a building that is a memorial to Shogun Tokugawa Ieyasu, a small Toshogu shrine which Ishin Suden built in 1628 following the instructions in Ieyasu's will. It is a strange combination of a black-lacquered Buddhist building in front and a yellow-and-vermilion-painted Shinto building with plaque cutouts of birds and animals to the rear. The interior of the front portion has a painted dragon on the ceiling and pictures of the shoguns painted across the beam before the altar area. Eight *arhats* (Buddhist hermits or holy men) are on either side of the front room while the inner room has the main image of Ieyasu. Behind the Main Hall is a noted teahouse with eight windows.

BIWAKO-SOSUI CANAL

One leaves the Nanzen-ji complex by the road on the south side of the huge main gateway and continues to the highway where one turns left to the Biwako-sosui canal and Sanjo-dori. The Biwako-sosui canal and incline are on the eastern side of Kyoto and can be observed between the intersection of Niomon-dori/Shirakawa-dori and the Keage stop of the Keihan Keishin Rail Line (below the Miyako Hotel) as the incline comes from the southeast where it emerges from the mountain tunnel.

From the early days of Kyoto, thought had been given to the creation of a water link between Lake Biwa (to the east of Kyoto and beyond the Higashiyama mountains) and the city of Kyoto. A plan had been drafted by Taira-no-Kiyomori in the twelfth century, and Toyotomi Hideyoshi found it of interest in the late 1500s as well. Its consummation, however, had to await the use of modern technology after the Meiji Restoration of the late nineteenth century. Work began in 1885 and the project was completed by 1904.

A canal seven miles long with a drop of eleven feet was created from Lake Biwa (in the Mii-dera railway station area) to the western side of the Higashiyama mountains in Kyoto. At the Keage area in Kyoto (the eastern end of Sanjo-dori at the mountains) a rail incline of 1,820 feet was created between the canal and the level of the Kyoto plain. Boats that had crossed the canal could be loaded onto steel trucks and thus safely lowered onto the rails for the 118-foot drop between the canal and the city. The power generated by the fall of the water was used by a hydroelectric plant near the bottom of the incline (at the eastern end of Niomon-dori) to generate enough energy to haul the boats as well as electricity for general use in the city. This hydroelectric plant was the first one built in Japan (1891), and it still operates on a limited basis—and as a museum as well. It made possible the use of the first electric trams (streetcars) in Kyoto from 1901 until the late 1960s when the trams were discontinued and the cars were sold to the city of Hiroshima.

For a number of years, the canal was used to transport both people and goods between the cities of Otsu and Kyoto. Some two hundred boats used the canal, carrying 157,000 passengers a year by the end of its first five years in operation. Part of the water that was brought to Kyoto in the canal was sent over a brick viaduct through the Nanzen-ji grounds and then through pipes across the eastern part of the city, under the Kamogawa river, and to the Horikawa river for use in the irrigation of farms. The water serves as fire protection for the Hongan-ji complexes in central Kyoto, as well as for other purposes within the city.

Obviously, the advent of rail and automotive transportation brought an end to the use of the canal for transportation purposes, but the water from Lake Biwa still serves the city.

The Miyako Hotel is on the nearby hill if refreshments are desired, or a visit can be made to the Kyoto International Center, mentioned in Tour 6. Otherwise transportation can be taken back to the heart of the city. The surface rail line runs from the corner of Shirokawa-dori to the Sanjo-dori terminal at the Kamogawa river and the Sanjo-dori Bridge. Buses to all parts of the city can be obtained at this terminal.

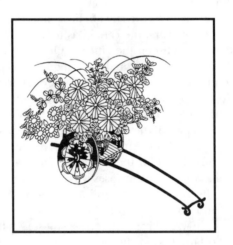

TOUR
9

The Esoteric Temple and the Shimabara Pleasure Quarters

島原　東寺

THE HILLS to the north, east, and west of Kyoto have always provided a natural barrier around the city, but the way to the south toward Osaka and the Inland Sea has always been open. The original southern boundary of Heiankyo (Kyoto) lay at Kujo-dori (Ninth Street) where the great Rasho-mon gate provided a grand entrance to the city. The capital to the north of the gate was protected by the placement of the To-ji (East Temple) and the Sai-ji (West Temple) to either side of the Rasho-mon. The temples may have offered the city spiritual protection, but for practical and political purposes they were no barrier to any armed foe.

This lack of protection in the area to the south of Kyoto was remedied at the end of the 1500s when Toyotomi Hideyoshi built his great Fushimi Castle a few miles below Kyoto to guard the city from the south. The area below Kujo-dori in Hideyoshi's day, and even later, was still open countryside interspersed with a few shrines and temples. In time, the Tokugawas were to dismantle Fushimi Castle, for under their strict rule there was little chance of revolt against the shogunal government. Then, in the late nineteenth century, the railroad came to Kyoto, and, with its eventual realignment and the addition of the Kintetsu and the Shinkansen rail lines, the Kyoto Central Station and the raised railroad tracks formed a new "barrier" at Hachijo-dori (Eighth Street). This new barrier, however, has been no more effective than the Sai-ji or the To-ji temples were, and the sprawl of the modern city now spreads to the south, engulfing old temples and shrines as the growth of modern Kyoto continues.

When Kyoto was established in 794, there was one experience the emperor Kammu had faced in the former capital of Nara which he did not wish to encounter again: the interference in governance of the nation by the Buddhist clergy. Thus, he planned his new capital so that the Buddhist temples would be outside the city gates rather than within the capital itself. Of course, a city and its people needed the religious and supernatural protection which Buddhism could offer. Thus, he designated a site to the east and to the west of the main city gate for two temples, the To-ji and the Sai-ji.

TO-JI

Before too many years had passed, the To-ji, at the order of the next emperor, had come under the leadership of Kukai (774–835). Kukai brought Mikkyo (Esoteric Buddhism) doctrines from China where he had studied the latest in Buddhist thought. He proposed that the temple should observe the Shingon rules of Buddhism the better to protect the state and city. The temple was thus known as the Kyo-o-gokoku-ji, "The Temple for the Transmission of the Teachings to the King and for the Protection of the State." This purpose suited the needs of the emperor and the court, and thus the To-ji flourished under imperial patronage.

The Sai-ji, on the other hand, had no leadership such as Kukai offered at the To-ji, and so the temple suffered. A fire in 990 damaged the temple buildings severely, and when the pagoda burned in 1233 (the sole structure of the temple still standing by that time), the Sai-ji became merely a memory. A memorial stone to the west of Shichi-honmatsu-dori (nine streets west of the To-ji temple and three streets north of Kujo-dori) is all that remains as a remembrance of the Sai-ji. In the same manner, a stone marker at the intersection of Kujo-dori and Senbon-dori is the only reminder of the Rasho-mon gate which was once traversed by aristocrats, priests, merchants, and beggars entering the noble city of Heiankyo.

The To-ji, however, survived and continues to flourish due to the efforts of Kukai who rejuvenated the temple and turned it into a bastion of Shingon belief. Shingon has a mystic bent to it (it is related to Tantric Buddhism which had its strength in Tibet), and Kukai's To-ji lecture hall (Kodo) was filled with Buddhist images arranged in the pattern of a mystic mandala or picture.

The To-ji lies to the north of Kujo-dori (Ninth Street) and west of Omiya-dori, a walk of approximately ten to fifteen minutes southwest of Kyoto Central Station. Bus 19, 20, or 208 to To-ji - minami-mon-mae (the south gate on Kujo-dori) or 207 to To-ji-higashi-mon-mae (the east gate on Omiya-dori) go to the temple which is open from 9:00 a.m. to 4:30 p.m. Most of the grounds can be entered without charge, but there is an entry fee to the area of the main buildings and a separate fee to the treasury.

In 796, shortly after the founding of the new capital of Heiankyo (Kyoto) by the emperor Kammu, the To-ji was erected. Then in 823 the emperor Saga (reigned 809–23), successor to Emperor Kammu, appointed Priest Kukai as the superior of the To-ji. The Shingon doctrines of Buddhism which Kukai had brought to Japan provided a new emphasis for the Buddhism of his day. They held that anyone could attain buddhahood after this life through faith and actions instead of having to wait until the end of the present cycle of time.

When Buddhism was first propagated in Japan, it was considered applicable only to the ruling classes, a situation that still prevailed at the founding of Heiankyo (Kyoto) at the end of the eighth century. Kukai, on the contrary, believed that buddhahood was available to women as well as men, to commoners as well as nobles; thus, he fashioned his approach to daily life with a concern for all levels of society, doing all he could to improve the condition of the average person. He opened a school for commoners, compiled the first Japanese dictionary in order to assist in the educational process, made medicines available to all, introduced new techniques in agriculture, improved roads, and built bridges to assist farmers.

Kodo   As Superior of the To-ji, Kukai made the temple's Kodo (Lecture Hall) the center both of his beliefs and of the visual realization of the mystic or magical significance of the mandala (a representation of the various Buddhist deities centered around the image of Dainichi Nyorai, the central Buddha) in paintings or tapestries. The physical alignment of the three-dimensional images which he placed in the Kodo reflected their arrangement in the painted representations of the Womb and Diamond Mandalas which he had brought back from China. For Kukai, art was a visible aspect of religion; thus, religious statues, paintings, and manuscripts enriched the temple and monastery under his leadership. Here in the Kodo was located his seminary for Mikkyo Buddhism. The Kodo, accordingly, was the most important building in this Shingon temple.

The layout of the To-ji followed the pattern that had been employed in the construction of temples in Nara when it was the earlier capital of the nation. Buildings were aligned from the Great South Gate (Nandai-mon or Minami Dai-mon) northwards. Behind the gateway was the Kondo or Hondo (Main Hall), followed by the Kodo, with the Jiki-do (Refectory) at the rear. Additional buildings to the left (from the southwest to the northwest) of the main structures included the Konchi-in (where priests were ordained as masters of Tantric Buddhism) in the southwest portion of the compound, then the Kyaku-den (Guest House), and finally the Taishi-do or Mie-do (Founder's Hall) created after Kukai's death. The pagoda was erected to the east of the main axis of the temple, and a small Shinto shrine to protect the temple lands was placed to the west of the pagoda.

As with virtually all temples in the city, the To-ji suffered destruction in the Onin Wars of 1467–77; thus, the present buildings are not the original ones. The temple's spacious gardens and three ponds remain, but the original extent of the To-ji was four times its present size. Today, the temple is the headquarters of the To-ji branch of Shingon Buddhism, and it consists of a twenty-four-acre area with walls and gates on all four sides.

Although it is possible to enter the grounds of the To-ji through any of its four gates, the main entrance is through the Great South Gate (Nandai-mon or Minami Dai-mon). The original great gateway to the To-ji on its southern side was lost with time. Earlier replacements were destroyed by fire, and then in

1894 the gate was replaced by the present eight-pillared Great South Gate which had formerly been the West Gate of the Sanjusangen-do temple. The Renge-mon gate on the western side of the temple grounds was built in 1191 and is the temple's oldest unit. To the east of the Great South Gate stands the temple pagoda with three small ponds to its north. The tallest pagoda of any temple in Japan, it stands 187 feet high in the southeast area of the temple compound. Originally constructed at Kukai's order, it has burned down five times since its construction in 826. Its present replacement was created in 1644 by Shogun Tokugawa Iemitsu. The Four Buddhas are on the *shumidan* (dais for a Buddhist image) and the Eight Great Bodhisattvas are painted on the wooden walls of the interior. This pagoda does not contain a relic of the Buddha (the original purpose of pagodas), but it stands as a symbol of the Mandala of the Two Worlds.

The Kodo is the most important building of the temple, rather than the Kondo as is the usual case, for the images within this building conform to the Tantric pattern based on Mikkyo Buddhist principles. (Such a pattern usually appears on mandalas, Buddhist pictures, or representations of a perfect, enlightened universe.) With images of twenty-one major deities, the figures are of great importance since they provide a three-dimensional version of the pictorial mandalas in which Dainichi Nyorai is the central figure surrounded by other Buddhas in a circular pattern. These images served as the central focus of ceremonies meant to protect the state.

As called for in the Shingon sutra, and as seen in the mandalas, the central figure is the seated Dainichi Nyorai Buddha, seven feet tall, with the four Kongokai (Diamond World) or Supreme Buddhas (Ashuku, Hosho, Fuku, and Amida) about him. The Diamond World symbolizes the wisdom of the Buddha which is as hard as a diamond and capable of crushing all illusions.

To the west (left when facing the main images) are the Godai Myo-o (the Five Radiant Kings, or the Five Great Kings of Light and Wisdom) all from about 839; one of them, Daitokuji, is seated on a bull. All are centered upon a seated Fudo Myo-o with an upright sword in his left hand. Ferocious-looking as they are, these kings are only ferocious in appearance. They are intended to frighten away evil, the better to protect mankind; multiple arms and heads add to the mystic nature of their powers. The Five Great Kings and the Five Bodhisattvas were new concepts, brought back from Tang China by Kukai, for they were not known to the Buddhism of Nara prior to the late 700s.

At the four corners of the complex stand the Shitenno, the Four Deva who protect the world of Buddha from evil. Between the pairs of Shitenno are Taishaku-ten on the west and Bon-ten on the east, both of painted wood. They show their Indian nature in that Bon-ten has four heads (one atop its main coiffure) and four arms and is seated on a group of four geese. Taishaku-ten is seated upon a white elephant. Neither of these India-inspired stylistic approaches with the unusual steeds were to be accepted in the Japanese iconography in the long run. The images in the Kodo are said to have been commissioned by Kukai in 825, and tradition claims that Kukai carved these images himself, a rather doubtful possibility. While these statues are physical representations of the painted mandala that symbolically present the truths of the world, the actual Mandalas of the Two Worlds which Kukai brought from China with him were so worn (through use) that by 821 they had disintegrated and had to be replaced by copies. The present copies done in colors on silk were painted between 1688 and 1703.

Kondo Directly to the north of the Great South Gate is the Kondo, the main hall of the To-ji. The Kondo was first erected in 796 at the inception of the temple. It burned down in 1486, and was replaced about 1606 by the present structure which has a double roof in the *irimoya* (hipped and gabled roof) style. An extra small roof above the lower roof marks the main entry to the Kondo. It is the largest structure in the To-ji and one of the largest Momoyama-period (1568–1603) buildings extant in Kyoto.

The main image in the faded vermilion-and-white interior of the Kondo is that of Yakushi Nyorai, the Buddha of Healing or Medicine. A huge golden aureole is behind the image. This ten-foot-tall seated image is a Muromachi-period (1336–1568) copy of the original Heian statue which was lost to fire in the late 1400s. On either side are his attendants Gakko and Nikko, all three images with a gilt aureole behind them. Under the draperies of Yakushi are the Twelve Godly Generals, attributed to the sculptor Kosho. Huge bronze urns with gilt lotuses stand on either side of these images. The altar table before the images is vermilion while a table and the other furniture on the floor in front of the images are black lacquer.

Jiki-do The original refectory, the Jiki-do, dated from the beginning of the temple in the 790s, but it has burned down twice since then. The present structure was erected in 1930. Rather than a dining room, it has served as a place of study. Traditionally, the main image in this building is Bishamon-ten, protector of the

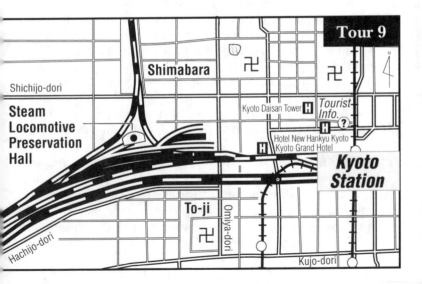

north, who carries a pagoda in one hand and a spear in the other. The Jiki-do image originally stood in the Rasho-mon when that gate was the main entryway to the city of Heiankyo (Kyoto), and the image served to protect the city which lay to its north. When the gate disintegrated, the image was brought to the To-ji. This Bishamon-ten image from the ninth century is dressed in Chinese armor with a helmet which has a phoenix representing the four directions from which it protects the city on each of its four sides. The hall also has a golden Kannon who is holding a bottle-shaped vase containing a lotus bud. To the left of the main image is a large mandala while to the right is a scroll depicting a Myo-o. *Ihai* (mortuary tablets) are to the far right and left.

Kanjo-in   The Kanjo-in (Supreme Purification Hall) lies in the southwest corner of the temple grounds (not open to the public). It was originally built in 1069 after the pattern of the Seiryu-ji temple in China at which Kukai had studied Mikkyo Buddhism. Destroyed by fire on several occasions, the present structure dates from 1634. The Kanjo-in serves as the locus for the *kancho* (or *kanjo*) service, a lustration rite performed as an initiation into the higher mysteries of Shingon Buddhism at which time monks are granted the title of Master of Esoteric Buddhism. The walls of the Kanjo-in contain portraits of the eight great priests of Mikkyo Buddhism as well as Sanskrit characters. Since 1882, by imperial order, prayers for the emperor's health and national peace have taken place here. (The *kancho* rite is not a "baptism" rite, as some Western authors state in their attempt to define a Buddhist form with Christian terminology.)

Mie-do/Taishi-do   The Mie-do or Taishi-do is located to the west of the Kodo and Jiki-do and is situated within its own walled precinct. The onetime site of Kukai's residence, the present building was constructed in 1380. Within is the painted-wood, seated image of Kukai created by Kosho in 1233. The image holds a rosary in his lap with his right hand while his left hand holds a *vajra* (a symbolic thunderbolt) to his chest. His shoes are in front of him and a water jar is to his side. With a round and plump face, the image is a realistic if symbolic representation of Kukai and is enhanced by the skillfully carved drapery folds of his robe; it is not an actual likeness since it was created some two hundred years after Kukai's death. It is thus an idealized portrait meant to serve as an inspiration to the worshipers viewing it, and it is so well composed that it became the model for later images of Kukai. Among other images in the Mie-do is a Fudo Myo-o from about 850, upright sword in his right hand and a rope in his left hand, a pigtail hanging down his chest on the left. On the twenty-first of each month, the Mie-do is open to the public, and becomes thronged with worshipers who come to pray before the image of Kukai.

Homotsukan   Originally, there were two *azekura*-style (log construction) treasure houses to the north and south of the temple buildings. One burned in the year 1000 and the other in 1127. In these original treasuries were said to be all of the treasures that Kukai brought back from China with him, including some of the ashes of the Buddha. The surviving and later treasures which the temple accrued through the centuries are now kept in a fireproof, concrete treasury building, the Homotsukan, situated at the northern end of the temple precinct. Here a portion of the temple's treasures are shown twice a year, from approximately March to May and then from September to November (check at the Tourist Information Center in downtown Kyoto for the actual dates of the showing of the temple's treasures). The treasury is open from 10:00 a.m. to 4:00 p.m. at these times. Entry fee.

The treasures of the To-ji include, among many other items: paintings of the patriarchs of the Shingon sect of Buddhism which Kukai brought back from China in 806; the Ryokai mandala of the ninth century; manuscript letters in Kukai's hand as well as those written by the great priest Saicho of the Tendai sect of Buddhism, a contemporary of Kukai; land records going back to 752, prior to Kukai's time; a Senju (One-Thousand-Arm) Kannon image of 877, the largest wooden statue in Japan; a Jizo from the Heian period (794–1185); and a set of gilt-bronze Buddhist ritual implements of Esoteric Buddhism from Tang China.

The treasury also holds the Kodo's three Shinto images from the ninth century: the oldest known Hachiman image in which the deity is represented as a seated Buddhist priest, and two Shinto goddesses. These are but a sampling of the treasures which are shown on a rotating basis. Some of the finest sculptures remain in the Kodo, arranged in the pattern of a mandala as planned by Kukai in the early 800s.

The To-ji holds many traditional ceremonies throughout the year, but one event that occurs monthly is worthy of mention. Kukai died on the twenty-first of the month, and on this day each month, a memorial service is held in the Mie-do in front of his image. In addition, one of the great fairs of Kyoto is held on this date monthly. Open-air stalls sell food, beverages, clothing, antiques, tools, kitchen items, dried seaweed and dried fish, ceramics, baskets, textiles—and anything else that one may desire. Some fifteen hundred vendors, some of whose families have been selling at these monthly markets for centuries, set up their stalls.

From the intricacies of Buddhist esotericism, it is possible to move to areas of a lighter note. One of these is a museum of both model and life-sized railway trains while the other offers a view of the onetime secondary pleasure quarter of Kyoto.

STEAM LOCOMOTIVE PRESERVATION HALL

Leaving the To-ji through its east side to Omiya-dori and continuing along Omiya-dori to the north and under the railroad overpass, a turn to the left on the second street on the left after the rail line will, after four streets, bring one to Senbon-dori. The Steam Locomotive Preservation Hall is across the street on the left. The Hall is open from 9:00 a.m. to 4:30 p.m., except on

Mondays. When a holiday falls on a Monday, the closing day is shifted to Tuesday for that week. Entry fee.

The Steam Locomotive Preservation Hall is a railroad museum which was created at the edge of a portion of the rail yards to the west of Kyoto Central Station. Actual trains as well as model trains of Japan Rail rolling stock are on display. Not only are steam locomotives displayed, but they are operated at 11:00 a.m., 1:00 p.m., and at 3:00 p.m. The place is a delight for train buffs.

Returning to Shichijo-dori (the east-west street previously taken) and walking back toward the east, a turn to the left after the north-south rail line overpass brings one to the Shimabara district.

SHIMABARA, WESTERN PLEASURE QUARTERS

The Shimabara, or Western Pleasure Quarters, as opposed to the Gion or Eastern Pleasure Quarters, was located between Gojo-dori and Shichijo-dori, west of Omiya-dori and extended to the present north-south right of way of the San-in Main Line railway. The Shimabara district still lies to the west of the Omiya-dori, although today its life as a pleasure quarter has come to an end.

In contrast to the To-ji, which is a center of piety and holds examples of exquisite art, the not-too-distant Shimabara district stands in apposition to the religious life. In 1641 there were two pleasure quarters in the Shijo-dori area of Kyoto. The Tokugawa shogunate worried about the effect of the pleasure quarters on the morals of its military followers and about potential disturbances by rowdy commoners, as well as about having the two pleasure quarters too close to Nijo Castle and the heart of the city. The government thus ordered the westernmost of the two districts moved to the southwest near the Tanbaguchi exit to the city.

In its new precinct, the relocated pleasure quarter became known as the Shimabara district, a name taken in defiance of the government since the shogunate had, with much trouble, only recently put down an insurrection in Kyushu at Shimabara. The new "licensed" district catered to all the pleasures, ranging from the theater, to drink, to the pleasures of the flesh. (It and the Yoshiwara district in Tokyo were the two major "red-light" districts in Japan in the Edo era [1603–1868].)

Shimabara was a district crowded with brothels, and it flourished for three centuries until its "houses of pleasure" were closed in 1958 when the national government outlawed prostitution and the "licensed" districts came to an end. Today, the rather run-down sector between the Nishi Hongan-ji to the east and the wholesale food markets (on the other side of the San-in rail line) on its western borders is of historic interest alone.

Shimabara originally had one street that ran through it from east to west while three streets ran north to south, thereby creating six blocks in the district, each of which had its own name. Set off by a ten-foot-wide moat beyond which an earthen wall separated the district from the rest of the city, it had but two entrances, the Dai-mon or Omon (Great Gate) which still exists on its eastern side, the old houses beyond it giving a flavor of the onetime district, and a smaller gate on its western side. Within the walls, the main places of pleasure were divided into two parts: *ageya,* where men were entertained, and the *okiya* or residence where the entertainers awaited a summons to the *ageya.*

In a hierarchical society, even the demimonde had its social levels. At the top were the *tayu,* women who were educated and who were gifted in the arts, music, poetry, and repartee. At a lower level were women with lesser talents who could not command the higher class of clientele (or fees) attracted to the *tayu;* those of lesser talents offered attractions more of a carnal nature. Thus Shimabara was a place of pleasure in every sense—from intellectual to alcoholic to sexual gratification for those with money. The area with its brothels flourished from 1641, when the Pleasure Quarter was removed from central Kyoto to this district, until 1958 when prostitution was outlawed. Its main raison d'être having disappeared under a new morality, the district declined, and today Shimabara has become a backwater of social history.

Two historic buildings still exist: the Sumiya, an *ageya* or place of entertainment, and the Wachigaiya, an *okiya* (storehouse) or residence from which the women were summoned.

The Sumiya (1670s, revamped in 1787) is a two-story wooden building; its shoji-screened windows are protected by wooden grills. One of the more important buildings of the former Pleasure Quarter, it is today a private building available as an *ochaya*, a teahouse, by private reservation for sedate modern entertainment and, as such, is not open for general viewing. (Arrangements may be made through the Tourist Information Center for a private view of the interior of the building.) It has been preserved fairly closely to its original condition. The interior of the building was richly decorated with finely painted *fusuma* (sliding panels) and *ramma* (transoms) with cut-out work in the form of hearts or fans. Some ceilings boast painted fans. One enters the Sumiya through the front gate which leads into a courtyard. The entry alcove is on the right. Ahead is the entrance to the kitchens. As in any proper villa, some of the rooms have a raised platform *(jodan)*, a built-in desk, cusped (bell-shaped) windows, a tokonoma, and *chigaidana* (staggered shelves), all of which show the influence of Zen architecture even in the Pleasure Quarters. One of the more sumptuous rooms on the upper floor has its decorative elements inlaid with mother-of-pearl. In other words, the stylized ideal for aristocratic residences and teahouses was the model for these houses of pleasure.

The Wachigaiya, originally an *okiya* or residence for the *tayu* of Shimabara, has been greatly remodeled since it first appeared on a 1716 map of Shimabara, but it still exists as a building even if its interior no longer reflects the layout it once enjoyed. As with the Sumiya, the Wachigaiya is now a private teahouse which is generally not open to the public. (Inquiries can be made at the Tourist Information Office.)

Another aspect of the past remains; since the theater was always an important part of the pleasure quarters, the Kaburenjo Theater was built in Shimabara and continues to exist.

Three annual events recall the era when the Shimabara was a flourishing and popular institution:

The Dochu (Tayu Procession) is held on the third Sunday in April at the Josho-ji temple in northern Kyoto. When a *tayu* was summoned to an *ageya*, she made her way regally through the streets on her high wooden geta (clogs), a richly decorated robe worn over her kimono with the large knot of its obi turned to the front. Her fancy, oiled umbrella protected an elegant hairstyle which was enhanced with hairpins and tortoise-shell combs. She was accompanied by a more simply dressed female attendant. In April, the spectacle of Shimabara's past is partially revived in a festival held at the Josho-ji in which the Dochu or procession of *tayu* is reenacted. (The Josho-ji is in the northern part of Kyoto and is not in the Shimabara district. The ceremony takes place here since a noted *tayu* was connected with the temple, donated the cost of its main gateway, and was buried here.)

Shimabara Kaburenjo performances by geisha are held on the third weekend in December at the Kaburenjo Theater.

The New Year Festival is held on December 25. There is a pounding of *mochi* (steamed rice) for the making of rice cakes for the New Year Festival. Geisha and *maiko* (apprentice geisha) participate in the singing and dancing which takes place at this time.

A return to Omiya-dori, or to the intersection of Shichijo-dori and Omiya-dori, or to the intersection of Omiya-dori and Gojo-dori brings one to various bus lines for all parts of the city.

TOUR
10

A Temple of
Momoyama Magnificence
and an Abbot's Garden

東本願寺 西本願寺

NOT FAR from Kyoto Station are two temples and a garden which can attest to the faith of the believers in one of the largest of the Buddhist sects in Japan while at the same time exhibiting the richness of the art of the period in which the original structures were created. The Nishi (West) Hongan-ji temple is the older of the two temples and the one that is worth concentrating upon, for it exemplifies the structure of the temples of this sect and is also the recipient of some of the most magnificent Momoyama-period (1568–1603) examples of architecture and interior design. Its special rooms may only be seen by appointment; thus, it is essential that reservations be made upon arrival in Kyoto so as to assure a possible visit to these extravagantly decorated chambers.

The Higashi (East) Hongan-ji is the second temple of this sect. It will be touched upon but briefly since it lost many of its treasures in a late nineteenth-century fire. However, it still retains its lovely garden a few streets to the east, a garden that exemplifies an earlier Japanese landscape and which is thus frequently used by film crews when creating samurai dramas for television and the movie screen. It is easiest to start this walk from the plaza on the northern side of Kyoto Station. Directly ahead is Kyoto Tower, a monstrous lighthouse-like structure whose only virtue is that it can permit (for a fee) a bird's-eye view of the city from its observation floor. At the eastern side of the building is a place of more importance: the Kyoto branch of the National Tourist Office where maps, information, travel advice, and even some reservation information can be obtained without charge. With a recent map of the city in hand, supplied by the tourist office, one can then head toward the Nishi Hongan-ji temple.

NISHI HONGAN-JI

The Nishi Hongan-ji is located northwest of Kyoto Station on Horikawa-dori. It is approximately a ten- to fifteen-minute walk from the station. Starting from in front of the Kyoto Tower

Building, one walks six streets to the west to Horikawa-dori and there turns to the right. Three streets further on, the Nishi Hongan-ji grounds will be on the left. The entrance to the temple is in the middle of the long Horikawa side of the complex. Bus 7, 28, or 78 can be taken to the Nishi Hongan-ji-mae bus stop on Horikawa-dori in front of the temple. The temple buildings are open from 8:00 a.m. to 5:30 p.m. without charge. Tours of the special Momoyama buildings occur at 10:00 a.m., 11:00 a.m., 1:30 p.m., and 2:30 p.m. weekdays and at 10:00 a.m. and 11:00 a.m. on Saturdays from the temple office in the southwest quarter of the main compound. (Requests for tours should generally be made at this office a week in advance of the date of the proposed visit.) The tours are conducted in Japanese. There is no fee.

The Nishi Hongan-ji temple is the headquarters of the Jodo Shinshu sect of Buddhism which is based on the teachings of Priest Shinran (1173–1263). Shinran had come under the influence of the priest Honen who had simplified Buddhist doctrine to the repetition of the *nenbutsu* (*Namu Amida Butsu*—Praise to the Buddha Amida) as being sufficient to bring one to Amida's Paradise, and Shinran was to develop this doctrine even further than had Honen. While Honen's doctrines seemed radical to the monks of his day, the teachings of Shinran, Honen's disciple, were to become even more radical. As his faith developed, he conceived that Amida's promise of salvation to all (the "Primal Vow," which is what *hongan* means—Amida's pledge to save all beings from suffering through faith in him) was sufficient in and of itself, and that the various practices that had developed in Buddhism were not essential. Thus, he discarded the idea of celibacy for the Buddhist priesthood and was induced by Honen to marry, taking as his wife the daughter of Fujiwara-no-Kanezane. He abandoned other precepts such as that calling for the abstinence from the eating of meat.

From Shinran's teachings, his followers developed a new sect, the Jodo Shinshu branch of Buddhism—the True Pure Land Sect as opposed to the Jodo-shu (the Pure Land Sect) of Honen.

Shinran died in his ninetieth year in 1263, and although his followers and those of Honen continued to increase, both sects underwent years of persecution until in 1591 Toyotomi Hideyoshi granted the Jodo Shinshu sect some eighty acres of land in central Kyoto where it finally found a permanent home. Jodo Shinshu spoke to the concerns of the farmers and the poor, and thus it continued to increase its membership.

Jodo Shinshu flourished in the years of peace that came with its establishment in Kyoto, but the religious sect was considered a possible threat by Tokugawa Ieyasu when he came to power in the early 1600s. Thus, in 1603 Ieyasu split the sect into two branches, the newer unit being located to the east of the original; the East Hongan Temple and the West Hongan Temple came into being as a result. Fire destroyed the Nishi Hongan-ji in 1617, and the new complex which arose from the ashes between 1630 and 1657 was embellished with some of the finest rooms from the former Fushimi Castle and the Jurakudai Palace of Hideyoshi, granted to the temple by the Tokugawa shogunate in the continued attempt to obliterate Hideyoshi's name and physical remembrances in Kyoto. In 1639, the temple opened Ryukoku University for scholarly study, a university that today offers an academic program through to the Ph.D.

With the end of the Tokugawa shogunate and the beginning of the Meiji period (1868), the Nishi Hongan-ji suffered persecution such as was levied by the newly militant Shinto-oriented imperial government against all forms of Buddhism. Some of its land was seized, leaving but twenty-seven acres of the original eighty granted by Hideyoshi, and it was oppressed by government attempts at regulation of religion. The *monshu* (head of the sect) struggled against governmental control of religion, and this created a new impetus for religious growth of the sect.

In 1872 the *monshu* sent students abroad to investigate how other religions were faring, and new ideas and practices were brought back to enrich the faith. In 1888 a journal was begun in English to reach beyond Japanese shores, and in 1897 missionaries were sent overseas, particularly to Hawaii and the United States and eventually to South America and elsewhere.

As the headquarters of the Hongan-ji School of the Jodo Shinshu sect, the Nishi Hongan-ji became one of the largest and most wealthy of Kyoto temples. Today, the sect has more than twenty thousand priests, twelve million believers worldwide, and 10,500 temples. Its monks may marry and may wear lay clothing if they so desire. The chanting of their services has been enriched by its contact with Western music and practices (witness the small organ in the Amida-do and Daishi-do), and its most solemn festivals are marked by high color in costumes and ceremonials. European customs have affected the life of the church, and it now supports Sunday schools, kindergartens, women's organizations, Scout groups, as well as up-to-date schools, universities, and language institutes, the latter being aimed at overseas mission work.

Higurashi-mon   So much for the background of the sect, information that helps in understanding the importance of the Joaɔ Shinshu branch of Buddhism. We can begin by viewing the non-working but ornamental Kara-mon (Chinese-style gateway) on the south side of the grounds on Shichijo-dori (Seventh Street). It is the most noted gateway of the temple and, as its name implies, was done in the Chinese *(kara)* style, a phrase which in Momoyama times (1568–1603) meant flamboyance. It is so embellished with decoration that it has been called the Higurashi-mon, the "Sunset Gate" or "Day-Long Gate"—on the premise that one could spend so much time in admiration of it that dusk would overtake the viewer before one realized it. With its gabled, overarching roof, its black lacquered and colorful enameled sections, its gilded metal work, its carvings of Chinese lions frolicking on the panels of the doors of the gate, and its figures of dragons, tigers, peacocks, and humans against a background of clouds, pine trees, peonies, and bamboo, it is a splendid work of art.

The openwork carvings on the sides of the gate reflect events in Chinese history; for example, Hsu-yu, the legendary Chinese hero, washes from his ears the obscene suggestion of the emperor that he accept a governmental position. Opposite stands a herdsman protesting Hsu-yu's action—since Hsu-yu is thereby polluting the water from which the herdsman's cattle must drink. The gate with its cypress-bark roof supported by six pillars originated in Hideyoshi's Fushimi Castle as the Chokushi-mon (Imperial Messenger's Gate) before it was moved here in 1632.

Sei-mon/Hondo-mon   There are two gates on the Horikawa-dori side of the temple grounds, the entry side to the complex: the Sei-mon (West Gate), one of the finer gateways of Kyoto temples (rebuilt in 1645), and the Hondo-mon (Main Hall Gate). The former has a wall behind the opening, no doubt going back to the ancient belief that this could help prevent the entry of evil forces into the compound. Unsightly wire netting about the gate has been erected in an attempt to deter nesting birds and the flocks about the temple grounds.

Daishi-do/Goei-do   The Daishi-do or Goei-do (Founder's Hall), built in 1632, is the southernmost of the two main buildings of the temple, the left-hand side as one faces the complex being the more honorable position. The Amida-do (Amida Hall) is to its right to the north. Constructed in 1636, the Daishi-do is 189 feet long by 147 feet deep by 90 feet tall, and it has a 477-mat main space. The sanctuary area *(gejin)* has two large rooms on either side with gilt pillars and walls decorated with lotus flowers and leaves. The front of the sanctuary is completely decorated in gilt with gilt trellis folding doors. The gilt *ramma* (transoms) above the doors are enriched with carved flowers which also are gilded. To the right and left of the trellised doors are *fusuma* (sliding panels), the right side showing a painting of pines covered with snow while the left side shows bamboo trees and a tree with birds. A small organ sits to the far right of the worshiper's area.

In the center of the inner sanctuary *(naijin)* is the altar with its two-foot-tall seated image of Shinran (1173–1263), a wooden image said to have been carved by Shinran when he was seventy (in 1243). After his death, the image was varnished, a portion of Shinran's ashes being mingled with the varnish. (The remainder of his ashes was divided between the Higashi Otani and the Nishi Otani burial grounds where it was placed in special tombs.) As a result, the image is held in great esteem by Jodo Shinshu members. On either side of this main altar section are portraits of the abbots who succeeded Shinran. Above the center part of the sanctuary are two characters painted in gold on a dark background. The characters are those for Kenshin (The Truth Realized), an honorary title granted Shinran by the emperor Meiji. The *ramma* above the doorway of the sanctuary are delicately carved and gilded. In the side rooms to the left and right are two large, old *kakemono* (hanging scrolls) with invocations to Amida written in large gold characters on a blue background.

Amida-do   The Amida-do is a 1760 building that replaced its 1591 predecessor which had been destroyed by fire. It is 138 feet long by 126 feet wide and stands 78 feet high. The central shrine of slender gilt pillars and a design of the chrysanthemum flower and leaf contains the wooden image of Amida Nyorai by an artist of the Kasuga school. Memorial tablets to emperors and scroll portraits of several illustrious priests of the temple are hung to the right and left of the Amida image. In the room to the left of the altar is a portrait of Prince Shotoku (574–622), while in the room to the right is a portrait of Honen (1133–1212). Additional portraits of great priests of India, China, and Japan hang here as well: Nagarjuna, Vasubandhu, T'an Luan (Donran), Tao Ch'o (Doshaku), Shan-tao (Zendo), and Genshin. All of the interior of the building is elaborately decorated; the sliding panels have a gold background on which are painted a peacock and a peahen sitting on a peach tree amid white blossoms, the work of an artist of the Kano school. Over the gilt carvings of peonies in the *ramma* are carvings of angels in full relief.

Kyodo Between the Amida-do and Horikawa-dori, to the north, is the Kyodo (Sutra Library). This double-roofed structure was built in 1678 and contains a complete set of the Buddhist scriptures.

Shoro The Shoro (Bell Tower) is in the southeast area of the temple grounds next to the Soro Pond. This 1620 unit contains the bell that had formerly been at the Koryu-ji temple in Kyoto, and it has an inscription upon it by Fujiwara-no-Michinori (died 1160).

In the north corner of the grounds is the drum tower housing a pair of very old drums which once belonged to the Saidai-ji temple in Nara. A large ginkgo tree behind the Hondo-mon gate was once thought to have been a protection against fire. Tradition holds that in case of fire, the tree would emit sprays of water to quench the flames.

While the amount of gilding makes the public worship rooms of the temple outstanding, these pale in comparison to the richness of the other semi-public buildings and rooms granted to the temple by the Tokugawa shogun in 1632. Not only was the marvelous Momoyama-period (1568–1603) Kara-mon given to the temple, but many of the exquisite rooms that once formed a portion of Toyotomi Hideyoshi's Jurakudai Palace and his castle/ residence at Fushimi were moved to the temple as well. These elements make the Nishi Hongan-ji one of the richest temples in Japan in architectural and interior design, for these rooms were decorated by the finest artistic masters of their time. The rooms are particularly rich in the paintings of the Kano school, a family of painters descended from Kano Masonobu (1434–1530) who came to Kyoto and initiated a family of artists who developed a distinct style and who flourished during the sixteenth and seventeenth centuries.

Dai Shoin The rooms of the Dai Shoin (State or Abbot's Apartments) were enriched with the work of various Kano artists: Eitoku, Hidenobu, Koi, Ryokei, Ryotaku, and Tanyu. The work of Maruyama Okyo and Maruyama Ozui also enhance the rooms. These paintings lack the element of mystery or symbolism of Zen paintings; instead they hark back to traditional scenes of a decorative nature taken from Chinese paintings—designs and subjects that appealed to the military rulers of the day.

The Dai Shoin complex is shown at specific times of the day (see the entry above). The complex includes a large entrance hall with three rooms that lead to the Taimenjo or Hideyoshi's Audience Hall with its garden, several private rooms called the Shiro Shoin, two Noh stages, and the separate Hiunkaku (Floating Cloud Pavilion).

Many of the interior paintings were created after the buildings had been reassembled at the Nishi Hongan-ji. However, they all exemplify the spirit of the Momoyama period of the late 1500s when the buildings were first erected.

The Noh stage south of the Dai Shoin was a gift from the shogun in 1674, and it once stood in Sumpu Castle in Shizuoka where it had been modeled after a 1594 stage. The Noh stage in the courtyard north of the Shiro Shoin (White Study) is the oldest Noh stage in Japan (1587); it was brought from Fushimi Castle. It was created with great simplicity, as befits the Noh tradition, rather than in the ornate style of the Momoyama period (1568–1603) when it was built. The Noh drama could be watched from the corridor of the Shiro Shoin. A Noh play is given on this stage on May 21 each year in memory of Shinran.

The Dai Shoin is entered from the south through a large entrance hall which has a cypress roof and a traditional, curved Chinese gate. The rooms within are as follows:

Room 1: Nami-no-ma (Wave Room). The room is so named from the ceiling panels and *fusuma* (sliding panels) decorated with paintings of waves.

Room 2: To the north of the Wave Room is the Tora-no-ma, (Old Tiger Room—"Old" to distinguish it from another "Tiger" set of paintings elsewhere in the complex). These paintings of tigers by Kano Eitoku have, unfortunately, lost their brilliance and are not as readily discernible as they once were.

Room 3: Between the Tiger Room and the Wave Room is the Taiko-no-ma (Drum Room), named from the original and extant painted drums in the ceiling panels. There is a small tokonoma which is covered with gold paper of a later date (as are the walls). The room was used by Hideyoshi to examine the heads of his defeated enemies. (It is claimed by some that the red in the ceiling was painted with blood!) The *ramma* between the Wave and Drum Rooms is a carved fretwork of grapes and squirrels.

To the south is a long porch leading to the Audience Room. The porch has a creaking *uguisubari* (nightingale floor) which announces anyone who is approaching the hall.

Room 4: The Audience Room (Taimenjo, which also is known as the Oshoin, Kon-no-ma, or Stork Room) was Hideyoshi's council hall, and it is the finest and largest of all the rooms in the Dai Shoin. Today, it is used by the abbot of the Nishi Hongan-ji who preaches here twice a month. Originally from the Fushimi Castle, it is floored with 203 tatami mats and is approximately 395 square yards in size. Having forty-five pillars, it is divided into three sections, each succeeding unit at a slightly higher level than the previous one. The pillars at the north (far) end of the room are closer together than those at the front of the room so as to give the illusion that the room is longer than it actually is. The ceiling is a coffered one with painted decorations.

Lower Section: The lower section is the larger portion of the Audience Hall, and the paintings on the *fusuma* on the east and west sides are by Kano Ryokei. The walls and *fusuma* are decorated with pine and plum trees and cranes while the ceiling has birds and flowers, all by Ryokei. A window in the shape of a ceremonial fan in the northeast portion of the lower section opens into the upper section to the north.

Middle Section: The shorter middle section is separated by a floor plank between the tatami of the lower and middle sections of the hall. This unit has painted murals on its western and northern (rear) walls. The north wall has a painting by Kano Tanyu of "The Four Aged Sages on Mount Shang," wise men who were summoned by Emperor Hui of the Han for consultation. The *fusuma* on the west wall have a painting of "The Queen Mother of the West," obviously taken from Chinese history. Huge red tassels on two of the panels of the north wall indicate that the area beyond these doors housed the guards who were always on duty for the protection of Hideyoshi.

Upper Section: At the northeast part of the portion is the small raised upper section in which Hideyoshi sat when holding audiences. The north wall has a scene of the interview by the emperor Wu Ti with a female wizard presenting the emperor with the peaches of immortality, the painting being a backdrop to a set of shelves (*chigaidana*). At the east side of this area, the *ramma* has the carved flying storks, rushes, and clouds attributed to Hidari Jingoro. This eastern portion of the upper section has all the elements of a *shoin* (study): a raised floor, a writing shelf with shoji window screens, and a *chigaidana*. The *fusuma* at this northeastern section have paintings by Kano Tanyu of children at play. A long corridor runs along the eastern side of the Audience Hall, and, when the *fusuma* of the hall are rolled aside, a view of the garden can be seen. Even the ceiling of this corridor is painted with pictures by Kaiho Yusetsu of books and has a wisteria-blossom frieze. The dry rock garden is called Kokei (Tiger Glen) and was designed by Asagiri Shimanosuke. This 65-foot-wide by 95-foot-long dry rock garden has a "lake" of white sand which is supplied with its "water" from a stone "waterfall." The traditional crane and tortoise islands are connected to the rest of the garden by a single arched stone which forms the bridge. The garden differs from most such dry gardens in that it uses sago palms which were brought to Japan by the Portuguese. In winter, they have to be wrapped with straw to protect them from a climate which is colder than what they enjoy in their normal habitat.

Room 5: West of the Audience Hall, behind the *fusuma,* are the Sparrow Room, Wild Geese Room, and the Chrysanthemum Room. The Suzume-no-ma (Sparrow Room) at the southern end of the Dai Shoin (southwest corner) is a lovely small room with *fusuma* and wall panels painted by Maruyama Ozui with sparrows, bamboo branches, and chrysanthemums on a gold ground. Ozui was most skillful in the use of gold and silver powder in his paintings. He has also decorated the coffered ceiling with flowers. The cedar doors were decorated by Kano Ryokei with monkeys and flower baskets of peonies, wisteria, cherry, and other blossoms on a cart.

Room 6: The Gan-no-ma (Wild Geese Room) is similar in size to and north of the Sparrow Room (eighteen mats), and is named for the somewhat damaged wild geese painted by Kano Ryokei on a gold background. The *ramma* between this and the adjoining room is carved with wild geese. Ryokei's paintings on the ceiling are of a species of clematis.

Room 7: The Kiku-no-ma (Chrysanthemum Room) is the last

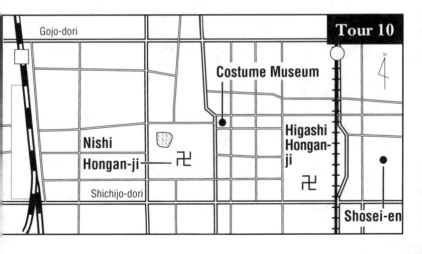

of the three rooms in a row on the western side of the Dai Shoin and was used as a waiting room for guests. This room has yellow and white chrysanthemums, several types of fences, and autumn grasses on a gold ground painted by Kaiho Yusetsu (1598–1677) on the *fusuma;* he also painted fans on the coffered ceiling. There are fans on the veranda as well, painted by Yusetsu and Kano Koi (died 1630). The cedar doors have a cat asleep under peonies on one side and a willow tree and herons on the other side, painted by Kano Ryotaku.

Room 8: Shiro Shoin (White Study). To the north of the Audience Hall are Hideyoshi's apartments of state which he used with his cabinet. They consist of three rooms divided by *fusuma* panels: the Shimei-no-ma or Jodan-no-ma, the Ni-no-ma, and the San-no-ma. The Shiro Shoin (White Study) received its name since the newly installed, planed cypress timbers had a light, natural look—which eventually darkened to the present color.

Room 9: The Shimei-no-ma or Ichi-no-ma (Purple or First Room) was probably Hideyoshi's private chamber, and it has the typical elements of an elegant *shoin:* a floor with two levels, the ten-mat upper level (Jodan-no-ma) having a tokonoma and *chigaidana* shelf arrangement, and a writing shelf with an ogee (arched) shoji window. The room is decorated with murals by Kano Koi and Kano Tanyu taken from legendary accounts of Chinese imperial history concerning the exemplary emperors Yao and Shun. Metal fastenings chased with designs of lions and peonies cover the nail heads on posts, the ceiling is coffered, and the *ramma* are carved with peonies and phoenixes.

Room 10: The Ni-no-ma (Second Room) is similar to the first room (it and the third room being eighteen-mat rooms), although it does not have the raised platform and tokonoma and shelf of the first room. It too was painted by Kano Koi and Kano Tanyu, again with murals of legendary accounts from Chinese history illustrating a Ming text of Confucius' admonitions as to imperial behavior. The paneled ceiling is of the type normally found in noble residences.

Room 11: The decorations of the San-no-ma (Third Room or Peacock Chamber), the cherry trees, the peonies, and the peacocks, are by Kaiho Yusetsu. The *ramma* in all three rooms are attributed to Hidari Jingoro; those between the second and third rooms are of peonies and long-tailed fowl. This eighteen-mat room becomes a Noh stage when the tatami are removed, and the other two rooms become the area for the audience (the intervening *fusuma* having been removed and all three rooms being made into one for the performance).

Room 12: The Shozoku-no-ma (Costume or Dressing Room) behind the Shiro Shoin is a small room with a tokonoma, *chigaidana* shelves, and a bell-shaped window. The decoration on the rear wall is of a hunting scene by Kaiho Yusetsu, while a mural of the historic fight between Atsumori and Naozane in 1184 is on another wall of the room.

Room 13: The abbot's private chambers, built in 1657, are located in the Kuro Shoin to the north of the Dai Shoin, and these are not open to the public. These are rooms in which the abbot can hold private meetings or be at ease. They provide a less formal unit than the Dai Shoin and have the usual features of *shoin* architecture: a tokonoma, a built-in desk with a bell-shaped ogee window, shelves, and shoji. These rooms are called Kuro Shoin (Black Apartment) since the pillars and ceiling were darkened with black lacquer. The alcove walls and *fusuma* have ink paintings by Kano Tanyu (1602–76) of Chinese figures. The Kuro Shoin also has a tea-room complex of two rooms of three and seven mats. The ink paintings of mountain scenery in these rooms are by Kano Tansaku, a grandson of Kano Tanyu.

Hiunkaku Hideyoshi had built his Jurakudai (Palace of Assembled Pleasures) in the northern part of Kyoto as an extravagant showplace. Within it, in 1587, he created his Hiunkaku "Pavilion of Floating Clouds," a three-story structure with a tea room (Okujaku-tei), a bath house (Kokakudai), and a chamber for resting. The pavilion was removed to Fushimi Castle when

Hideyoshi decided to destroy the Jurakudai, and it was probably moved about 1615 to the Nishi Hongan-ji when Fushimi Castle was demolished by order of the Tokugawa shogun.

At the Nishi Hongan-ji, the pavilion was placed in the southeast corner of the temple grounds. It stands in the middle of the Soro Pond, and at one time the only approach to this pleasure pavilion was by boat to its "boat docking room" which has a sliding trapdoor to the steps from the first floor. Today, the Ryuhaikyo (Devil's Back Bridge), the longest single stone bridge in Japan, connects it to the rest of the precinct. This pavilion, along with the Ginkaku-ji and the Kinkaku-ji, is known as one of the "Three Pavilions of Japan." It is eighty-five feet across the façade and forty feet deep.

The pavilion is decorated in a subdued style, given Hideyoshi's taste for the extravagant. On the first floor is an entrance hall and three rooms. In the central room is a painting of the "Eight Views of Lake Hsiao-Hsiang" in China by Kano Tanyu and Zensetsu Tokuriki (1591–1680), as well as one of "Willow Trees Under Snow" by Kano Eitoku in a second room which has three levels.

Okujaku-tei Adjacent to the pavilion is the Okujaku-tei, a teahouse with a three-and-one-third-mat main room, a washing/storage room for utensils, and a corridor. The second floor has the Kasen-no-ma (Hall of Famous Poets) with the painting of the "Thirty Six Famous Poets," while the ceiling has paintings of grape vines and squirrels, both by Kano Sanraku (1559–1635); this room also has an elevated section of eight mats. The second floor has a veranda with a low railing on all sides. On the third floor is the painting of Mount Fuji by Kano Motonobu. This picture is sketched on gold ground, and one can only obtain a full view of the scene by kneeling before it. (The painting has thus been called *Gyogi Fuji* ["Good Manners Fuji"] since one has to kneel in front of it. Unfortunately, it is now very faded.) An adjacent caricatural drawing of a grove of trees is thought to have been a *jeu d'esprit* by Hideyoshi himself. The third floor once provided a fine view of the Higashiyama mountains, but modern construction now interferes with the former view.

Kokakudai   The bathroom of the pavilion (Kokakudai) is connected by a covered corridor to the pavilion. It contains paintings by Kano Eitoku (1543–1590) in the upper room. Stairs lead down to a steam bath and to baths for hot and cold water. Near the bathhouse is a toilet.

Kocho-tei and Seirensha   In the garden is the Kocho-tei, a rest house, and the Seirensha, a teahouse. A pool called Shogetsusha and a spring called "Waking from Sleep Spring" in an area of plum trees also enrich the grounds.

COSTUME MUSEUM

On leaving the Nishi Hongan-ji and returning to Omiya-dori, a walk to the north to the far end of the walled grounds brings one across the street from the interesting Costume Museum which is located in an office building.

The Costume Museum is on the fifth floor of the Izutsu Office Building at the corner of Horikawa-dori and Shinhanaya-dori, across the street from the northeastern corner of the Nishi Hongan-ji. It is open from 9:00 a.m. to 5:00 p.m., except on Sundays and during changes of exhibitions. An entry fee is charged. (The museum is about a ten- to fifteen-minute walk from the Kyoto Central Station. Bus 7, 28, or 78 can be taken to the bus stop at the north end of the Nishi Hongan-ji.)

The Costume Museum shows examples of Japanese costumes from the earliest of times to the present. Beautiful costumes are handsomely mounted on appropriate mannequins in modern display cases. These costume exhibitions are changed two or three times a year. An English-language pamphlet is available, and costumes are labeled in English as well as in Japanese. A souvenir/postcard counter is provided.

Across from the Nishi Hongan-ji lies Monzenmachi, "The

District Outside the Temple Gates." A large gateway at the Horikawa-dori entry to a street which runs between Nishi Hongan-ji and Higashi Hongan-ji marks the beginning of the district. Particularly at its western end, along and just off Horikawa-dori, are shops selling all those items connected with Buddhism which range from small rosaries to the large *butsudan* chests for family altars placed within the home. Incense, candles, altar cloths, and small gongs are among the numerous items that can be purchased. The area has been host to pilgrims to the temples as well as visitors to the city for centuries, and small *ryokan* (inns) can be found throughout the district.

HIGASHI HONGAN-JI

To proceed to the Higashi Hongan-ji temple, it is best to return south on Horikawa-dori to Shichijo-dori at the southern edge of the Nishi Hongan-ji. A turn to the left and a return to Karasuma-dori and to the east side of the Kyoto Tower Building where one turns to the left (past the National Tourist Office) will bring one to the southern edge of the Higashi Hongan-ji temple. The main entrance is in mid-block on Karasuma-dori. The Higashi Hongan-ji is the headquarters of the Otani branch of Jodo Shinshu. The Taishi-do and Amida-do are open from 6:00 a.m. to 5:00 p.m. No entry fee.

The two branches of Jodo Shinshu (at the Nishi Hongan-ji and the Higashi Hongan-ji) followed the same line of history until the 1600s. Thus, the pre-1600 background to the Higashi Hongan-ji can be found under the description of the Nishi Hongan-ji. The division of the sect into two parts was a political ploy by Tokugawa Ieyasu after he came to power at the beginning of the 1600s. He needed only to look at the attitude of the sect in the period after 1550 to feel that the monks offered a possible threat to the peace of the realm. In the time of Oda Nobunaga, the head of the then unified Hongan-ji temple and his older son fortified themselves in Osaka and withstood a siege by Nobunaga's forces. Therefore, when Hideyoshi succeeded Nobunaga in 1582, he bypassed Kosa, the head of the temple, and his older son by appointing another of Kosa's sons as abbot and granted the sect land in Kyoto (the present Nishi Hongan-ji) for their headquarters.

Shogun Tokugawa Ieyasu, who succeeded Hideyoshi, used the device of "divide and conquer" when it came to the Jodo Shinshu. He had a second temple on a thirty-acre site in central Kyoto built for the son Hideyoshi had bypassed, thereby assuring a lack of unified action on the part of the sect; thus, the original temple became Nishi Hongan-ji while the new unit became Higashi Hongan-ji.

Fires have plagued Higashi Hongan-ji on four occasions, and the last, decisive fire in 1864 (caused by an attempt by imperial adherents to overthrow the Tokugawa shogunate) wiped out all of the buildings of the temple. The disaster was brought on by the daimyo of Choshu in his attempt to seize the emperor in the struggle between the rising imperial forces and the last Tokugawa shogun. The temple buildings were rebuilt between 1879 and 1911; they were restored in 1984. Only the Taishi-do and the Amida-do are open to the public. The remainder of the buildings are not open since their treasures were lost in the last fire. It is possible to visit these other structures by request a day in advance through the Japan Travel Bureau or one's hotel, or by application at the temple office.

The rebuilding of the temple occurred at a less than propitious time since, after the restoration of imperial power in 1868, Buddhism was severely slighted by the new Meiji government with its Shinto leanings. The fact that the temple was rebuilt through public appeals by the abbot indicates that Buddhist beliefs and practices could not easily be eradicated by a militant Shinto government. Not only did gifts of money flow in, but women cut their long hair and sent it to the temple as an offering to be made into ropes which could be used to pull the beams of the buildings into place during construction. Fifty-two such giant ropes, the longest of which is 36 feet long and 1.3 feet in circumference (weighing 2,334 pounds), were created from these donations and are still on display in the corridor between the Taishi-do and the Amida-do.

Hondo-mon/Amida-do-mon   The temple grounds are entered through a gate which is known by two names: the Hondo-mon (Gate to the Main Hall) or Amida-do-mon (Gate to the Amida Hall). This gateway originally belonged to Fushimi Castle and was given to the temple by Shogun Ieyasu. The original gate was lost in the 1864 fire, and this identical replacement was built in 1909.

The Hondo is an Amida-do, hall of the Buddha Amida, the primary deity of the Jodo Shinshu sect and is located in the southern part of the temple grounds. In front of the Hondo to the southeast is the Shoro (Bell Tower), the original having come from Hideyoshi's castle at Fushimi. Lost to fire, a duplicate was constructed in 1893. A gigantic, bronze water vase in the shape of a lotus flower stands in a circular pond, 144 feet in circumference, in front of the hall. The water flowing into it comes from Lake Biwa, the same water being available in various places as fire protection for the temple. Two very large, excellent bronze lanterns stand before the Hondo and Taishi-do.

The Hondo/Amida-do is a 401-mat structure which is supported by seventy columns; it is 170 feet wide by 150 feet long and is 90 feet high and divided into two parts: the sanctuary and the place of worship. The sanctuary has three sections: the *naijin* or central sanctuary and the two *yoma* or side sanctuaries. The central portion holds the *shumidan*, the altar which symbolizes Mount Sumeru, the central mountain in the Buddhist universe, with the image of a thirteenth-century Amida Nyorai placed in a shrine. Behind, on the right, is an image of Prince Shotoku, while on the left is one of Priest Honen, founder of the original Jodo sect. An imperial tablet by the emperor Kameyama is hung to the right of the shrine.

In the left sanctuary are images of the Six Patriarchs of the

Jodo Shinshu sect: Nagarjuna, Vasubandhu, T'an Luan (Donran), Tai Ch'o (Doshaku), Shan-tao (Zendo), and Genshin. Golden-trellised folding doors separate the sanctuary from the worship area. This latter section has a tatami-matted floor for worshipers, and large, gilt lamps are suspended from the ceiling. The Hondo and Taishi-do are connected by a passageway in which, under glass, are displayed the ropes made from human hair which were employed in constructing the building.

The gateway at the street in front of the Taishi-do is a two-story, double-roofed structure. The plaque on the gate reads *Shinshu Honbyo* (Shin Sect Main Temple) in the handwriting of Prince Fushimi. The second floor holds images of the Shaka Buddha with Maitreya and Ananda, carved by Rennyo Shonin. The ceiling has paintings by Seiho Takeuchi of celestial beings in flight. The gate, which was begun in 1907 and completed by 1911, is 100 feet wide, 88 feet long, and 90 feet tall. An interior stairway leads to the second floor (generally not open to the public).

Taishi-do/Goei-do The 927-mat Taishi-do or Goei-do is the largest wooden building in Kyoto and the second largest such building in Japan. It is 190 feet long by 240 feet wide and stands 125 feet tall, and the structure is supported by ninety columns. It is connected to the Hondo by a covered bridge.

The sanctuary is subdivided in the same manner as the Hondo, and the interior is lavishly decorated in gilt and metal-work with gilt trellis doors between the sanctuary and the worshipers' area. Gilt chandeliers hang in the public area. An image of Shinran, founder of Jodo Shinshu, reputedly carved by him, is in the shrine in the center of the altar, which, as in the Hondo, is mounted on a symbolic Mount Sumeru. The statue was given to Priest Jonenbo by Shinran as a parting gesture when Shinran left Shimosa Province during the course of his exile. An image of the twenty-second patriarch, Rennyo Shonin, is behind the altar, and on the left are images of successive patriarchs of the sect. Buddha's name appears on tablets on either side, and in the upper front of the central sanctuary is a tablet with the characters for Kenshin (The Truth Realized), the posthumous name given to Shinran by the emperor Meiji. The calligraphy is in the emperor's hand. The *ramma* above the gilt folding doors at the front of the sanctuary are carved with angels playing musical instruments. The worshipers' area is tatami-matted, and large golden lighting fixtures hang from the ceiling. The architect for the Taishi-do was Ito Heizaemon.

Chrysanthemum Gate/Chokushi-mon The Chrysanthemum Gate or Chokushi-mon (Imperial Messenger's Gate), slightly to the north of the Taishi-do at the street, derives its name from the two sixteen-petal imperial chrysanthemum crests, one on each of its doors. The original gate came from the Fushimi Castle, but it too was lost in the 1864 fire. In 1913 the new gate was dedicated, having been rebuilt in the style of the Momoyama period (1568–1603).

Oshin-den The Oshin-den, to the north, is a ceremonial hall, but it and the other temple buildings are not generally open to the public except by request beforehand.

The abbots of the Higashi Hongan-ji enjoyed a villa set within its own park grounds, a residence but a few streets from the temple. Although the major buildings have disappeared, the garden remains a delightful park.

Shosei-en The Shosei-en garden is located two streets east of the Higashi Hongan-ji, one street north of Shichijo-dori, and one street south of Rokujo-dori. It is bounded on its eastern side by Kawaramachi-dori. (It is between the two east-west streets Kamijuzuyamachi-dori and Shimojuzuyamachi-dori.) The gardens are open from 9:00 a.m. to 4:00 p.m. Entry fee.

A former villa of the abbots of the Higashi Hongan-ji, the alternate name of the Shosei-en or Kikoku-tei comes from the name of the plant used for the hedge which once surrounded it. Originally the site of a villa of Minamoto-no-Toru (822–895), Minister of the Left and a son of the emperor Saga, in 1631 the grounds were given by Shogun Tokugawa Iemitsu to the thirteenth abbot, Sennyo, of the Higashi Hongan-ji . A portion of Hideyoshi's Fushimi Castle buildings was brought here. Completed in 1657, it had various buildings around the central lake, the Ingetsu-chi, a lake originally supplied with salt water (from Osaka) monthly and where salt was made so as to imitate life on the seashore. These buildings were destroyed by fire in 1864 in a civil disturbance in an attempt to overthrow the Tokugawa shogunate, the same fire that destroyed the Higashi Hongan-ji.

The garden was in part designed by the noted poet and landscape designer Ishikawa Jozan (1583–1672) and in part by Kobori Enshu (1579–1647). It was renowned for its "Thirteen Beautiful Landscapes" which were featured in numerous tanka poems. Unfortunately, many of these landscapes were destroyed in the same fire that demolished the villa.

In the center of the garden is the pond Ingetsu-chi which is adorned with islands and large trees. To-no-shima (Tower Island), a small islet, has a nine-layer lantern which is believed to mark the tomb of Minamoto-no-Toru, and to its east is a smaller isle of stones. The main island is approached from the west over an arched wooden bridge or by means of an arched stone bridge from the east; a covered bridge (see below) leads from the island to the north. On a hill on the island among trees is the Shukuen-tei, a two-mat teahouse with ancillary small rooms, one of which holds a stove for the making of tea. The covered bridge which leads from the teahouse island to the north has a moon-viewing platform at its center. The Sochinkyo, a small two-and-a-half-mat tea room with an entry area, is at the edge of the pond to the southwest.

On the east of the garden is a trellised wisteria vine which was a gift of Emperor Go-Mizuno-o (reigned 1611–29). The Bokaku-mon, a two-story gate with side stairways, leads to a family shrine with screens painted by Munakata Shiko (1903–75). To the north of the gateway is a grove of cherry trees and then two buildings connected by a bridge. To the east of these units is an L-shaped building with a pond before it, and further to the east is the Tairetsuseki, a one-story building. Various other buildings lie beyond; the main villa buildings are behind a wall.

A return to the plaza in front of Kyoto Station offers various bus lines, the subway, and taxis for transportation within or beyond the city.

TOUR
11

The Immovable Kannon
and the Nijo-jo

二
条
城

六
角
堂

I N THE heart of modern Kyoto is an ancient temple, one naturally attributed to Prince Shotoku as is any very old temple. Rokkaku-do's association with the Ikenobo flower-arranging school, its lovely pond and swans, and the fact that it dates back to the 1200s, if not earlier, all make it of particular interest. The flower-arranging school initially began within the temple, and today the Ikenobo school both literally and physically overshadows the source from which it sprang. The Ikenobo office building housing the school is a skyscraper at whose ground level is an open plaza and pool, both of which were created by the architect to complement Rokkaku-do and return to it the pond which legend claims as reason for its origin.

To the north of Rokkaku-do is the Heian Museum, one of those delightful examples of early Japanese "modern" buildings designed in the Western mode of architectural style created at the end of the nineteenth century. Once the home of the Bank of Japan, it now houses an institute whose display rooms illustrate the early history of Kyoto.

Two places in this part of Kyoto bring to mind the tales of medieval samurai and ninja "guerrillas." One is the Nijo Jinya (Nijo Manor), a private home on the outside, but a fortress of secret passageways and disappearing staircases on the inside such as would delight any aficionado of samurai derring-do. The other is the impressive Nijo-jo (Nijo Castle) of the Tokugawa shoguns, more a fortified palace than a castle as such. Its rooms remain a showpiece of splendor and richness almost four hundred years after they were first conceived and constructed, and it is a sight that few visitors would wish to miss. We begin at the southern side of the visit to these various sites of interest and start with the Rokkaku-do temple.

Rokkaku-do (also sometimes known as Choho-ji) temple is situated east of Karasuma-dori on Rokkaku-dori, midway between Shijo-dori and Oike-dori. It is set back behind the tall, modern building mentioned above (the Ikenobo headquarters).

The Shijo Station of the city subway or the Hankyu Electric

Railway (here an underground line) is just south of Rokkaku-dori and the temple. Buses 5, 28, 59, 203, 205, and 207 stop at Karasuma-Shijo. The temple is open from 9:00 a.m. to 5:00 p.m. No entry fee.

It is claimed that the temple was founded by Prince Shotoku in 587, a somewhat unlikely date since the prince would have been but fifteen years of age. In the prince's time there was a pond where the temple now stands. (The modern Ikenobo office building to the north and west of the temple has tried to recreate this pond in a contemporary manner.) According to legend, the prince bathed in the pond when this was open countryside, first putting on the ground at the edge of the water the two-inch-tall, gold Nyorin Kannon image he carried with him as a talisman. When he tried to pick up the Kannon on coming out of the water, it had become far too heavy to lift. That night Kannon appeared to him in a dream and informed the prince that he wished to remain at the pond. Thus, it is said, the prince built the temple to Kannon at this spot.

It is also reported that when the emperor Kammu laid out the plan for his new capital of Heiankyo (Kyoto) in 794, almost two hundred years later, the Rokkaku-do stood in the way of one of his projected main streets of the new city. The emperor sent a messenger to explain the problem to the Kannon image in the temple, and thus a cloud enveloped the temple and moved it just far enough so as not to interfere with the new city street plan. The Heso-ishi (Bellybutton Stone) on the temple grounds has often been referred to as the "navel" of Kyoto since it is popularly supposed to be a base point used in the planning of the city layout and thus ostensibly marks the center of the city.

It was to this temple that Priest Shinran, the eventual founder of the Shin Jodo sect of Buddhism, is said to have made a retreat for one hundred days as he sought a greater satisfaction within Buddhism than could be offered by the Tendai Buddhist teachings with which he had grown up and under which he lived at the Enryaku-ji on Mount Hiei. At dawn on the ninety-fifth day of his retreat, Prince Shotoku (who was believed to be a reincarnation of Kannon) appeared to Shinran in a dream and suggested that he consult with Priest Honen, the founder of the Jodo (Amida) Buddhist sect. This Shinran did, becoming one of Honen's disciples. (In time, Shinran instituted the new Buddhistic teachings that became the basis for the Jodo Shinshu sect—see "Nishi Hongan-ji.")

In the fifteenth century, the twelfth abbot of the Rokkaku-do, Sankei Ikenobo, created a flower-arrangement method *(ikebana)* in the Ikenobo (the "Priests' Lodging Beside the Pond") when preparing flowers to be placed before the temple's image of Kannon. The school of flower-arranging which developed from his floral art was continued by a family who lived in a building behind the temple, and today the school continues to flourish in its headquarters in the tall, modern building adjacent to the temple on the northwest.

ROKKAKU-DO

The Rokkaku-do temple lies hidden away behind the modern Ikenobo office building on Karasuma-dori. Its entry is to the east of Karasuma-dori on Rokkaku-dori. Although overshadowed by its towering neighbor, the temple enjoys a delightful setting even in this crowded center of commercial Kyoto—through the courtesy and generosity of the owners of the Ikenobo office building. Mindful of the ancient legend that a pond existed here in which Prince Shotoku bathed and at whose side he built the temple, the architects of the Ikenobo office building created a covered plaza (screened-off from busy Karusama-dori) in lieu of what should have been part of the building's ground floor. Here a pond has been recreated, partly within the Rokkaku-do precincts and partly under the open first floor of the Ikenobo structure. The pond is filled with large carp of various colors—as well as being the home of both a white and a black swan. Thus, the pond provides a most pleasant setting for the temple.

Hondo The Rokkaku-do temple was rebuilt in 1876, and its Hondo is hexagonal in shape. Above the Hondo proper is a second pyramidal roof topped with a large, gilt-bronze "jewel" of a memorial nature. This second roof not only covers the main temple building, but offers a covered area in front of the temple as well. In front of this double-roofed structure, once the entry gate on Rokkaku-dori has been passed, are two large stone lanterns on either side of the path leading to the Hondo. To the left of the path is a life-sized, bronze figure of the priest Shinran, a rosary in his left hand and a pilgrim's staff in his right hand, as he makes his pilgrimage to the Rokkaku-do in search of religious understanding. To the right of the path is the roofed water basin. The water issuing from the mouth of a bronze dragon is used for purification purposes before one enters the temple.

The second roof over the temple provides a "porch" before the hexagonal Hondo, and hanging from this roof is a huge, red paper lantern. Beneath and before the lantern is a large Chinese-style, bronze incense pot on six legs, a holder for the incense sticks which worshipers light and place in the sand within the pot before praying. There is also a Chinese-style table.

The front wall of the enclosed Hondo is open above a three-foot-high wall that separates the worshiper from the inner sanctuary. The interior of this small Hondo is resplendent with its gilt-covered pillars and rear wall. Two long, pendant, gilt baldachins *(tengai)* cascade from the interior ceiling. The altar table and adjacent religious furniture placed before the image area are in black lacquer with gold highlighting and stand out in contrast to the gilt of the area behind them. Triangular-shaped votive candle holders stand on either side of the altar. Beyond the altar table, on the left, is an image of the two-year-old Prince Shotoku at his first prayers. In the center of the rear portion of the Rokkaku-do Hondo is the main image of the temple, that of Kannon. A dark figure with multiple arms, the Kannon stands out against its gilt surroundings. It is obviously not the Kannon of the Shotoku legend.

Heso-ishi On the western side of the temple grounds, a covered shrine beside the precinct wall holds the large Heso-ishi which has water flowing over it and a small Fudo Myo-o image before it. Strings of colorful origami cranes hang on either side of the stone. To the north of this shrine are numerous images of the Buddha and other Buddhist beings sculpted on flat stones two feet tall, all set within the framework of a very small garden. Next comes a small structure with a Buddha image accompanied by guardian deities. Beyond this is the modern Ikenobo office building and the attractive contemporary pond. The pond, a reminder of the pool in which Prince Shotoku bathed, lies to the northwest and is partially behind the Hondo. A section of the pond flows under the open plaza of the first floor of the Ikenobo structure, huge carp and two swans enlivening the otherwise still waters. Directly behind the Hondo is a life-sized image of Kannon and then a small garden which lies in front of a one-story temple building.

In the northeast portion of the precinct is a memorial umbrella spire atop a pagoda. To the right of this and against the eastern wall of the temple grounds is a memorial building with a flaming jewel on its rooftop, a symbol that it is a memorial to a Buddhist saint, in this case to Prince Shotoku. The main image within is of the sixteen-year-old prince praying for his dying father, the emperor Yomei, and above and behind the image is a figure of the two-year-old Shotoku, his hands clasped in his first prayer. Between the two images is a round mirror such as is usually seen in Shinto shrines. At the right rear is an image of the prince on horseback, representative of the late sixth-century battle of Shigisan hill fought against the court officials who opposed Buddhism.

To the south of this memorial building is a modern, seated, many-armed Kannon with the traditional image of Amida on his crown. Two rows of attractive metal screens form an arc behind this Kannon, the modern screen being composed of the traditional "one thousand images of the Buddha." Further south is a vermilion-fenced area with two small Shinto shrines. The south-ernmost of these two shrines is composed of three units, each with a sacred mirror within. Over these three is a gabled roof of the *kara* (Chinese) style. The intricate carving on the roof beams includes a figure of a man carrying rice sheaves as well as carved animals and birds. All of these small Shinto shrines have thatched roofs and are covered by an additional protective roof.

IKENOBO SOCIETY AND SCHOOL OF FLOWER ARRANGING

The Ikenobo Society and School of Flower Arranging headquarters is on Karasuma-dori just north of Rokkaku-dori in an attractive, tall, modern building. It is thus around the corner from the Rokkaku-do temple. The Ikenobo school teaches both classical and modern forms of *ikebana*, and it has branches in other countries as well as in Japan. English is spoken at the school for those wishing to learn more about the Ikenobo Society. An exhibition is held at the society's headquarters in November.

Not far from the Ikenobo Society building is the Heian Museum which features a permanent display devoted to the early years of Kyoto's existence.

HEIAN MUSEUM

The Heian Museum of Ancient History is on Takakura-dori (two streets east of Karasuma-dori) and just south of Oike-dori. It is thus one street north of the Ikenobo office building and then two streets to the east. It is open from 9:00 a.m. to 4:00 p.m. Closed Sundays, national holidays, and the New Year period. Entry fee.

The Heian Museum, a branch of the Ministry of Education, is primarily an archeological research institute rather than a museum, but it does have public exhibits concerned with the past of the ancient capital. A very fine pamphlet in English gives a full description of the five major rooms/exhibits.

The Paleological Association of Japan, which is located here, was created in 1951 and moved into this building in 1966. The three-story brick structure (whose bricks were imported from England) is typical of Meiji architecture (1868–1912) of the Western mode. At one time, the building housed the Kyoto branch of the Bank of Japan.

The exhibits consist of the following units:

- ROOM **1**: The pre-history of Japan through the Jomon and Yayoi periods.
- ROOM **2**: Yamashiro province (Kyoto) before the establishment of Heiankyo (Kyoto)—before 794.
- ROOM **3**: The Heian capital from 794 to 1185.
- CENTRAL HALL: A restoration of an interior scene from the Seiryo-den (the Imperial Sleeping Quarters of the imperial palace) of the Heian period.
- ROOM **4**: Literature and life of the Heian period.
- ROOM **5**: Lady Murasaki Shikibu and *The Tale of Genji*.

Thus, the collection consists of archeological finds, reproductions of Heian paintings and costumes, and a scale model of the Seiryo-den.

On leaving the Heian Museum a walk along Oike-dori (one street to the north of the Heian Museum) to the west eventually brings one to the next major north-south street, that of Horikawa-dori. Four streets beyond this and then a turn to the left (south) brings one to the Nijo Jinya.

NIJO JINYA

The Nijo Jinya (Nijo Manor) is situated on Omiya-dori, north of Anekoji-dori. Take bus 9, 12, 50, 52, 61, 62, or 63 to Horikawa-Oike, walk west four streets to Omiya-dori and south to the building in mid-street. Reservations must be made one day in advance. Tours are at 10:00 a.m., 11:00 a.m., 2:00 p.m., and 3:00 p.m. with a limit of fifteen to a tour (no children under high school age). Tours are in Japanese only. Entry fee.

The Nijo Jinya is one of those anomalies of history, a house that became an inn for daimyo making their required courtesy call to the shogun's Kyoto headquarters. It is an anomaly since this ancient building is the type in which Japanese soap operas of medieval, swashbuckling sword play and intrigue are filmed; a house with secret passages, disappearing staircases, hidden rooms, and trapdoors, all the necessary props for samurai epics. This fascinating building can be visited by appointment. However, for a complete understanding of the secrets of Nijo Jinya, a translator may be required since the guide lectures only in Japanese.

Ogawa Hiraemon, a former daimyo who became a rice merchant, built this private residence in the early 1600s just to the south of the Nijo Castle and the Shinsen-en garden, a house still owned by his descendants. Thirty years were spent in the construction of this fortified *jinya*. Some of the daimyo who came to Kyoto on official business stayed with Ogawa, and his home gradually became an inn as well as a private residence. He built the house with such stability and so many safety features that it has survived the many catastrophes nature has visited on Kyoto. It even withstood the three-day Great Tenmei Fire of 1788 when all else about it and the center of the city went up in flames. Its specially covered roof, its windows with fireproof blinds which could drop into place, its clay doors, its complex water system of twelve interconnected wells—all these novel elements helped to protect it from the uncertainties of the times following the death of Toyotomi Hideyoshi.

The Nijo Jinya looks like a one-story building from the outside; inside it is a three-story structure. The building has some eleven downstairs rooms and thirteen upstairs rooms, all heavily decorated. A Noh hall and a tea-ceremony room make it a grand residence, better suited for a nobleman than a merchant. A fortress within, it has all the elements that make for a Japanese television spectacular with black-clothed spies scaling walls, disappearing behind seemingly solid partitions, and performing improbable feats in impossible situations. There are hidden and disappearing staircases, hollow spaces in the ceilings and walls from which bodyguards could appear, walls constructed so as to allow for eavesdropping, and shoji that permit the shadows of intruders to give them away. Secret tunnels under a garden pond, rope ladders—all the paraphernalia of mystery, intrigue, bravery, and treachery are present. Whether these devices were ever needed or used is not the question. They exist to tickle the imagination of readers of Japanese stories or viewers of medieval soap operas.

In contrast to this veritable private fortress is the nearby Shinsen-en garden. In the year 794 the emperor Kammu had his palace built in the north-central portion of Kyoto. In time, fires destroyed the complex on more than one occasion, and eventually the site was abandoned. Alone of all the magnificence which once enhanced this section of Kyoto, there remains the small Shinsen-en, a tiny portion of the pleasure grounds once enjoyed by emperors and empresses, princes and princesses, and members of the courtier class. Given to the To-ji temple in recent centuries for a detached sub-temple, the tiny garden is still a pleasant forepiece to the temple building and restaurant that overlook the pond and its vermilion bridges and small Shinto shrine. It is yet another place for quiet relaxation in the heart of the commercial portion of the city.

SHINSEN-EN

The Shinsen-en (Sacred Spring Garden) lies just to the south of the Nijo Castle and on the north side of Oike-dori. It is three streets west of Horikawa-dori. Take bus 75 to Shinsen-en-mae or take buses 9, 12, 50, 52, 61, 62, or 63 to the Nijo-jo-mae bus stop. The garden is open without charge during daylight hours.

All that remains of the impressive imperial palace that was built in 794 for the emperor Kammu and his entourage is the tiny Shinsen-en garden. When the palace was built, the emperor decreed that a walled pleasure garden be created to the south of it, a garden of eight *cho* (a *cho* being 1,073 square feet)—some thirty-three acres in size. It extended from Nijo (Second Street) to Sanjo (Third Street). When the palace burned in 1177 (it had burned down some seventeen times in two centuries), the then emperor moved his residence to Kobe for a period of time and, thus, the garden was abandoned.

In the 1600s the Tokugawa government gave permission to the To-ji temple to build a sub-temple on what remained of the garden site, and the northeast corner of the original garden (about one acre) was saved from further development. A small Buddhist temple and three tiny Shinto shrines thus came into being.

When the garden existed in the palmy days of the Heian court with the full complement of its thirty-three acres, all the delights of the Heian-period (794–1185) aristocracy were practiced in this Chinese-style park: there were imperial boating parties; vermilion, Chinese-style moon-viewing and flower-viewing pavilions; and the floating of cups of wine down a stream. (Guests would pick up the cups and, between sips, compose an impromptu poem on a given subject.) Pleasure pavilions in vermilion lacquer dotted the park and were even created at the edge of the pond to permit for the fishing expeditions of the nobility. It was said that dragons lived in the pond, and at one period of drought in 824 even Kobo Daishi (Kukai) prayed successfully to the resident dragon for rain. The power of Buddhism was thus proven effective—but the composition of a poem by a noted poetess on another occasion of drought also brought relief. In reverse, there were times in the late 800s when the dragon had to be prayed to for dry weather so as to preserve the crops and prevent flooding. It is not surprising, therefore, that the small island in the middle of the pond has a shrine to the Dragon Queen. No doubt the only real dragons, however, were the dragon-headed boats used by courtiers. The street leading to the west from the Shinsen-en is called Oike-dori (Honorable Pond Road), a reminder of the pond's better days.

The garden has been restored to an approximation of its

original Chinese style, albeit it is but one-tenth its earlier size. The pond, called the Hojoju-ike, has an island which is reached by a stone bridge from the south and by a delightful, arched, vermilion bridge from the west. A shrine to the Pious Woman Dragon Queen (Zennyo-ryuo) is on the island in the pond as is a stage for ceremonies or events of a religious nature. An attractive, large, squat stone lantern enhances the northeast section of the pond. Since this garden was given to the To-ji temple, the main hall of the sub-temple, the Shinsen-den, contains an image of Kobo Daishi. In 1963 a new north wall and gate were erected, and the Hojo, a fairly large building from the To-ji, was placed next to the Shinsen-den.

There is a belfry in the northeast corner of the garden and a group of stone Jizo images (the guardian deity of children) in the southeast area. On the east bank of the pond is a shrine to Benten and an Inari (god of harvests) shrine with many torii, both shrines being quite small. A restaurant serving traditional Japanese food is on the west side of the garden; its sliding panels offer diners a view over the garden and the pond.

One of the garden's ceremonies should be noted: in late April or early May the Shinsen-en Kyogen, masked pantomime plays, are presented in the garden from 1:30 p.m. to 6:00 p.m. on the first two scheduled days and from 1:30 p.m. to 10:00 p.m. on the last two scheduled days. There is no charge for viewing the performances.

NIJO-JO

The centerpiece of this district, however, is the Nijo-jo (Nijo Castle), the luxurious palace of the Tokugawa shoguns meant to overawe both the Inside Lords (*fudai-daimyo*) and the Outside Lords (*tozama-daimyo*) who came here to do obeisance to the shoguns—after delivery of the required and expensive gifts. Five interconnected buildings, each of greater interior splendor and extravagance of decoration, recall the glory of the Tokugawa court. Shoguns they may only have been, merely representatives of the imperial power, but their palace (since it is not really a defensible castle) has imperial tastes and overtones. Historically important as a residence meant to impress all with the power and wealth of the Tokugawa court, it is remembered as the locus for the surrender of the shogun's power to the fifteen-year-old Meiji emperor by the last Tokugawa shogun in 1867.

The entry to Nijo-jo is on Horikawa-dori just to the north of Oike-dori. Take bus 9, 12, 50, 52, 61, or 67 to the Nijo-jo-mae bus stop. The castle is open from 8:45 a.m. to 4:00 p.m. in summer, from 9:00 a.m. to 3:30 p.m. in the winter, but is closed on Mondays. If a national holiday falls on a Monday, the castle is open that day, but then is closed the next day. It is not open from December 26 to January 3 each year. The entry fee is paid at the ticket booths on Horikawa-dori just outside the main gates to the castle.

In Kyoto's earliest days, after the founding of the city in 794, the imperial palace grounds encompassed a large area which included the site of the later Nijo-jo. After a number of fires, the palace was moved to Kobe for a brief period, but on the return of the capital to Kyoto, the original palace site was abandoned and a different location was occupied by the imperial residence.

In 1569, a mansion for Ashikaga Yoshiaki, the last of the Ashikaga shoguns, was built on a portion of the site of the original palace by Oda Nobunaga. With the deposition of the Ashikaga in time by Nobunaga, the mansion became vacant, and in 1601 when Tokugawa Ieyasu became shogun, he took over the land to build Nijo-jo, ordering all the feudal lords of western Japan to undertake the construction of the castle at their expense. Ieyasu's administrative headquarters for Kyoto remained at Fushimi Castle south of Kyoto at this time, just as his permanent seat of governance was established in Edo (Tokyo). Thus, the Nijo Castle was seldom used by the Tokugawas but served primarily as a showcase for Tokugawa power and wealth rather than as a residence.

The partially completed castle was first occupied by Ieyasu in March of 1603, and he did not return to it again until 1611. It was used again briefly in 1617 by his successor, and then in 1624–26 it was expanded and enriched with the completion of the Honmaru (the castle keep), the Ninomaru, and the dungeon so as to serve as the locus in that latter year for an extravagant reception for the emperor Go-Mizuno-o. In order to impress the court and the nobles, the five-story Tenshukaku tower of Fushimi Castle was moved to the Honmaru area of the Nijo grounds; it was destroyed by lightning in 1750. The Ninomaru, completed at this time, is an excellent example of the *shoin* style carried to the extremes that unlimited wealth and little regard for austere beauty permitted. Elements that once marked the seriousness or austerity of Zen architecture were here enhanced with gold and precious metals. Thus, tatami flooring, painted *fusuma* (sliding panels), the tokonoma alcove, and staggered *chigaidana* shelves moved from temple architecture (as had happened at the Silver Pavilion earlier) were here enhanced so as to become a part of secular Japanese architecture.

Between 1624 and 1626 the finest artists were employed to create the most beautiful secular building in Japan, and the overall supervision of the project came under the direction of Kobori Enshu (1579–1647). The loveliest elements of the Fushimi Castle were relocated here and helped to enhance the overall decoration of the Nijo-jo—truly a palace rather than a military stronghold. A special Noh theater was even built outside the Ohiroma (Grand Hall) of the Ninomaru for performances during the emperor's visit, as was a residential palace for the emperor, structures which were removed thereafter.

Fire and the gradual removal of parts of the complex to other sites left only the Ninomaru of five buildings *in situ* along with the main East Gate and North Gate. (The five-story dungeon was destroyed when hit by lightning in 1750, and then in 1788 the Honmaru burned to the ground in the Tenmei Fire.) Today only the second building of the Ninomaru dates back to the earlier years of the castle, and much of the present structure reflects an 1855 restoration.

In 1863 Shogun Tokugawa Iemochi came from Edo (Tokyo) to the castle to consult with the emperor, the first such visit in two centuries, an unheard-of action during the previous 260 years. Here he received the emperor Komei's instructions to "expel the barbarians" who were attempting to open Japan to international commerce. Unable to expel these foreigners who were infringing on Japan's sovereignty, and with shogunal authority collapsing, the last Tokugawa shogun, Yoshinobu, here resigned his office in October 1867 in favor of the restoration of imperial rule. In early 1868, an Extraordinary Council of State met in the presence of the new, fifteen-year-old emperor Meiji in the Grand Audience Hall of the Nijo-jo to witness the emperor abolish the shogunate at the suggestion of his advisors. The castle became the temporary seat of the new imperial government until it moved shortly thereafter to Edo which was renamed Tokyo (Eastern Capital).

With the relocation of the capital to Tokyo, the castle was made available to the Kyoto prefectural government for offices. Many of the paintings of the castle were rolled up and stored between 1868 and 1883 while the castle was occupied by various local governmental offices, but some painted doors and metalwork in the building were vandalized by local officials who, once the craze for Westernization began, had little appreciation of Japan's past. In July of 1884 the castle was returned to the imperial family and was designated an imperial detached palace, and the restoration of its structure and interior finishings was begun. The sixteen-petal chrysanthemum was substituted for the Tokugawa crest of three hollyhock leaves which previously had proclaimed their ownership of the castle. In 1939 the historic complex was given to the city of Kyoto (and renamed the Nijo-jo) which today preserves it and has opened it to the public since 1940.

In 1893 the mansion of Prince Katsura in the grounds of the

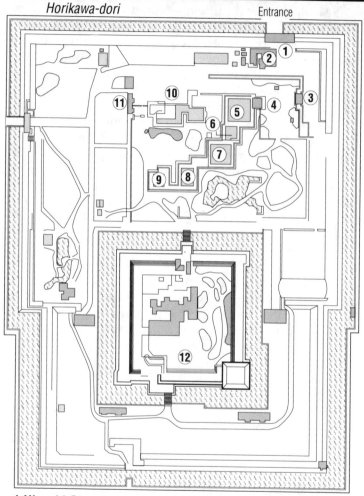

Horikawa-dori

Entrance

1 Higashi Ote-mon
2 Administration
3 Kara-mon (gate)
4 Kurumayose

5 Tozamurai
6 Shikidai
7 Ohiroma
8 Kuro Shoin

9 Shiro Shoin
10 Kitchen
11 Rice Storage
12 Honmaru

imperial palace was removed to the site of the Main Keep of the original Nijo-jo, that area having been destroyed in the Great Tenmei Fire of 1788. In 1928, at the enthronement of the emperor Showa (Hirohito), the great banquet which formed part of the enthronement ceremony was held in this building. Then, in 1965, the Seiryu-en garden was created to serve as a reception area for public functions of the city as well as being made available to the public.

The castle grounds cover about twenty-eight hectares (seventy acres, over three million square feet), of which 78,580 square feet are buildings. The grounds are surrounded by moats and by imposing stone walls with turrets at the southeast and southwest corners. The main entrance is through the iron-bound Higashi Ote-mon (Eastern Main Gate) on Horikawa-dori just north of Oike-dori. Entry tickets may be purchased at the booth outside the castle walls. (In all, there are four gateways to the grounds.)

Bansho   Within the castle's outer walls is the Bansho, the guardhouse, which regulated the entry of official visitors to the castle. Built in 1608, from 1634 to 1868, when the shogun was in Edo, the guardhouse was staffed by fifty men at a time. Today, the building has mannequins representing guards of the Tokugawa era as they would have appeared on duty in the past.

Kara-mon   The Kara-mon or Shikyaku-mon gate is the second gate traversed. This gate is a delight with its imposing curved, gabled roof of *hinoki* (cypress) bark and its carved wood and fine metal work; the outer panels of the gate have carved cranes, butterflies, and flowers while the inner panels offer Chinese lions, tigers, and a dragon. Said to have been the work of Hidari Jingoro, it once stood at the Fushimi Castle of Hideyoshi. In Hideyoshi's day, it held his paulownia crest which was later replaced by the Tokugawa hollyhock leaves, and since the Imperial Restoration of 1868, it boasts the sixteen-petal imperial chrysanthemum. Beyond the gate is a walled courtyard with pine trees, a courtyard that leads to the five buildings of the Ninomaru.

Ninomaru   The courtyard before the Ninomaru complex ends at the Kurumayose (Carriage Approach Gate) with its carvings of peonies and phoenixes enriched with color and gold, also attributed to Hidari Jingoro. The gate offers access to the Ninomaru, a series of five buildings with thirty-three rooms (and eight hundred tatami mats) connected with corridors, corridors with the *uguisubari* (nightingale floors) that squeak when walked upon—a security measure that would keep anyone from entering the inner areas of the castle buildings unnoticed. The ceilings of the connecting corridors between the buildings were originally quite plain, but after 1867 were painted. The Ninomaru is a *bukefushoin*, a Samurai-style residence with Momoyama-period (1568–1615) decoration.

Status and rank were hierarchical and rigidly fixed in Tokugawa times, and the Ninomaru of Nijo-jo reflects such stratification through the height of its floors. Each of the five buildings, as one progresses through them, has a floor slightly higher than the previous one, and access was by rank: imperial messengers were received at the lowest level (First Building), the Outside Lords *(tozama daimyo)* of the realm being greeted at the Third (and higher) Building, while Inside Lords *(fudai daimyo)* were received at the next higher Fourth Building. The last building, where the shogun resided when at the castle, was at the highest level. Seating in the Audience Hall was hierarchical as well; the title and rank of each lord determined the seating arrangements in the hall.

All the precautions necessary to protect the shogun were taken: no swords were permitted within the Ninomaru, all doors between the five buildings were kept locked from the upper to the lower level, and doors with ornate tassels mark the locations where guards were on duty at all times when visitors were present. Within the buildings, all was extravagantly luxurious. Each room was named from the mural-size painted scenes on the *fusuma,* and the nails and bolts of construction were hidden behind elaborately chased and ornamented gold-plated copper covers (*kugikakushi*). Each audience chamber had a raised portion where the shogun sat when in attendance, and ornate carvings on the transoms at the ceiling between levels were crafted with different scenes on either side. Coffered ceilings were delicately painted, such ceilings indicating the importance of the rooms. The *fusuma* paintings were done by the Kano school artists: Kano Sanraku (1559–1635), Kano Koi (1569–1636), and Koi's two pupils, the brothers Kano Tanyu (1602–74) and Kano Naonobu (1607–50).

Tozamurai—The First Building The first building (Tozamurai) is the largest of the five units, and it is thought that this and the next two buildings were brought from Fushimi Castle in 1625 while the fourth and fifth buildings were constructed in place the same year. The entry room is the twenty-four-mat Willow Room (Yanagi-no-ma) from its paintings of willows on a gold ground. Behind it is the Young Pine Room (Wakamatsu-no-ma) also of twenty-four mats with young pines and cherry trees on the *fusuma.* Its coffered ceiling has painted grapevines. (The artist who did the paintings in these two rooms is not known.) These first two rooms were used by shogunal inspectors to verify the identity of visiting feudal lords. The next rooms to the west of the Willow Room along the corridor are the two-part waiting rooms for samurai (Tozamurai-no-ma) of forty mats and of thirty-six mats, also called the Tiger Rooms because of the *fusuma* paintings of tigers and bamboo on gold ground. The tigers are not realistic, such animals being known only at second hand by the artists of the Kano school who depicted them. These rooms have coffered ceilings and *ramma* (transoms) of floral carvings.

All the rooms are surrounded by corridors, these corridors connecting the five buildings at their corners. All rooms, in a sense, are "inside rooms" since they are behind the corridors, although the *fusuma* could be opened to the corridors and the outside if so desired. Rooms at the rear of these chambers are seen on the return passage through the buildings, and thus they are described at that time.

Shikidai—The Second Building The gallery from the First Building leads to the west to the Second Building (Shikidai) of four rooms, the most important of which is the south-facing Room of Decorum and Salutations of forty-five mats. Just upon reaching this unit there were a pair of cedar doors with a Korean-style lion whose eyes seemed to stare at the viewer no matter where one stood. (These doors are now free-standing exhibits.) This building was used for the reception of daimyo by the shogun's ministers, and here they accepted those gifts which custom decreed had to be offered by the daimyo to the shogun. Two large pine trees on a gold ground are painted on its north wall, while the lower portions of the *fusuma* depict geese in a rice field, flowers, and bamboo trees. These paintings are by the then twenty-five-year-old Kano Tanyu.

Ohiroma—The Third Building The third building, which has cedar doors at its entryway with a painting of a goat and a pine-tree branch, is the Ohiroma (the Grand Chamber or Audience Chamber) of four rooms. The first room is the Ohiromasan-no-ma (Third Grand Chamber) which was a forty-mat anteroom for visiting *tozama-daimyo* or Outside Lords, those who became Tokugawa Ieyasu's vassals after he won the overlordship of Japan as victor of the Battle of Sekigahara on October 21, 1600. Its *fusuma* are decorated with a large pine tree by Kano Tanyu. The *ramma* by Hidari Jingoro are said to have come from Hideyoshi's Fushimi Castle and each of the carved panels is made from one block of wood fourteen inches thick. The nail heads in the woodwork of the room are covered with copper which has been plated with gold, each one different in design and shape from all others.

The Second and First Grand Chambers really form one unit, although they can be divided by *fusuma*. The Second Grand Chamber is on a lower level (for the daimyo) than is the raised inner room (for the shogun). This room is a forty-four-mat room with *fusuma* and with wooden doors having paintings of a peacock in a pine tree, the carved ceiling being elaborately decorated with flower patterns on a dark blue and gold background. The carved, openwork *ramma* between the room for the daimyo (Second Grand Chamber) and the shogun's room (First Grand Chamber) of pine and peacocks is credited to Hidari Jingoro. Today, the room is peopled with mannequins dressed in the costumes of the Edo period (1603–1868); they represent the daimyo, seated by rank, in attendance upon the shogun.

The First Grand Chamber in the northwest of the building is the upper portion (Jodan) of the Grand Audience Hall (Ohiroma). Of forty-eight mats, it is where the shogun sat on a raised platform where he could overlook the daimyo in the room below him when holding an audience for these Outside Lords. Here a shogun sits, today in the form of a mannequin dressed in shogunal finery. The tokonoma of this section is made from a single *keyaki* (zelkova) board eighteen feet long by seven inches thick and three feet wide. The rear *fusuma* are painted with a huge pine tree while the *chigaidana* have a few slender stalks of bamboo and various flowers as background. The doors of the east walls, behind which the guards were stationed, are decorated with beach scenes. The large red tassels on the doors always indicated the Mushakakushi-no-ma (Bodyguards' Room) where guards were on alert duty, ready to act if needed to protect the shogun, thus being both decoration and warning. The paintings in the room are by Kano Tanyu. The ceiling has elaborate designs against a gold ground similar to those of the previous room. All of this grandeur was meant to impress upon the Outside Lords the power, authority, and wealth of the shogunate. (It was in this chamber, seated in the center of the room on October 14, 1867, that the fifteenth and last Tokugawa shogun, Yoshinobu, returned the administrative power of government to the very young emperor Meiji.)

Kuro Shoin—The Fourth Building   The Fourth Building (Kuro Shoin or Black Study) is a smaller but luxuriously decorated unit, for it was here that the shogun granted audiences to the Inner Lords, those who had been his vassals before the 1600 Battle of Sekigahara. The building has five rooms plus the inner guard room; four of the rooms form a square with the fifth room being a wide hallway (used by visitors today on the return to the main entrance/exit). On the cedar wooden doors *(nuresagi no sugito)* at the entry to this building is the famous "heron in the rain, perched on the edge of a boat" by Kano Naonobu (1607–50), the younger brother of Kano Tanyu.

The first room in this building is the Pine Beach Room (Hamamatsu-no-ma) of thirty-five mats. Here the Inner Lords awaited their invitation into the audience chamber. Its northern and eastern upper walls depict a beach with pine trees painted by Mochizuki Guokusen, while its *fusuma* of pines and heron are by Kano Naonobu. The coffered ceiling has a phoenix pattern.

The two rooms on the western side of the building compose the audience chamber. The northernmost half is the twenty-four-mat room where the shogun sat. The tokonoma, as in the previous audience chamber, is unusual in that it also has a *keyaki* plank fifteen feet long and eight inches thick by two feet wide. The paintings in the tokonoma are by Kano Naonobu of a snow-covered pine tree with three birds in it. The tokonoma shelves offer examples of early cloisonné work *(shippo-yaki)*. The walls and sliding doors of the *chigaidana* are painted with bamboo while the eastern *fusuma* are painted with cherry blossoms and pheasants in a tree. A horizontal timber *(nageshi)* around the walls, about seven feet above the floor over the north and east walls, holds more than three dozen Tokugawa family crests made of antique cloisonné and fine metal work. It is said that it was here that the last Tokugawa shogun made the decision to resign authority to the emperor. The lower room of thirty-one mats where the Inner Lords sat has paintings of birds and cherry blossoms over a rustic fence with a scene of a seashore painted over the *nageshi*. A pattern of phoenixes is depicted on the coffered ceiling.

Shiro Shoin—The Fifth Building The Fifth Building (Shiro Shoin, White Study, or Oza-no-ma, Throne Room) in the final portion of the Ninomaru was the private living quarters of the shogun. Here he was served only by women who were trained in self-defense and to protect the shogun if need be, but even so there is an inside room for guards. The Shiro Shoin consists of four rooms (plus the inner guard space). The room in the northwest corner, the main room of fifteen mats and tokonoma, is the most attractive and important room in the castle. This was the shogun's personal room and, therefore, it had a raised floor. The eighteen-mat room preceding it on a lower level was for his attendants. The *fusuma* of the Shiro Shoin by Kano Koi are almost monochromatic Chinese scenes of mountains and rivers under snow. The coffered ceilings of black lacquered squares have flowers painted on them.

The room to the east of the lower room, designated for the attendants of the shogun, is the Mountain Water Room (Sansui-no-ma) of eighteen mats. The *fusuma* paintings continue the theme of the room to the north with Chinese snow scenes. To the east of the Sansui-no-ma, in the southeast corner, is the Southeast Room (Tonan-no-ma) with cedar doors painted with flowers and with painted geese in the hallway corner. The last and innermost room is the northeast room, the Sleeping Sparrows Room, (Nemuru Suzume-no-ma) whose *fusuma* depict two sparrows asleep on snow-covered bamboo on a gold ground; the floral design on the coffered ceiling is on a brown ground.

Here one returns to the main entrance by means of corridors along the eastern side of the four preceding buildings.

Fourth Building (Rear Rooms)   The first room in the northeast corner of the Fourth Building is a twenty-eight-mat room known as the Chrysanthemum Room (Kiku-no-ma) with embossed chrysanthemum flowers over a rustic fence by Kano Naonobu. The upper panels offer various kinds of fans while the ceiling has floral circles on a gold ground. The adjacent hallway is called the Peony Room (Botan-no-ma) or the Waiting Room (Tamari-no-ma) of sixty-six mats. Its *fusuma* and walls have peonies and white plum blossoms by Kano Naonobu; it too has a coffered ceiling.

Third Building (Rear Rooms)   The first room at the rear of the Third Building is the Spear Room (Yari-no-ma) or the Hawk Room (Taka-no-ma) of fifty-two mats which at one time held spears used as a part of the shogun's armory. It is decorated with massive pines and hawks by Kano Tanyu.

The last room of this unit is the Sago Palm Room (Sotetsu-no-ma) of fifty mats which serves as a corridor. It is this room which was so badly damaged in the 1870s when the prefectural government had offices here; the original paintings have been effaced. Plain gold paper replaces what had once been a noted portrayal of the fernlike sago palm.

Second Building (Rear Rooms)   The Elder Counselors' Rooms (Rochu-no-ma) consist of three rooms behind the main hall of the Second Building which were used by the counselors for business purposes. The first room of twelve mats and second room of fourteen mats have painted *fusuma* depicting a rice field after harvest, reeds, oak trees, and geese in the snow. The *fusuma* in the third room of twelve mats are painted with herons on a snow-covered willow tree, cherry blossoms, and long-tailed birds, reputedly by Kano Tanyu.

First Building (Rear Rooms)   Around the corner of the corridor, the Imperial Messenger Waiting Room (Chokushi-no-ma) of fifty-six mats is next, decorated with paintings of tigers and bamboo. It was here that messengers from the emperor were received by the shogun or his emissaries. There are two levels in the Chokushi-no-ma, an upper level and a lower level. The upper level (Jodan-no-ma) of twenty-one mats has a raised platform of honor for the imperial messenger, while the shogun would have sat below him. The room has a tokonoma and *chigaidana* decorated with maples in autumn colors, while the doors of the small closets placed above are ornamented with plum and cherry trees, globe flowers, and mallows. The coffered ceiling is highly decorated. The second level (Ni-no-ma) of thirty-five mats was also for the imperial messenger and has fir trees on a gold ground painted on its *fusuma* by Kano Sanraku.

There is an interior room, the Fuyo-no-ma (Changeable Mallow Room) of twenty-four mats with paintings of peaches, flowers, hydrangeas, and a bamboo grove with sparrows, among other subjects. It is also known as the Dark Room (Kuragari-no-ma) since it is an internal room. Its doors are painted with peonies, bamboo, tigers, sheep, hares, and geese. Most of the paintings (other than in the Fuyo-no-ma) are by Kano Tanyu and his pupils.

Grounds of the Ninomaru   To the north of the Ninomaru are two kitchens, one for the preparation of the shogun's food, and one for the preparation of the food for the other occupants of the castle. A storage building for rice also remains intact. The many other buildings that once were on the grounds were either moved to other locations in Kyoto, razed, or destroyed by fire.

The gardens of the Ninomaru lie to the southwest of the Ohiroma and the Kuro Shoin. The task of developing the gardens was given to Kobori Enshu by Shogun Iemitsu in 1624. This garden and a few temporary buildings were erected in honor of the 1626 visit to the palace by Emperor Go-Mizuno-o (1596–1680). The Gyokugo-ten, a temporary palace connected to the Ninomaru, was created for the emperor's residence, as was a Noh stage. Both were razed after his visit.

The garden is close to the moat of the original keep. According to tradition, this one-acre garden was originally designed so as to avoid the thought of the change of seasons and the passing of time. No trees were to be planted since they inevitably drop their leaves and give rise to thoughts of the transitoriness of life. (The present trees were planted at a much later time.) The garden is centered on a large pond a quarter of an acre in size, a pond that is enhanced by waterlilies, groupings of fine stones, and plantings. Three islands, connected by four bridges of natural stone, lie within the waters: Horai (representing the Island of Eternal Happiness), the traditional Crane Isle (Tsuru-jima) on the left, and Turtle Isle (Kame-jima) on the right, the latter two both symbols of longevity. In its original state, the pond was probably dry, and the rocks and stones that composed it were gifts of great rarity brought to the castle by Tokugawa daimyo. Altered frequently through the centuries, the garden is now in *tsukiyama-sansui* (go-round style), rocks and ponds against a backdrop of pine, maple, and other trees. The plantings have been so arranged as to permit for flowering or color throughout the year: January–February, camellias; February–March, apricot blossoms; April, cherry and dogwood blossoms; May, azaleas; June, azaleas and cape jasmine; July–August, Indian lilac; September–October, bush clover; November, maple; and December, firethorn.

The Honmaru, consisting of a square, walled castle or main keep of five stories, was destroyed by lightning in 1750; the palace to house the shogun and his retainers was destroyed by fire in 1788. Both units were originally from Hideyoshi's Fushimi Castle. The present Honmaru was the 1847 town villa of Prince Katsura which stood in the grounds of the imperial palace, and it is the only existing building of imperial style. With the removal of the imperial family to Tokyo after 1868, the villas of the palace grounds were removed, the Katsura villa being relocated here in

1893 as a gift from Prince Katsura. At the time, it was thought that the dowager empress would reside within, but she died before being able to occupy the mansion. It is open to the public for two days toward the end of November each year.

SEIRYU-EN

The Seiryu-en (Seiryu Garden) was constructed in 1965 for official receptions of city guests and for cultural events. Here are located two teahouses, the Koun-tei and the Waraku-an. The garden has over one thousand stones of which eight hundred stones and one teahouse were originally part of the early-1600s residence of Ryoi Suminokura (the merchant and engineer responsible for the Takagase Canal and the opening of the Oi River to navigation) which sat near the Takagase Canal in the Pontocho (Shijo-dori) area of Kyoto. The gardens are of both traditional (in the western half) and modern style (in the eastern half), and they encompass 177,604 square feet.

A few ceremonies are worth mentioning: in mid-April, the castle cherry blossoms are in bloom; and in early June and again in early November, an annual tea ceremony is held. At that time, from 9:30 a.m. to 3:00 p.m., tea masters perform tea ceremony for the public in the Seiryu-en. Tea is served in alternate years by masters from various tea schools. In late November, the opening of the Honmaru occurs. From 9:30 a.m. to 3:30 p.m., the villa is open during the third weekend of November. Entry fee.

A return to other sectors of the city can be made by means of the many buses that stop at the main entrance area of the castle on Horikawa-dori and Oike-dori.

TOUR
12

Temples, Palaces,
and
Pavilions of Delight

金閣寺　竜安寺　仁和寺

I N THE north-central portion of Kyoto, along Kitasuji-dori at the foot of Kitayama (North Mountain), is a crescent of noteworthy temples. At the southwestern end of the group is the Ninna-ji temple in which are preserved not only the temple buildings but also the restored complex of what once was the Omuro Palace, consisting of a series of buildings interconnected by roofed, wooden corridors which look out upon lovely gardens and bring into reality exactly what one would anticipate imperial palaces of early Kyoto to have been like.

Two more famous (and crowded) temples are also located in this area: the Ryoan-ji and the Kinkaku-ji. The former is noted for its dry garden of fifteen stones set within a walled courtyard, but it also can claim a series of imperial tombs on the hillside behind it as well as a pond and a rest house where tofu and tea can be ordered. Further to the east is the Domoto Insho Art Museum and finally the Kinkaku-ji, the Temple of the Gold Pavilion, famed for the gold-clad pleasure villa of the Ashikaga-period shogun Yoshimitsu. Turned into a temple after his death, nothing original remains; the Gold Pavilion itself is a 1955 reconstruction after its destruction in a fire set by a deranged monk in 1950.

We begin a visit to these temples at the Ninna-ji, the Temple of Benevolent Harmony, and its lovely Omuro Palace (Omuro Gosho).

NINNA-JI AND OMURO PALACE

The Ninna-ji temple can be reached by means of buses 26, 28, and 59, which stop outside the temple grounds at the Omuro Ninna-ji bus stop. It can also be reached from the Omuro Station of the Kitano Line of the Keifuku Electric Railway. The temple is to the north of the station. The Ninna-ji lies about a half-mile south of the Ryoan-ji. (The sites in this group are at approximately a half-mile distances from each other.) The temple is open from 9:00 a.m. to 5:00 p.m. in summer and from 9:00 a.m.

to 4:00 p.m. in winter. Entry to the temple is free, but there is a fee to the Omuro Palace complex.

In 886 the emperor Koko ordered the construction of the Omuro Gosho (Omuro Palace) but died shortly before the palace was finished. His son, Emperor Uda, ascended the throne when he was twenty-one, and in 888 he completed the palace as a temple, the Ninna-ji, since his father had wished it to become a temple after his death. In 901, when he was thirty-three, Emperor Uda abdicated in favor of his son Daigo, and Uda became the superior of the Ninna-ji. Here he reigned as ex-emperor and monk-emperor from the Suzaku-in of the Ninna-ji. He was the first emperor to become a monk in Heian times, and he started the *monzeki* tradition whereby a member of the imperial family became the superior of a major temple. From his death in 931 until 1868, the first or the second son of the emperor became the superior of the Ninna-ji for the next thirty generations. (Uda was also the first emperor to be buried behind the Ryoan-ji temple.)

Although his son Daigo was succeeded by another of Uda's sons, Suzaku, Uda continued to rule behind the scenes. He gathered about him the associates of Sugawara-no-Michizane, a group of those who were delighted with Chinese learning and art. Thus, the Ninna-ji became an artistic center since Uda claimed that he had abdicated in order to live primarily for his artistic interests.

Prior to the Onin War (1467–77), the Ninna-ji had sixty subtemples on its grounds, but the temple was destroyed in 1467, and it was not until more than one hundred years had passed that it was rebuilt with the assistance of the emperor Go-Mizuno-o and the Tokugawa shogun in the 1630s. Among the units of the reconstructed temple, the Amida Hall was created from the Shishin-den of the imperial palace, which Hideyoshi had built for the emperor in the late 1590s, while the Miei-do was once the Seiryo-den palace.

In 1887 fire again struck the temple, and twenty-five of its buildings were destroyed. Only the Hito-tei and the Ryokaku-tei, the two teahouses, survived in the Omuro Palace area. Reconstruction began at the turn of the century, and by 1915 the Omuro Palace had been recreated in the Heian-period (794–1185) style, albeit it follows the building plan of the sixteenth- and seventeenth-century buildings since the earlier pattern is not known.

Today, the Ninna-ji is visited both as a temple and for its noted reconstructed Omuro Palace. In springtime, it is visited for its cherry trees which have short, thick trunks and multipetaled blossoms appearing from mid- to late April in a normal season.

San-mon The grounds of the temple are entered by steps leading to the rebuilt (1630s) San-mon, the Mountain Gate, a two-story structure with a tiled roof. On either side of the three-portal entry stand the huge eleven-foot-tall Kongo Rikishi (Nio), guardian deities of the temple entrance. Two *koma-inu* (Korean lion-dogs) stand in the gateway. Within the precincts of the temple, to the left of the main path which stretches from the San-mon gate north to the Chu-mon (Central Gate), is the reconstructed Omuro Palace, the two historic teahouses, and the palace gardens behind walls (see below). To the right of this main path is the Omuro Kaikan (Omuro Hall), the 1935 Reihokan (Treasury), the Omuro Schools of Flower Arranging, and the priests' apartments.

Chu-mon Beyond the San-mon, a graveled courtyard with walls and gateways on either side leads to the steps of the one-story, vermilion Chu-mon. A Deva King stands guard on either side of the passage through the gate; on the left is Bishamon-ten with a stupa in his right hand and a rod in his left hand, while on the right is Zocho-ten with a *vajra* (symbolic thunderbolt) in his left hand and a rod in his right hand. Both have wheel-shaped halos behind their heads and each has two small figures before him.

To the right of and beyond the Chu-mon is the graceful five-story pagoda, 108 feet tall and 18 feet square. It was erected in

1637 with the assistance of Shogun Iemitsu. To the right of it is the Kusho Myojin Shrine, the Shinto shrine that protects the temple, of three thatch-roofed, one-story buildings standing behind a solid wooden fence.

Hondo   Directly behind the Chu-mon at the rear of this inner compound is the Hondo, formerly the Shishin-den (Throne Hall) of the imperial palace and moved here in 1676. Within, the main image is that of a gilt Amida with Seishi and Kannon on either side, each with a gold aureole. To the right of the Hondo is the Kyodo (Sutra Library).

Miei-do   In the northwest corner, to the left of the Hondo, is the Miei-do (Founder's Hall) in its own walled enclosure with a flaming jewel symbolizing its memorial purpose atop its pyramidal cypress roof. The hall was made from the wood of the Seiryo-den of the imperial palace and later, through a gift of Shogun Iemitsu, of wood from the Nanden Palace. The image within, behind a small mirror, is that of Kukai (Kobo Daishi) with an elaborate arrangement of altar tables and gold brocade decoration before it. To the right of the Miei-do is the very small Fudo Myo-o-do (Fudo Myo-o Hall) with an image of Fudo. Long bamboo dippers are available for the pouring of water over the Fudo as an act of worship.

South of the Miei-do is the Kannon-do with an image of Kannon, and south of that is the grove of the famous cherry trees of the Ninna-ji temple.

Omuro Palace   Upon returning to the entry courtyard behind the San-mon, one can see the reconstruction of the Omuro Palace to the west. First rebuilt in 1630, the Otsune-goten (Everyday Palace) of the imperial palace was relocated here to replace the Omuro Palace which had been destroyed in the Onin War. Destroyed once more by fire in the late 1800s, it was rebuilt in the Shinden-style architecture of the Heian period.

The entry to the palace complex is through a gate in the wall just beyond the San-mon. (The large Chokushi-mon [Imperial Messenger's Gate] in the middle of the walled area is a ceremonial gate and not a passageway.) In the entry courtyard of the palace precincts is a magnificent, horizontally trained pine tree which serves as the focal point for this area. The entryway into the palace buildings has a gabled roof of the Chinese style, and all of the structures that make up the palace are interconnected with covered passageways, each offering views from differing perspectives onto the gardens of the palace. The first covered corridor leads from the entry building to the Shiro Shoin.

Shiro Shoin   The Shiro Shoin (White Study) which looks out on a raked gravel garden and the Chokushi-mon gateway is the first building beyond the entryway. The Shiro Shoin served as an informal meeting hall for the *monzeki* princes. It is divided into three rooms. The *fusuma* (sliding panels) of the three walls of the first room have paintings of cranes and pines in the snow; the second room has cranes on the left, a huge, thick pine tree in the center which extends to the left wall *fusuma,* and on the *fusuma* of the right wall are waves breaking over large rocks. In the third room, the *fusuma* on the left wall is decorated with squirrels and small flowers beneath a pine tree; two tokonoma, a *chigaidana* (staggered shelves), and two very large scrolls are on the center wall, while the *fusuma* of the right wall has another painting of two large pine trees. All of the *fusuma* were painted by Seihan Fukunaga in the years after its 1914 reconstruction.

Shinden   Corridors connect the Shiro Shoin with the cedar-bark, thatch-roofed Shinden, the very large main residence. The corridor or veranda around the Shinden first takes one along the south side of the building, the side looking out onto the raked sand garden and the Chokushi-mon gate, as does the Shiro Shoin. At the entry to the Shinden are two wooden panels of dark brown natural wood. One panel is painted with a pine tree covered with snow, while the second panel shows birds in flight. When one turns the corner, one can see the white and yellow chrysanthemums on the reverse side of the latter panel. The room behind this veranda is backed by half-wood, half-shoji sliding panels.

Continuing to the east veranda and to the north side of the Shinden, one has a full view of the lovely garden onto which the three rooms of the north side of the building face. A raked sand garden is in the foreground, and rising beyond it is a hillside with plantings, ponds, rocks, a waterfall spilling into a pond, its two teahouses, the Hito-tei to the right and the Ryokaku-tei to the far left beyond the Remei-den (see below), and a view of a distant pagoda rising above the trees.

The northern side of the Shinden is divided into three rooms. The rear wall of the first room is composed of half-*fusuma* of painted flowers on a gold base, as is the left wall. The right wall has a colorful scene of men of the Heian court on horseback with a lake to the right and mountains to the left rear. The second room has a scene of the Arashiyama Boat Festival on the *fusuma* of the left wall, while the *fusuma* of the right wall depict a Heian procession through the countryside. The third room has *chigaidana* and a tokonoma on the right-hand wall. The background of the tokonoma has a scene of hills and trees. The rear wall is made up of four doors with a painting of peacocks on a tree, while the left wall has a huge tree in white bloom. The paintings of this 1914 reconstruction of the Shinden were done by Suekichi Kameoka while the paintings of the four seasons are by Zuisen Hara. The richly decorated building was originally used for formal meetings and ceremonies.

Kuro Shoin The next range of corridors leads to the Kuro Shoin (Black Study), the hall used for formal meetings by the *monzeki*. It has *fusuma* painted by Insho Domoto, and its six rooms are arranged in three rooms back-to-back, separated by *fusuma* on the north and south sides. To the north of the Kuro Shoin, connected with it by a roofed corridor, is the Remei-den which was built in memory of the emperor Uda who completed the temple and was its first superior. Memorials to the *monzeki* and other members of the imperial family are within; an altar with small tables is arranged before an Amida trio, while thirty books in Kukai's handwriting have traditionally been kept in this memorial building. The decorations of the hall were done by Suekichi Kameoka in 1914.

Reihokan   The temple Reihokan (Treasure House) lies to the east of the main courtyard between the San-mon and Chu-mon gates. It is open from the first to the third Sundays in October from 9:00 a.m. to 5:00 p.m. The treasury includes images of Amida, bodhisattvas, and Shitenno (Deva Kings); scrolls in the hand of Kobo Daishi; Chinese and Japanese furniture; textiles; musical instruments; and other treasures. The temple also holds a statue of the young Prince Siddhartha by Inchi from 1252. The figure is in the style of images of Prince Shotoku although the draperies are in the Sung manner. A symbol in the shape of the corona of the moon on his chest is the sign of absolute purity. It is a collection that is worth seeing during the short period the treasure house is open each year.

Omuro Kaikan   To the rear of the precinct in which the Reihokan is located is the Omuro Kaikan (Omuro Hall) designed for various religious and secular purposes of the temple and the sect. The Omuro School of Flower Arranging is in the temple precincts also, and information concerning the school can be obtained from the temple office.

RYOAN-JI

The Ryoan-ji (Temple of the Peaceful Dragon) is located in the northwest-central portion of Kyoto, a half-mile northeast of the Omuro Kaikan, between the Ninna-ji and the Kinkaku-ji (Temple of the Gold Pavilion). It can be reached by taking bus 59 to the Ryoan-ji-mae bus stop. Alternatively, the subway can be taken to Imadegawa Station and then bus 59 can be taken to the Ryoan-ji-mae bus stop. Between March 1 and November 30, the temple is open from 8:00 a.m. to 5:00 p.m., and from 8:30 a.m. to 4:30 p.m. from December 1 to the end of February. Entry fee.

This very popular Rinzai Zen temple is primarily noted for its stone and sand garden for which there are numerous interpretations—all equally valid or not, as the viewer wishes to believe. It is best to see the temple in the early morning before the hordes of visitors appear or at the end of the day when they have gone on to other sites or back to their hotels.

The temple site was originally the Heian-period (794–1185) estate of a branch of the Fujiwara family who ruled the country under the emperor. It served as well on occasion as the home of a retired emperor, and then became a temple, the Tokudai-ji (also known as Enyu-ji). Hosokawa Katsumoto (1430–73) created his estate on the ruins of the Tokudai-ji temple, but in 1473 he died in the ongoing Onin War and left his 120-acre estate to become a temple, the Ryoan-ji. The original buildings were destroyed in the Onin War which left most of Kyoto in ashes. Reconstructed in 1499, the temple burned again in 1790, and in the rebuilding of 1800 not all of its structures were re-created.

The temple's present renown has made it an inevitable tourist destination so that the calm of the stone garden, claimed to be a help in meditation, is frequently broken by the amplified descriptions (in Japanese) being delivered by tour guides. Its present popularity is all the more remarkable since until 1930 not much attention was paid to its dry garden, a garden that today is one of the most important tourist sites in Kyoto.

Kyoyo-chi   The outer grounds of the temple, in front of its main building and its walled enclave, have as their focus the twelfth-century Kyoyo-chi (Mirror-Shaped Pond) with its two small islands. The larger island is Benten-jima which has a small causeway and bridge leading to a shrine to Benten, the Shinto goddess of good luck (the only female among the Seven Gods of Good Luck). The smaller island is named Fushitora-jima (Hiding Tiger Isle). To the west of Benten-jima is the Daishu-in (Big Pearl) Temple and then the Seigen-in, a resting and refreshment place where tofu, vegetarian fare, and tea can be enjoyed.

For many years prior to the tenth century, mandarin ducks *(oshidori)* made the pond their home, and thus the Ryoan-ji was also known as the Mandarin Duck Temple (Oshidori-dera). The water that creates the pond arises around two rocks in the southern part of the Kyoyo-chi pond, and the stroll garden around the pond was created in the late 1100s. It is usually visited after one leaves the Ryoan-ji buildings.

Kuri One enters the Ryoan-ji temple by means of a broad flight of steps leading to the Kuri (Priests' Quarters) with its Kara-mon (Chinese-style gateway). The Kuri is the major building of the

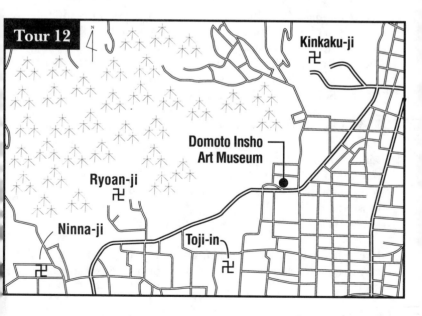

temple, the temple's many other buildings, as noted above, not having been rebuilt in the 1800 reconstruction. A small bell under the eaves is used for the call to services. To the rear of the Kuri is the Zoroku-an, the Tortoise Arbor Tea Room (not open to the public). The tea room is in the early seventeenth-century style which was favored by Kishuza, a tea master of that time.

Hojo The Kuri is attached to the Hojo (Superior's Quarters) of 1797 by a wide corridor. The Hojo consists of six rooms (three rooms back-to-back), each opening onto a veranda, the altar room being the rear center room of these connected chambers. The center room to the front has ascending and descending dragons painted on its *fusuma,* while at the rear of the room is a painted tree so composed as to resemble a dragon. Behind this front room is a second room which serves as a preliminary area to the altar room itself, a small area which extends beyond the rear of the Hojo. The altar room has a dragon painted by Chodensu (1352–1431) on the ceiling, while the altar has an image of Shaka (Buddha) as its primary object of veneration. To Shaka's left is an image of Monju, an image of Hosokawa Katsumoto (general of the Muromachi period, 1136-1568), and the *ihai* (mortuary tablet) to Giten, first abbot of the temple. To the right of Shaka are images of Fugen, Abbot Giten, and Abbot Chuko. Before the Shaka image are *ihai* for the Hosokawa family and prayer tablets for the current emperor.

Of the other rooms in the Hojo, the twenty-mat front room on the west has *fusuma* of the Diamond Mountains of Korea in winter, while the companion east room has *fusuma* of the Diamond Mountains of Korea in summer. The 12.5-mat rear, east room has *fusuma* painted with scenes of the Diamond Mountains of Korea in spring. These *fusuma* paintings are modern, having been created in the 1950s by Kakuo Satsuke.

Ryoan-ji Garden The garden, created at the end of the fifteenth century, consists of fifteen stones on a sand bed, a number symbolizing wholeness or completeness since the Buddhist world consists of seven continents and eight oceans. These fifteen stones (only fourteen of which can be seen at any one time no matter the angle of viewing) are in groups of five, two, three, two, and three on a base of sand which is raked daily in a set pattern. Moss about the base of the stones provides the only greenery in the garden. This 50-foot-wide by 102-foot-long *karesansui* (dry garden) is attributed to Soami (1455–1525) by some authorities, while others say it is by an unknown designer. It was restored in 1499 and was later endowed by two Tokugawa shoguns, Ieyasu and Iemitsu.

Originally, the garden was open to the Kyoyo-chi pond below it, but at a later date it was enclosed by the present wall. An earthen wall composed of clay boiled in oil encompasses the garden on three sides while the temple Hojo forms a fourth side. The varied color of the wall is occasioned by the seepage of the oil from the clay. Prior to the construction of the enclosing wall in the seventeenth century, the emphasis of the garden was not so much on the stones as on the vista beyond—an intent that has obviously been altered.

What is the significance of the garden? No one knows, but theories abound, all promulgated with great authority by those explaining their version of the symbolism. Perhaps the motto on the Tsukubai, the stone water basin in the shape of an old coin for washing hands before tea ceremony in the Zoroku-an, best sums it up: "The knowledge that is given is sufficient," or "I learn only to be contented." In Zen, learning or knowledge is sufficient unto itself and is not for "use" in a popular sense. The Tsukubai was a gift of Tokugawa-no-Mitsukuni (1628–1700), the compiler of the *Dai Nippon-shi* (The Great History of Japan).

To the west of the Hojo is a moss garden, and behind it garden and a small pond with the Tsukubai nearby.

The path from the entry/exit of the Ryoan-ji building the landscaped garden, to the *nokotso* (crypt), and to in refreshment pavilion alongside the Kyoyo-chi

A path and steps at the west side of the Kyoyo-chi pond, before the temple, lead through the Imperial Gate to an area of tombs that lies behind (to the north of and above) the Ryoan-ji on the hillside to its rear. Directly behind the Hojo on an extension of this path are the Hosokawa tombs, and across the path are the graves of Emperor Go-Suzaku (1009–45) and his sons, the emperors Go-Sanjo (1034–73) and Go-Reizei (1025–68). Beyond these are the tombs of the emperors Horikawa (1079–1107) and Ichijo (980–1011). All these imperial graves were enhanced in the later nineteenth century by the Meiji government. The first emperor to be buried here was Emperor Uda in 931.

A view of Kyoto can be had from this higher ground.

DOMOTO INSHO ART MUSEUM

The Domoto Insho Art Museum lies between the Ryoan-ji and the Kinkaku-ji temples on Kitasuji-dori; thus, it can be visited en route to the Gold Pavilion. The Domoto Insho Art Museum is open from 10:00 a.m. to 5:00 p.m., but the entry is closed at 4:30; it is closed on Mondays and the New Year holidays as well as from March 25–31 and from September 25–31. Bus 59 takes one to the museum stop. Entry fee.

Domoto Insho (1891–1975) was a versatile artist who created paintings, ceramics, stained glass, and tapestries. In his early years, he painted in a traditional Japanese style but later showed the influence of French art on his work. The museum is devoted solely to his work and the museum mounts two main exhibitions a year from April to September and from October to March.

asuji-dori to the northeast is the

**E TEMPLE OF THE
PAVILION)**

ern part of the city of Kyoto at the
be reached by means of bus 12, 59,

s a
s leads to
the Seigen-
ond.

204, or 205 to the Kinkaku-ji-michi bus stop or bus 50 to the Kinkaku-ji-mae stop. The temple is open from 9:00 a.m. to 5:30 p.m. in summer and from 9:00 a.m. to 5:00 p.m. between October and March. Entry fee.

Originally the mountain villa of Saionji Kintsune (1171–1244), the grounds included the Saionji temple and the Kita Yama-den villa with its forty-five-foot-high waterfall. In time, the temple and villa fell to ruin, and the 4.5-acre site was eventually obtained by Shogun Ashikaga Yoshimitsu (1358–1408). In the manner of emperors, for Yoshimitsu was not shy in his pretensions, he retired at age thirty-eight, turning the role of shogun over to his nine-year-old son, Yoshimochi. As with retired emperors, he remained the power behind the shogunate and used his mountainside retreat, which he began in 1397, as a place from which his political power could still be employed.

Here in 1408 he entertained the emperor Go-Komatsu with a boating party, an occasion of the greatest display of ostentation inasmuch as it was the first time an emperor had deigned to stay at a villa of one who was not of noble status. Here, too, he held a reception for ambassadors from China, for Yoshimitsu was captivated by the aesthetics of that great country.

The Gold Pavilion (originally called the Shari-den or Relic Hall) and its pond were designed to evoke the image of the Seven Treasure Pond found in Buddhist Paradise scenes. The pond was originally filled with flowering lotus plants, symbol of the pure flower of the truth of Buddhism rising from the mud of this world.

This retirement retreat was rather impressive since it contained a variety of buildings: an eight-gabled Shishin-den hall which resembled that of the same building in the imperial palace (replete with a throne at its center for this ex-shogun and with eight dragons in gold lacquer on its roof); the Hall of the Court of Nobles; the Pavilion of the Mirror of Heaven; the Hall of the Confessor of the Doctrine; the North-gazing Hall (toward the hills); the Snow-viewing Arbor; the Relic Hall; the Hall of the

Waters; the Hall of Fragrant Virtues; the Lesser Hall; the Jizo Hall; and, of course, the Gold Pavilion. All but one of these buildings have disappeared with time.

After Yoshimitsu's death, following the instructions in his will, his pleasure palace became the Rokuon-ji (Deer Park Temple) of the Rinzai sect of Buddhism, and the noted priest Muso Kokushi was invited to become the founding abbot. Despite the vicissitudes of war, earthquakes, and fires, the Gold Pavilion, the heart of Yoshimitsu's complex, survived until 1950 when a deranged monk set it on fire. It was rebuilt in 1955 as an exact replica of the original pavilion and has been regilded since its reconstruction.

The grounds of the Kinkaku-ji are entered through the So-mon gate and followed down a tree-lined path to an area before a yellow wall and the Chu-mon (Middle Gate). To the left of this entry path is the Shoro (Bell Tower), while to the right is a large boat-shaped stone. The camellia bush in the garden before the Kuri (Priests' Quarters) was planted by Emperor Go-Mizuno-o himself. The Hondo (Main Hall) of the Rokuon-ji temple, rebuilt in the early 1600s at the order of Emperor Go-Mizuno-o, and the Kuri lie to the right of the entry path. (These halls are generally not open to the public.)

Hondo   The main image in the Hondo is a seated Sho Kannon (a gift of Emperor Go-Mizuno-o) attributed to Jocho (eleventh century) with Bon-ten and Taishaku-ten, two Devas, on either side. To the right is a statue of Muso Kokushi, the first abbot of the temple, while to the left is a statue of Yoshimitsu in priestly garb. The *fusuma* in the hall bear sepia drawings by Kano Tanyu (1602–74). The main hall also has paintings by Chodensu (1352–1431) and by Kano Tsunenobu (1636–1713). In addition, there is a portrait of Yoshitsune with an inscription by his son.

Dai Shoin   The Dai Shoin (Large Study) to the rear of the Hondo (which extends toward the Gold Pavilion and its pond) has *fusuma* decorated by Sumiyoshi Hiromichi (1599–1670) and by Ito Jakuchu (1716–1800). A noted pine, named the "Land Boat Pine" from its boatlike shape, is in the north garden opposite the Gold Pavilion. At the end of the entry path, the Chu-mon or Kara-mon (Chinese-style gateway) leads to the precincts of the Gold Pavilion.

The renewal of contact with Sung China brought many new artistic influences to bear on Japanese life, and Yoshimitsu surrounded himself with cultural advisors who had been to China (since he had a major concern for the aesthetic aspects of life). As a result, the Gold Pavilion, the jewel in his retirement retreat, shows the influence of Sung architecture.

The Gold Pavilion   The three-story pavilion is 33 feet wide by 40 feet long and is 42 feet high; it is topped by a 3.7-foot-tall bronze phoenix with outspread wings (a 1955 reproduction of the original). The first floor of the pavilion, the Hosui-in was used as a reception hall where Yoshimitsu welcomed his guests. It contained an altar in the middle with the central image of Amida by Anami, a Kannon by Unkei, and a Seishi by Tankei. In addition, there were wood images of Yoshimitsu, of Muso Soseki, of Daruma, and of many Jizo. This first floor is in the Heian-period (794–1185) *shinden-zukuri* architectural style, the style of early palace buildings. The Tsuridono (Platform) juts from the side of the pavilion into the pond and provided a landing dock for the boating parties of ornate Chinese-style boats created by order of Yoshimitsu.

The second floor, the Cho-onkaku (Hall of Roaring Waves), was created in the *bukezukuri* style, that of the architectural style of a samurai house of the Kamakura period (1185–1333). This level was reserved for Yoshimitsu's private meetings with special guests, and here he held discussions of affairs of the day or of matters of an artistic nature. It had paintings by Kano Masanobu (1434–1530), a central altar with a Sho Kannon by Eshin, with Shitenno images on the right and left.

The third floor, the Kukyocho (Firmament Top), twenty-three

feet square with a ceiling of one piece of camphor wood eighteen feet square, served as a private retreat for ceremonial tea drinking and contemplation with his most intimate friends. It is in the Sung-inspired Chinese *(kara)* or Zen-temple style with its cusped (bell-shaped) windows. It once held a Jodo Shinshu-style Amida and twenty-five bodhisattvas.

The exterior of the first floor of the pavilion is of unpainted wood while the two upper floors are lacquered and then covered with gold foil. (The replacement of the foil in 1987 under a general reconstruction program cost $5,000,000.) At one time, the pavilion was probably on an island attached to the shore by means of a bridge. The carp-filled pond before the pavilion, Kagami-ike (Mirror Pond), covers 1.75 acres and has numerous islands within it, some with noted (and named) stones. These islands represent the nine mountains and the eight oceans of the Buddhist creation story.

Behind the pavilion and up a short flight of stone steps is a small shrine, the Shinun, dedicated to the god of the temple grounds, and then a spring, the Ginkasen, which supplied the water for Yoshimitsu's tea ceremony. The Ryumon-baku, a small waterfall, has a large stone, the Carp Stone, standing before it—to suggest the way carp can ascend a waterfall on the way to the spawning grounds. A noted style of bamboo fencing named for the pavilion, the Kinkaku-ji fence, leads up the hillside to the Kokei-bashi, a small stone bridge over an artificial valley and a pond, the Anmin-taku, which has a small island with a modest stone pagoda on it (with four Buddhas cut into the four sides of the stone base) dedicated to the White Dragon who controls the water supply.

Sekka-tei Stone steps up a winding path lead to the thatch-roofed Sekka-tei, a small tea-ceremony house built in honor of a visit by Emperor Go-Mizuno-o in the 1600s. Although destroyed in an 1874 fire, it was recreated in 1884. An old stone lantern, a stone basin, and a stool standing before the building came from the former Ashikaga-Muromachi-period (1336–1568) Hana-no-Gosho (Flower Palace). This simple teahouse has a crooked post of rare wood from the Nandin (*nanten* or heavenly bamboo) tree setting off its tokonoma, and the shelves are of bush clover *(hagi)* wood. To the rear of the teahouse is the post-1868 rebuilt Kyohoku-ro where Yoshimitsu carried out state business.

Fudo-do   The path eventually leads through a moss garden to the Fudo-do, a small temple to Fudo Myo-o with a stone image of the god and his attendants. The bushes about this tiny temple are covered with twisted strips of paper "fortunes" which have been obtained from an adjacent fortunetelling machine.

(The mountain behind the Kinkaku-ji, Mount Kinugasa [Silk Hat Mountain] is reputedly so-named since one hot July day the ex-emperor Uda ordered it spread with white silk so his eyes could enjoy a cool, wintry sensation.)

A return to the center of the city can be made by taxi or by bus from in front of the temple on Kitasuji-dori or by subway at the Kitaoji-eki-mae bus stop on Karasuma-dori.

TOUR
13

Brocades,
Samurai Movies, and the
Contemplative Bodhisattva

広隆寺　等持院　北野天満宮　大報恩寺

WARS CAN be disruptive to the crafts and to trade, but, strangely enough, war can sometimes lead to changes and improvements in these fields. So it was with the craft of weaving in the late 1400s. Luxurious fabrics that would grace their elegant and nonproductive lives were in demand by the imperial court. The aesthetic pleasures of fine clothing came to an end, however, as a result of the Onin Wars of the late 1400s, and even the weavers themselves were lost to Kyoto for a number of years. When they returned from their self-imposed exile, they settled in what had been the Western Army Camp (Nishijin) area of Kyoto, and there, with new techniques learned in Sakai (Osaka) in the 1470s, the weaving craft in Kyoto revived and earned fame both for its practical materials and for its rich brocades.

The central sector of Kyoto had not only the imperial palace and Nishijin, but to its west lay shrines and temples of note. One, the Senbon Shaka-do (Senbon Shaka Hall, also known as Daiho-on-ji or Daiho-on Temple) is known for its magnificent collection of Buddhist images which have been placed in a handsome treasury building, but it is perhaps more often remembered for the wife of its architect than for its treasured images. Within the temple is a memorial to Okame whose quick mind saved her architect husband from a serious architectural faux pas during the construction of the Senbon Shaka-do and whose smiling face has been duplicated in a humorous papier-mâché representation seen at festivals throughout Japan.

The memorial to this smiling spirit exists not too far from Kitano Shrine which had been created to appease the supposed unhappy and restless spirit of Sugawara-no-Michizane, a tenth-century poet and statesman. A student rendezvous for centuries, the Kitano Tenman-gu (Kitano Tenman Shrine) is still patronized by those aspiring to success in intellectual endeavors, for Michizane, among other attributes, is now regarded as a Shinto spirit who can assist students and scholars. Even the unliterary flock to the Kitano Shrine each month, for here is held one of the great monthly fairs of Kyoto where everything from antiques to food to knickknacks can be purchased.

The Koryu-ji, furthest west in this tour, is dedicated to the memory of the ever-reverenced prince Shotoku, the official proponent of Buddhism in early Japan. The temple was originally founded in the 620s on the death of the prince, and it is a mecca for those interested in early Buddhist artistry. Its attractive treasury contains finely crafted images from the 600s on, including a famed statue of a contemplative Miroku, the benevolent bodhisattva, which was created in Korea.

Another temple, the Toji-in (Toji Temple), has had the best of times and the worst of times. The Toji-in is the sepulchral temple of the Ashikaga shoguns, but today is enjoyed for its lovely garden and teahouse. It served as the family temple of the Ashikaga clan who numbered among their more noted members the creators of the Gold Pavilion and the Silver Pavilion. The Ashikaga were despised by the Meiji authorities after 1868, however, because of their disrespect paid to medieval emperors, and thus the temple fell upon difficult times. After 1870, some of the images (now restored) could be beaten (for a fee) to show one's dislike of those who had not honored earlier emperors.

All is not seriousness on this tour. The Toei Eigamura (Toei Film Village) provides the lightness of the entertainment world, for here one can visit the studio where films have been made for many years and where television soap operas originate today. The Toei Eigamura is a filming complex that recreates everything from medieval Japanese times with swashbuckling samurai epics and black-masked ninja to Edo-period (1603–1868) Japan with its political intrigues. To the delight of adolescents (and adults), one can see films being made or one can be photographed in the cityscape of old Edo.

While there will be some walking in this tour, public transportation (or taxis) will be found to come in handy, for the distances to be covered are fairly considerable, more than is normal in this guidebook. The first location to be visited is the Nishijin Textile Center.

NISHIJIN TEXTILE CENTER

Bus 9 or 12 taken along Horikawa-dori to the bus stop at the intersection of Imadegawa-dori or bus 203 or 59 taken along Imadegawa-dori to the same intersection puts one across from the modern Nishijin Textile Center on the west side of Horikawa-dori just south of Imadegawa-dori. The center is open daily from 9:00 a.m. to 5:00 p.m. without charge. Kimono shows (groups only) are held between 10:00 a.m. and 4:00 p.m. There is a fee.

The Nishijin area is a fairly large and somewhat amorphous one. It spreads from just south of the Daitoku-ji (Kita-oji-dori) down to Imadegawa-dori and from the Kitano Shrine area to Horikawa-dori. Since 1976, the Nishijin Textile Center has been in a new building on the west side of Horikawa-dori and south of Imadegawa-dori.

The Nishijin area received its name from the wars of the fifteenth century which laid waste this area as well as virtually all of Kyoto. Nishijin means Western Army Camp, for that was what was here in the late 1400s. When the Onin War ended, and as peace was restored to Kyoto, this area began to revive as a place of work and residence, and it was here that the weavers resettled. The weavers had moved to Sakai (the port of old Osaka) and to Yamaguchi during the wars of the fifteenth century, and there they learned some of the new (to them) Chinese techniques of weaving. Additional immigrants from the mainland who came to Japan as a result of Hideyoshi's Korean incursions in the late 1500s also added not only new techniques in weaving but also the secret to making gold thread. These techniques helped Kyoto weavers to develop more luxurious materials for their major customers. Much of their income came from the woven silk goods they supplied to the imperial court and to the aristocracy.

The weaving of silk in Kyoto was a tradition that began even before the city was established. Among the early settlers in the region were the Hata family who brought the technique of weaving silk from the continent when they immigrated to Japan in the 300s. Weaving thus became a major source of income in the new capital when it came into being in the 800s, and the craft continued to flourish until the Onin Wars. After the war, revival came slowly at first until the Nishijin weavers organized into a guild and obtained a monopoly in weaving so as to assure their future. Thus by the early 1700s there were five thousand weavers working in the private homes of the Nishijin area. (Much of the production was a home industry.)

All was not smooth sailing, however, for the fire of 1730 destroyed many of the houses and looms in the district. Some three thousand looms reputedly were lost. Then in the 1830s the government, in one of its anti-luxury moods, prohibited the weaving of silk much to the detriment of the Nishijin weavers. The move of the capital and the court to Tokyo in 1868 might also have adversely affected Nishijin production, but the relocation of the capital was offset by new technology which began to come from the West. The importation of Jacquard looms led to a mechanization of and an increase in production of handloomed cloth.

Since the 1980s the outlook for Nishijin has had other shadows cast over it: young people have other opportunities; the import of inexpensive woven goods from factories in newly industrialized countries of Asia poses a serious threat to the industry; and the diversification of weaving to other areas of Japan, which began at the time of the Onin War, inexorably continues. Therefore, although three thousand looms were said to be in use in the area in the 1980s, whether the Nishijin area will remain a textile center is an open question.

A center for display and sales of various Nishijin products began in 1925 with the opening of the textile museum. In 1976 a new and expanded center was opened which has three public floors:

First floor: Displays, Information Center, Japanese restaurant, confectionery sales.

Second floor: Jacquard and hand-operated looms in action. Sales area.

Third floor: Exhibits of old Nishijin weaving and kimono and obi modeling. Videotapes of the Nishijin weaving process may be seen.

On leaving the Nishijin Textile Center, the route continues by bus or taxi along Imadegawa-dori to the west to the Senbon Shaka-do temple.

SENBON SHAKA-DO (DAIHO-ON-JI)

The Senbon Shaka-do is 437 yards northeast of the Kitano Shrine. Take bus 52 or 203 from the Nishijin Textile Center to the Kamishichiken bus stop on Imadegawa-dori (the bus stop just before the north-south Nishi-oji-dori). A sign with an arrow on the north side of Imadegawa-dori at the Kamishichiken bus stop points north to Senbon Shaka-do (in English). The main entrance to the temple grounds is on Shichihonmachi-dori. The temple buildings are open from 9:00 a.m. to 5:00 p.m. Entry fee.

Hondo According to tradition, the Senbon Shaka-do was founded by Emperor Yomei (reigned 585–87), a fairly unlikely event since the emperor only accepted Buddhism on his deathbed, and the first Buddhist temples (the Shitenno-ji in Osaka and the Hoko-ji in Asuka) were built a few years later. The present

Hondo (Main Hall) was built in 1227 and miraculously survived the Onin War (1467–77), which destroyed so many of the other structures in the city.

The architect of the Hondo was Nagai Takatsugi who, unfortunately, miscalculated the measurements for the main pillars and came up with posts too short. It was his wife Okame's suggestion that saved his reputation; she proposed adding brackets to the top of the posts to reach the correct height. This was done, but Okame died before she could see the success of her proposal. When the last beams were put into place, the workmen, in her honor, placed a mask of her round, plump, cheerful face on the ridge pole. Thus, the cult of Okame began and spread throughout Japan, and she became the deity of good luck, the grantor of desires, and the patroness of business prosperity. As a mask, her round face has red cheeks and small, round eyebrows. In her honor, a statue of Okame sits to the right of the Hondo when one faces the building.

The main gate to the Senbon Shaka-do is on its south side; the path to the Hondo leads past minor buildings. To the right, before reaching the Hondo, is the statue of the round-cheeked Okame. To the left is the temple office and ticket booth where one pays the entry fee to the modern treasury located behind the Hondo.

The Hondo was originally created in the *shinden-zukuri* style with a thatched roof. Although the roof was tiled in 1670, in recent times the roof has been returned to its earlier thatched status. The central image on the main altar of the Hondo, kept in a closed case but opened for public viewing on August 8 each year, is that of Shaka Nyorai. Created in wood by Gyokai, the senior apprentice to the noted artist Kaikei, this thirteenth-century image is thirty-six inches tall and is covered with gold leaf. It is seated upon a lotus and has an elaborate aureole of fine fretwork with small Buddha images behind it. This image is the only surviving work by Gyokai.

The four pillars about the Shaka image case are decorated

with colorful but faded images. Two poles stand at either side, each topped by round, fanlike units bearing the image of Okame's face. Representations of Okame in all sizes and shapes fill the cases lining the corridor on the east side of the veranda, and at the rear of this corridor is a large wooden image of Okame.

Reihokan The fairly compact precincts of the temple include a number of buildings, the most important being the Reihokan, one of the finest treasure houses in Kyoto, known both for its interior and its treasures. A 1973, fireproof, concrete building, it has walls and ceiling of attractive wood with magnificent sculptures arranged around three of its walls. On the left wall are an early Buddha image, the Shitenno (Four Deva Kings), a Jizo, a seated Dainichi with a large crown, and the standing, painted wood Judai-deshi (Ten Great Disciples) carved by Kaikei in 1218. These vigorous portraits of real individuals once stood about the Shaka image in the Hondo.

At the rear center is a bronze "Birthday Buddha," a figure of the newborn Buddha with one hand pointing to heaven and one to the earth to indicate his sovereignty over both realms, a Heian-period (794–1185) Senju Kannon (One-Thousand-Arm Kannon), a Kamakura-period (1185–1336) Jizo, and a three-piece set of a seated Chinese sage and his two assistants. On the right-hand side are six magnificent representations of Kannon, deity of mercy, by Jokei II, dated 1224. They average seven feet in height. These exquisite, unpainted wood images are each backed by a full-length aureole of curved and delicately carved (fretted) wood. They show the influence of the fullness of Sung Chinese sculpture. Next to these are a Senju Kannon of the Heian period (794–1185) and two huge wooden frames, some twenty feet tall, each of which once held an immense drum. One is decorated with carved peacocks, while the other has carved dragons. On the fourth (entry) wall are two gigantic wheels from a court cart once used by Shogun Ashikaga Yoshimitsu (1358–1408), creator of the Temple of the Gold Pavilion (Kinkaku-ji).

KITANO TENMAN-GU

From the Senbon Shaka-do, the street on the southern perimeter of the temple should be taken to the west (turn right) for a few streets to the Kitano Tenman-gu shrine. The Kitano Tenman-gu is just north of Imadegawa-dori and one street east of Horikawa-dori in the northwestern portion of central Kyoto. The grounds are open during daylight hours. No entry fee is charged except for entrance to the treasury.

The Kitano Tenman-gu is dedicated to Sugawara-no-Michizane (845–903). A poet and statesman who was an advisor to the emperor Uda and then to his son the emperor Daigo, Michizane became the victim of a court intrigue, was disgraced and banished to Kyushu in 901, dying shortly thereafter in exile. His death was followed by tremendous storms, disastrous floods, epidemics, and even the loss of the Minister of the Left, Fujiwara-no-Tokihira who was responsible for the banishment of Michizane and who died in the 909 epidemic. Again, in 930, Kyoto suffered a series of calamitous storms, floods, and then droughts and epidemics. The palace was hit by lightning, and then the emperor Daigo fell ill and died.

Finally, in 942, a dream was interpreted and brought to the attention of the court. The interpretation held that the series of disasters inflicted on Kyoto were the action of Michizane's unhappy spirit, and that surcease could only be had if the Tenjin Shrine (dedicated to the god of thunder) were rededicated to Michizane. Michizane's spirit was therefore identified with that of the god of thunder, and in 947 a shrine was created to Michizane (at an existing shrine to the god of thunder) in order to bring relief to Kyoto. The shrine was also planted with Michizane's favorite tree, the apricot. In 959 a Fujiwara descendant, no doubt as a form of insurance, had the shrine enlarged. Meantime, to further allay Michizane's supposed angry spirit, his rank as Minister of the Right was restored. When problems still ensued in the land, he was elevated posthumously to the rank of

Minister of the Left, and, finally, in desperation, the court raised him posthumously to the prime ministry. From 1004 on, visits were even made to the shrine by various emperors. Through the years, the shrine gained in popularity, particularly since Michizane was also recognized as the patron of literature, of scholars, and of students. In this present century of universal education in Japan, the shrine is heavily frequented by students in need of spiritual or supernatural assistance at examination times.

It was at the Kitano Shrine in October 1587 that Toyotomi Hideyoshi held his famous tea party to which he invited everyone to attend, "even those from China." One had only to bring a mat to sit on and a tea cup. (In remembrance of this occasion, the Ochatsubo Hokensai [Tea Festival] is held every November 26.)

In 1607 Toyotomi Hideyori (Hideyoshi's son) had the shrine rebuilt to include three gates, a Honden (Spirit Hall), and a Haiden (Oratory). Their roofs were covered with cypress shingles. The shrine was further surrounded by a grove of apricot trees. (On February 25 each year, a festival is held in honor of the blooming of the trees).

The shrine's southern entrance at Imadegawa-dori is marked by a huge granite torii preceded by *koma-inu* (Korean lion-dogs) on either side. Small Shinto shrines and stone lanterns line the path through two more torii before coming to the main wooden gateway. En route are stone oxen, gifts of devotees of the shrine— in memory of the day of the ox in the ancient Chinese calendar since on that day (June 9, 847) the shrine was first dedicated to the god of thunder.

The shrine precincts are behind a wooden fence which is pierced by a plain, wooden, two-story Nan-mon (South Gate) which is touched with gold and which has a colorful Shinto guardian holding his bow in his lap on either side of the entryway. The Chu-mon (Central or Middle Gate) is also called the Sanko-no-mon (The Gate of the Three Luminaries) from the carvings of the sun, moon, and stars on its beams (now largely effaced). The tablet over the entryway reads *tenmangu* in the calligraphy of the emperor Go-Sai-in. Beyond the gate are the main buildings of the temple: the Ema-do (ex-voto gallery), the treasure house, the Haiden (Oratory), and the Honden (Spirit Hall). Directly beyond the gate to the right is the purification water fountain while a small log treasury building is further to the right. On the left is the Ema-do (a large wooden building raised on pillars), stocked with votive paintings donated by devotees.

The inner portion of the shrine precincts is enclosed by buildings and fences to form an inner courtyard; a path down its center is lined with lanterns, a pair of bronze bulls, and then a pair of *koma-inu* (Korean lion-dogs). The unit on the right side of the courtyard offers religious goods for sale, while on the left side there is a unit for the placement of prayer candles.

Haiden and Honden   The roofed Haiden (Oratory) is on the north side of the square, and between the Haiden and the Honden is an area paved with stone, so small that the two buildings are almost one. The Honden (which holds the spirit of Michizane) is decorated with carvings of birds and flowers on the lintel, attributed to the famed carver Hidari Jingoro. Before the oratory is a small, fenced-in apricot tree, a duplicate of the one which supposedly once stood here and which was so moved by the poem written by Michizane at the time of his exile that it is reputed to have flown to Kyushu to be with him. Behind the Honden is the Jinushi-no-yashiro, the Shinto shrine of the god of the temple grounds, said to date from 836, together with numerous other small shrines. East of the central courtyard is the *kagura* (sacred dance) stage and the storage building in which the shrine *mikoshi* (portable shrines) are kept.

The temple grove of apricot trees is noted, particularly for the trees' early spring bloom. The largest number of trees are along the Kamiyagawa stream on the western side of the grounds.

Homotsu-den   The Homotsu-den (Treasure House) is open on the twenty-fifth of each month, unless it is raining. In summer the hours are 10:00 a.m. to 6:00 p.m., while in the winter they are 10:00 a.m. to 4:30 p.m. Entry fee.

The treasures of the shrine include paintings, sculpture, lacquerwork, *ema* (votive tablets), court costumes, scrolls, screens, sutras, and examples of calligraphy. The thirteenth-century *Kitano Tenjin Engi* (Legends of the Kitano Shrine), which traces Michizane's life, is one of the temple's more famous holdings.

TOJI-IN

From the Kitano Tenman-gu, a return is made to Imadegawa-dori which is followed to the main north-south street, Nishi-oji-dori. The street is crossed to the terminal station of the Keifuku Electric Railway. Its trolleys lead to the remaining sites of this tour, the first of which is the Toji-in. The Toji-in lies four streets north of the Toji-in Station of the Keifuku Railways Kitano Line. (Bus 52 on Imadegawa-dori goes to the Toji-in-mae bus stop.) The temple is open from 8:00 a.m. to 5:00 p.m. Entry fee.

The Toji-in was founded in 1341 by Ashikaga Takauji (1305–58), the first of the Ashikaga shoguns. The previous Kamakura military government, which governed Japan from 1192 to 1333, had ruled from Kamakura and had thus separated actual governance from the seat of the imperial reign. It was Takauji's decision to return the seat of government to Kyoto once more, the better to oversee and to control the throne. Thus began the Muromachi period (1336–1568), named for the section of Kyoto in which the Ashikaga shoguns established their rule.

Takauji commissioned Muso Kokushi to design a family temple for the Ashikaga, and the Toji-in was the result, with Muso being named its first abbot. He was also responsible for the design of the temple garden and pond. Here many Ashikaga shoguns were to be memorialized for the next two hundred years, and here would be placed an image of most of the fifteen Ashikaga shoguns.

The temple was burned on several occasions, the 1467–77

Onin War being particularly disastrous, but it was rebuilt in 1606. The present buildings date to an 1818 restoration. In the nineteenth century, an anti-Ashikaga feeling developed among many Japanese, partially as a reaction against the ruling Tokugawa shoguns who could not be opposed openly and who had, in a sense, shunted the emperor aside as had the Ashikaga before them. In April 1863, a group of twenty samurai, pro-imperial partisans, six with swords, raided the temple, decapitated three of the shogunal images (Takauji, Yoshimitsu, and Yoshiakira), and planted their heads in the Kamogawa river, the treatment usually accorded traitors. Six of the assailants (those most responsible for the act) were eventually decapitated, while the others were jailed temporarily. While the six samurai permanently lost their heads, those of the wooden images of the shoguns were restored.

The temple suffered under the 1868 Meiji Restoration of imperial rule. That year, the temple treasury was looted and many of the temple records were burned. As late as 1887, almost twenty years after the restoration of imperial rule, people would pay five yen for the privilege of beating the image of Ashikaga Yoshimitsu (founder of the Gold Pavilion) in the Toji-in. Happily, the temple and its garden are today restored and preserved.

Hondo On entering the Hondo, one's shoes are replaced by the temple's slippers, and the entry ticket is obtained from the counter directly ahead. Beyond the ticket area to the right and then again to the left is a large tatami-matted hall facing a lovely garden which is the pride of the temple (see below). Here one can sit and contemplate the beauty of the garden. Directly ahead on the right of the ticket counter, at the end wall, is a large painted image of Daruma, the Chinese founder of the Zen sect of Buddhism (the temple was created as a Zen temple). The room behind this painting contains various artifacts: a suit of medieval armor, temple roof tiles, etc. Behind this artifact room, to the east, is the main worship area. A Buddha image stands in the rear center of the room with many *ihai* (mortuary tablets) to the souls of the dead on either side of it. To the south of the veranda (which surrounds the building) is a *karesansui* (dry garden) of sand, rocks, and moss with pines and maples offering a backdrop of greenery.

Ashikaga Shogun Images   An arched bridge leads from the east veranda of the Hondo (Main Hall) to the Ashikaga memorial building. Here in the front two rooms are the statues of all the Ashikaga shoguns except the fifth and the tenth. The *fusuma* (sliding panels) were painted by Kano Sanraku (1559–1635) in India ink, and they represent the "Twenty-Four Paragons of Filial Piety." The images of the Ashikaga shoguns include the figures of Yoshimitsu (1358–1408, third shogun and creator of the Gold Pavilion); Yoshimasa (1436–90, eighth shogun and creator of the Silver Pavilion); Yoshikatsu (1434–43, seventh shogun who died at the age of nine); Yoshiharu (1511–50, thirteenth shogun, a short and unpleasant-looking individual); and fat Yoshiaki (1537–97, fifteenth and last Ashikaga shogun). The images are considered to be fairly realistic, the wearing of the moustache and short, pointed beard being the custom of the time. In the middle chamber, there is a row of shoguns on either side of the passageway. The third (last) figure on the left is Ashikaga Takauji, seen here as a lacquered figure wearing a Chinese or court robe and the tall, black, ceremonial hat *(eboshi)* and carrying a wand of authority *(shaku)* in his hand. Opposite to him is a figure of Tokugawa Ieyasu (1543–1616), first shogun of the Tokugawa line. The third and innermost room has an image of Jizo, the patron of the Ashikaga, attributed to Saicho (Dengyo Daishi, 767–822).

From the memorial building, a path is taken to the garden to the north of the building. This garden by Muso Kokushi has been highly praised. In two parts, the eastern section is called Shinjichi (Heart Shaped Pond), while the western section is called the Fuyo-chi (Lotus Pond). The gardens have an informal nature to them with a stream wandering through the area and a stone bridge leading to the traditional Horai (Island of Eternal Youth) from Chinese mythology. At one time Mount Kinugasa to the north provided borrowed scenery; today, unfortunately, the modern buildings of Ritsumeikan University hide the mountain, in no way enhancing the distant view.

On a slight rise to the north of the Lotus Pond stands the thatched-roof Seiren-tei teahouse, a simple structure planned by Ashikaga Yoshimasa, the eighth shogun. In springtime, red, white, and pink camellia blossoms enliven the garden, while in autumn the yellows and reds of the leaves of the trees create a colorful palette. A memorial stone to Ashikaga Takauji on the south side of the pond marks the site of his grave.

By contrast, a return to the Keifuku Rail Line will eventually bring one to a temple whose fame, unlike that of the Toji-in, has never been demeaned: the Koryu-ji, created in memory of Prince Shotoku.

KORYU-JI

At the seventh station, the Keifuku Line trolley brings one to the Katabira-no-tsuji Station. Here one changes for a train headed back east on the adjacent tracks. The next station to the east is the Uzumasa Station which is the station for the Koryu-ji and Toei Eigamura. The Koryu-ji is located across the street from the Uzumasa Station of the Keifuku Railway. The main gate of the temple is 328 feet to the west of the station. The temple is open from 9:00 a.m. to 5:00 p.m. daily (9:00 a.m. to 4:30 p.m. from December to February), but is closed during the New Year holiday. Entry fee.

Although the Koryu-ji is reputed to have been begun by Prince Shotoku in the year 603, it was probably originally founded on the banks of the Katsura River by the Hata clan soon after their arrival in the fourth century from Silla (Korea). In 622 it was relocated to its present site by Hata-no-Kawakatsu for the peaceful repose of Prince Shotoku's soul since the prince had died the previous year. The Hata family had originally come from China via Korea, bringing with them the advanced technologies of the mainland (silk culture, weaving, agriculture, and distilling) which were to flourish in Japan and in Kyoto in particular. (The Shinto shrine behind the Koryu-ji honors the god of weaving and the silk cocoon. A different rendering of *hata* in ideograms can mean "loom.") The Hata were also responsible for the creation of other temples within the city as well. It has been suggested that their offer of land to the emperor Kammu in the late 700s was the

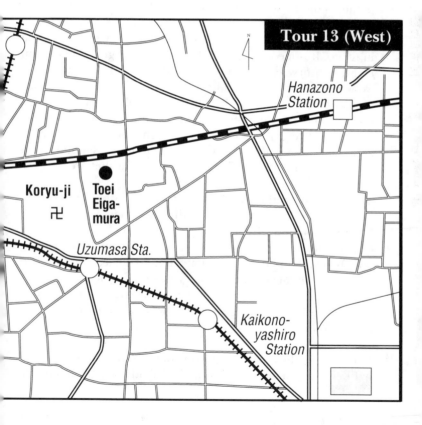

Tour 13 (West)

Hanazono Station

Koryu-ji 卍

Toei Eiga-mura

Uzumasa Sta.

Kaikono-yashiro Station

determining point in the emperor's decision to relocate the capital from Nagaoka to the future site of Heiankyo (Kyoto). It is further suggested that the actual imperial palace site was formerly the location of the home of Hata-no-Kawakatsu, the leader of the Hata clan in the 600s.

The temple precincts are entered through the large gateway at the southern side of the temple grounds. On either side of this gate, in the niches to the right and left, are the huge images of the Nio in wood, the protecting Buddhist deities of the temple.

Kodo   The first building on the right within the temple compound is the Kodo (Lecture Hall) which was originally built in 836, but which burned down in 1150 and was reconstructed in 1165 as a seven-bay structure. It is thus the second oldest building in Kyoto. Its wide altar area holds its main images, a triad of an eighth-century seated Amida flanked by a Kokuzo Kannon in wood from the 800s and an image of a seated Jizo from 868. Jizo holds the mystic jewel in his left hand, while his right hand is outstretched. An eleven-foot-tall Fukukensaku Kannon in wood from the late eighth century is to the right and behind the altar area, while a Senju Kannon (One-Thousand-Arm Kannon) from the ninth century is to the left and rear of the altar area.

Taishi-do   Behind the Kodo is the Taishi-do (Memorial Hall) to Prince Shotoku, built in 1720, with two huge stone lanterns before the building. Its main image is that of the prince at the age of thirty-three, reputedly a self-portrait created by Shotoku in the year 606. In this representation of the prince, according to tradition, the image was originally clothed in the prince's garments, these clothes being replaced by the court as they disintegrated with age. The image currently wears a yellow robe, a skirt, and a crown.

Keigu-in   In the northwest portion of the grounds is the octagonal Keigu-in (Keigu Temple) or Hakkakudo of 1251, each side measuring 7.5 feet. A one-story building with a cypress-bark roof, it contains a statue of Prince Shotoku as he looked at the age of sixteen. It also holds an early Nyorin Kannon presented by the king of Paekche (Korea) as well as an Amida Nyorai.

Reihokan   Behind the Taishi-do is the 1982 Reihokan, the new treasury building. (The old treasury building is to the left.) This recent, fireproof building is lined with wood in its interior, and provides a spacious and attractive center for one of the greatest collections of early Japanese Buddhist sculpture, its prize being the wooden Miroku bodhisattva dating from the Asuka period (552–646). This priceless image was given to the temple in 623 by the kingdom of Silla (Korea) at the earlier request of Prince Shotoku. It is similar to the image in the Chugu-ji nunnery next to the Horyu-ji south of Nara, and both images show the influence of Korean art of that day. Seated with its right leg crossed over its left leg, its left hand delicately held before its face, it has an enigmatic smile as it contemplates Buddhist truths with closed eyes. Created from one piece of wood, it is one of the most important sculptures in Japan.

Opposite the Miroku, on the south wall, are a standing Fukukensaku Kannon in wood (twelve feet tall) from the 600s; a seated, wood Senju Kannon from 1012; and a standing Senju Kannon in wood from the 800s. A seated Jizo image in wood from 868, a circlet behind his head, holds the magic jewel in his left hand, while his right hand is extended. Among the many other treasures are a thirteenth-century representation of Shotoku at sixteen years of age seated in a Chinese chair with a censer in his hands, an eighth-century wood Bishamon-ten, and a tenth-century image of Hata-no-Kawakatsu and his wife. The painted surface on these last two images is still quite evident. In addition, there are some fifty or more images and small treasures, including an eleventh-century, polychromed wood, Zao Gongen (The Incarnate Zao) brandishing a trident and balancing himself on his left leg.

The most noted festival of the Koryu-ji is the annual October 12 Ushi Matsuri when a priest dressed as Mandara, an Indian god, rides to the temple altar on an ox. He is accompanied by four priests representing the Shitenno (Four Deva Kings). At the temple, he intones a sacred sutra from an archaic Indian text.

From the main entry gate of the Koryu-ji, a turn to the left along the road to the north brings one to the entryway to the Toei Eigamura—a street usually crowded with people coming from the rail station.

TOEI EIGAMURA

The Toei Eigamura (Toei Film Village) lies to the north of Uzumasa Station on the Keifuku Arashiyama Railway. The street heading north, one street east of the station, leads to the studio which is just before the San-in Main Line Railway right of way. The studio is open from April to November from 9:00 a.m. to 5:00 p.m., and from December to March from 10:00 a.m. to 4:00 p.m. It is closed from December 21 to January 3. Entry fee.

The Toei Eigamura is a portion of the back set of the Japanese version of Hollywood—inasmuch as Kyoto was the birthplace of the Japanese film industry. This studio is still an active filming center, primarily for television. The seven-acre area contains not only the sets used in filming the "samurai swashbuckler" tales so dear to Japanese film and television audiences, but it also maintains sets representing aspects of the Meiji era (1868–1912). Here are old streets of medieval Japan, the arched Nihonbashi bridge of ancient Edo (the Tokyo of the shoguns), the domains of samurai and geisha entertainers—some twenty or more sets (both indoor and outdoor) are in continuous use by filmmakers. Actors in costumes of the feudal times add a sense of reality to these false-fronted buildings as they wander the streets of the past—including that of Edo's famed Yoshiwara "red light" district.

An entertainment world in its own right, there is everything from restaurants and souvenir counters to a dragon who rears his head from a pond to the delight of both youngsters and their elders. Special halls exhibit the history of Japanese filmmaking. An animation studio where the techniques of special effects are described, location studios for period scenes, and miniatures of settings of the past (castles, bridges, etc. of medieval or feudal Japan) all create a series of diversions for visitors of varying ages.

A return to the center of town can be made by taking the Keifuku Line trolley back eastward to its initial station and terminus at the intersection of Shijo-dori and Omiya-dori. Buses 11, 28, 203, 205, and 207 can thereafter be taken on Shijo-dori or one can walk to the east to Karasuma-dori for the city subway. The Hankyu Railway runs under Shijo-dori and has a station across from the Keifuku Line terminal.

TOUR
14

The Old Imperial Palace

京都御所

KYOTO GOSHO, the old imperial palace, was once the center of Kyoto as not only the emperor's residence, but as the seat of governance of all Japan as well. Relocated from its original 794 site after the fires of the 1200s, today it occupies a large area between Teramachi-dori on the east and Karasuma-dori on the west to the north of Marutamachi-dori and south of Imadegawa-dori. Within the palace's walled enclosure is the resurrected splendor of another age. Its halls, its painted *fusuma*, and its gardens all recall the glory of the Heian period (794–1185). Once the most sacred of areas in the capital, available only to those of noble rank, today it may be visited by foreign tourists who apply to the Imperial Household Agency office in the palace grounds just south of the Imadegawa subway station and just east of Karasuma-dori. The tour of the palace should not be missed, even though the buildings date only from a mid-nineteenth-century reconstruction following the latest decimating fire.

Kyoto Gosho can be reached by taking the subway to the Imadegawa Station or by bus 2, 30, 32, 36, 47, 204, or 206 taken to the intersection of Imadegawa-dori and Karasuma-dori. The palace tours (usually but not always in English) take place at 10:00 a.m. and 2:00 p.m. Tours of the grounds of the former Sento Palace are at 11:00 a.m. and 3:00 p.m. (Japanese language only). Tours are not given on Saturday afternoons, Sundays, public holidays, or between December 25 and January 5.

(The palace is open to the general Japanese public without reservations one week in April and one week in October—a good time to avoid the palace.) The office of the Imperial Household Agency is open from 9:00 a.m. to noon and then from 1:00 p.m. to 4:00 p.m. weekdays. Passports are generally requested. It is best to request admission for a date other than the day the request is made—although it is sometimes possible to join the next tour if one arrives at least twenty minutes early. Tours begin at the Seisho-mon gate to the grounds in the middle of the west side of the palace walls, easily recognized by the guard house and the group awaiting entry. One should be at the gate at least fifteen minutes in advance of the beginning of the tour.

THE OLD IMPERIAL PALACE

The original imperial palace was located in the north-central portion of Heiankyo (Kyoto). Today only the Daigoku-den stone marker is all that is left as a reminder of the original location. The marker stands between Senbon-dori on the east and Rokken-machi-dori on the west, north of Marutamachi-dori and about one mile southeast of the Kitano Shrine. The stone marker indicates the site of the Dai Dairi (Inner Enclosure) of the imperial palace of Heian times.

The imperial palace, built in 794, encompassed the entire north-central area of Heiankyo from Ichijo-dori (First Street) in the north to Nijo-dori (Second Street) to the south between Higashi Omiya-dori (East Palace Street) on the east and Nishi Omiya-dori (West Palace Street) on the west. It measured 4,600 feet from north to south and 3,800 feet from east to west, some three hundred acres. The walls of the "Nine-Fold Enclosure," as it was known, with their five white bands denoting imperial status, were pierced by twelve gates, and the grounds included not only the imperial residence (the Shishin-den [Hall for State Ceremonies] and the Seiryo-den [Imperial Sleeping Quarters]) but various governmental offices (Hassho-in) including the Daigoku-den (Great Hall of State) and various departments of state.

Fire destroyed the palace buildings on numerous occasions, and, after the 1177 fire, the currently reigning emperor moved to Kobe. When the imperial court returned to Kyoto, the palace was relocated to the area of the Tsuchimikado, the present palace grounds which had previously served as a temporary residence when the main palace was destroyed by fire or earthquake. The city itself had never developed its western half, and thus the new palace was moved to the east to a more central location in the city.

What today is Senbon-dori was, in Heian times, the location of the central long, grand, willow-lined Suzaku-oji (Red Sparrow) Boulevard, 250 feet wide, which went from the Rasho-mon gate on the southern edge of the city right to the imperial palace, dividing the city into its Sakyo (eastern or left) and Ukyo (western or right) portions. The original city of Heiankyo (Capital of Peace and Tranquillity) was a rectangle 3.5 miles from north to south and 2.5 miles from east to west. There were eight north-south streets, varying from 80 feet to 170 feet in width and parallel to Suzaku-oji Boulevard, and nine wide avenues running from east to west. Surrounded by a stone wall six feet high with a nine-foot-deep ditch on either side, the city was divided into 400 square-foot units called *cho*, which were then subdivided into 32 residential plots, each 50 by 100 feet. Six canalized streams ran through the city from north to south. With forty thousand houses and a population that soon reached one hundred thousand, it was second in size only to Constantinople and Cordova of the ninth and tenth centuries.

Work on the city was begun in March of 793 after the emperor Kammu sent a delegation of priests to inform the local Shinto deities of his intention to build the new capital and to request their favor. In addition, a clay figure of a warrior was buried fully armed on the height of the mountain (Shogun-zuka) to the east of the new capital to protect and to give warning of impending attack should Heiankyo ever be threatened. By October of 794, the emperor had moved into the new palace which eventually had thirty pavilions; however, the city continued under construction for thirteen more years, development being hampered by insufficient funds.

The emperor wished his new capital to outshine all other capitals (notably that of China) in its cultural attainments. He was named principal of the new university, an appropriate honor since he was a student of Chinese civilization. In time, his son, the emperor Saga, was to enhance the life of the court by introducing elaborate Chinese dress and etiquette. The luxurious life of the nobles had its negative side, however, in that the nobility had to be given tax-free lands to support their ceremonial ways, a situation that in time was to cause acute problems for the imperial government.

Unlike Chinese administration, education in Japan was not intended to select the most capable of individuals for positions of administration within the government. Rank, family, and nobility were foremost in selecting those who would attend university and who would govern. In time, the luxurious and effete nature of court society led to an aristocratic class that was not concerned with nor involved with the real problems of the nation. After 1185, a more hardy group would shoulder aside the nobles; reign the emperor might, but he and his court became peripheral to real governance and to actual rule.

By the time the Kamakura government took power in 1185, the Dai Dairi had burned some fourteen times in its four hundred years of existence. The original site, now remembered only by the Daigoku-den marker, was abandoned, and the palace was moved to its present location. Thus by 1228, fire had destroyed all the original buildings of the city, and by 1600, of the 260 feudal houses thhat had come into existence, only a dozen or so remained intact. A city of wood and thatch was always prone to catastrophe.

Known as Heiankyo (City of Peace and Tranquillity) during Heian times (794–1185), the city was called Miyako (Imperial Residence) after the year 1200, and then after 1870 it was renamed once more as Kyoto (Capital City), although Tokyo (Eastern Capital) was the actual seat of governance once the palace and governmental offices were established there in 1870.

The present site of the palace was originally the location of homes of the nobility, much of the ground belonging to the Fujiwara family. Fujiwara-no-Kunitsuna owned a historic mansion on the property, the Tsuchimikado Higashi-no-toin, a complex that was repeatedly used by the emperors as a temporary residence when their palace was destroyed by fire or earthquake. By 1308, the present location of the imperial palace had come under imperial ownership, and in 1336 the emperor Komyo made the site the official imperial palace, a status it held until 1868 when the capital and imperial residence were moved to Tokyo. Some twenty-eight emperors resided here for 531 years, despite the fact that the palace burned down more than a dozen times. After the depredations of the Onin War (1467–77) and the Sengoku Jidai (Period of the Warring States, 1467–1568), the palace was repaired and rebuilt by the conquering general Nobunaga, then by Hideyoshi, and subsequently by Tokugawa Ieyasu. A fire destroyed the palace in 1788, and it was rebuilt on its present site in 1790 by Matsudaira Sadanobu on the basis of ancient palace structures. Burned again in 1854, it was rebuilt by 1856 in the traditional style of early Kyoto.

The eighteen buildings of the old imperial palace, joined by covered corridors and separated by Japanese-style gardens, stand in the north-central part of the palace grounds on 27 acres out of the 220-acre imperial park. At one time it was a "Court Town," bordered by outer palace walls and with the residences of the noble families surrounding the palace. After the Meiji Restoration of 1868 and the removal of the court to Tokyo, the noble residences were either moved or taken down and Prince Katsura's mansion was moved to the Nijo Castle in 1898 as a gift to replace the buildings that were destroyed by fire in the Honmaru area of that castle.

The walls that surround the imperial palace grounds are pierced by twelve small gates: one to the south, five on the east, four on the west, and two on the north. The grounds of the imperial park (outside of the palace grounds themselves) are planted with pines, maples, oak, birch, and ginkgo trees. Some of the gardens once belonged to the mansions of noble court families, the Kujo, the Konoe, and the Saionji, prior to 1869. To the northern side of the palace, for example, stood the mansion of the Nakayama family, the family into which the emperor Meiji was born on November 3, 1852. The Sachi-no-i (Well of Divine Help), in which the future emperor was first bathed, is in this area, covered with a gabled lid and enclosed with iron bars.

The imperial palace buildings within the imperial palace park are surrounded by high, plastered walls 750 feet long to the east and west and 1,500 feet long to the north and south. These brown plastered walls *(tsuiji)* with five white stripes denoting imperial status are surmounted by a tiled roof. About the perimeter of the walls is a narrow channel through which fresh water constantly runs, water brought from Lake Biwa. At the northeast corner of the walls, the corner is inverted to make it a "non-wall," and there is also a small carving under the tiles of a monkey (reputedly created by Hidori Jingoro). Both of these additions serve as a protection against the evil that comes from the northeast. The adjacent minor gate, the Ki-mon, is sometimes referred to as the "Devil's Gate" since it faces northeast, the direction from which trouble flows.

The walled imperial palace grounds (within the walled imperial park) have four main gates: the Kenrei-mon gate to the south, a gate only used by the emperor and opened twice a year for viewing by the public; the Kenshun-mon to the east, formerly used by ministers of state and by the empress and the dowager empress; the Gishu-mon on the west, originally used by imperial princes and nobles; and the Sakuhei-mon on the north, originally used by imperial consorts and court ladies. North of the Gishu-mon is the Seisho-mon, designed for the lowest court ranks; today, it is the visitors' entrance from which tours begin. There are fourteen smaller gates for use in an emergency.

Having cleared a time for a visit to the palace from the Imperial Household Agency, visitors enter the grounds of the palace precincts through the Seisho-mon gate where a guard examines the entry passes. One is then escorted past the *kura* (fireproof storage buildings) on the west and past the Gishu-mon gate to approach the first of the eighteen palace buildings, all linked by covered corridors or galleries.

Shodaibu-no-ma   The first unit the guide escorts a group to is the Okurumayose (Carriage Porch), the original entryway for the emperor. Beyond is the Shodaibu-no-ma (Room of Dignitaries) which consists of three rooms where nobles awaited entrance into the palace. These rooms are arranged according to rank. As one faces the south side of the building, the room on the left, the Sakura-no-ma (Cherry Blossom Room) has *fusuma* decorated with cherry trees by Hara Zaisho. This room is for those of the lowest rank. The middle room is the Stork or Crane room decorated by Kano Eigaku. The tatami mats of these first two rooms are bound with a plain brown binding. The third room, to the right, is the Tora-no-ma (Tiger Room), which was reserved for those of highest noble rank. Its tatami are bound with silver ribbon with a flower pattern. The tigers on the *fusuma* of this third room were painted by Gantai.

Seiryo-den   From the Shodaibu-no-ma the tour passes the Shin Mikurumayose (New Carriage Porch), which was built in 1915 for the emperor Taisho (1879–1926). By 1915 the emperor was arriving at the palace by automobile and a new entrance to the palace was needed which would accommodate vehicles different from the traditional carriage pulled by oxen. The entry porch was designed with a traditional style on the outside, but a modern style inside, complete with glass windows and carpeted floors. This entrance is reserved for the emperor, empress, and the crown prince. Formerly, the Shunko-den, a sanctuary to hold the sacred mirror, stood here, but this building was granted to and moved to the Kashiwara Shrine south of Nara when the tomb of the legendary emperor Jimmu was constructed in the late nineteenth century under the influence of the rabid nationalism of the day. The Shin Mikurumayose leads to the Seiryo-den (Serene and Cool Chamber, so-named from the stream of water that runs under its steps). Between the Shin Mikurumayose and the Seiryo-den is the Hagi-no-tsubo, the Bush Clover Court. In the original palace, this was the imperial residence hall where the emperor lived. In time, its function changed and it became a ceremonial hall. This sixty-nine-foot-long by fifty-two-foot-wide 1850s reconstruction adheres closely to the original Seiryo-den. The structure is in the *shinden-zukuri* style, the style of sleeping quarters or residences from the period between the ninth and the thirteenth centuries. Of Japanese cypress, it has a cypress-bark *(hinoki)* roof. Double-hinged doors and heavy-hinged shutters suspended from the roof (and which are held open by iron rods) are noticeable elements of early court architecture. Within the ten-room hall (which can be thrown into one large room through the removal of any of its dividers: *fusuma*, silk curtains, screens, or bamboo blinds) is the *naruita*, a board at the entryway which emits a noise when trod upon, thus serving as an alarm to alert the guards.

The main room (Omoya) in the center of the building contains the *michodai*, the throne on which the emperor sat on ceremonial occasions. It is covered with a silk canopy with hangings of red, white, and black. To the right and left of the throne area are two stands meant to hold the imperial regalia on state occasions. Protective animals stand on either side of the throne unit as guardians against evil, the left-hand one being a *koma-inu* (Korean lion-dog) while the right-hand one is a *shishi* (lion). To the left of the Omoya is the *ishibaidan*, an unfloored area "cemented" with limestone. Here the emperor would stand, making symbolic contact with the earth, when worshipping his ancestors. The area was covered with sand before the emperor stepped upon it since white sand can cancel evil forces. A screen in strong colors depicting the four seasons is adjacent to this sacred sector.

The *fusuma* (sliding panels) in the hall are by Tosa Mitsukiyo and are accompanied by a Chinese or Japanese poem; appropriately enough since the Tosa school took their subjects from Japanese history, rather than that of China as did the Kano school of painters. The sixteen-petal imperial chrysanthemum symbol is ubiquitous in the decorations of this hall. It was in the

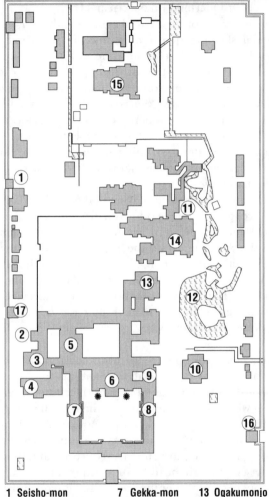

1 Seisho-mon
2 Okurumayose
3 Shodaibu-no-ma
4 Shin Mikurumayose
5 Seiryo-den
6 Shishin-den

7 Gekka-mon
8 Nikka-mon
9 Jinoza
10 Shunko-den
11 Kogosho
12 Oike-niwa

13 Ogakumonjo
14 Otsune-goten
15 Kogo-goten
16 Kenshun-mon
17 Gishu-mon

Seiryo-den that the emperor performed the Shihohai (Worship of the Four Quarters) on New Year's Day.

To the north of the central room was the Yon-no-otodo, the imperial sleeping quarters, composed of several rooms: the Fujitsubo, the Hagi-no-to, and the Kokiden for the emperor's consorts. A two-mat "closet" surrounded by screens depicting the Chinese emperors enclosed the emperor's sleeping area. The western portion of the Seiryo-den has five small rooms: the Ochozu-no-ma (the Emperor's Morning Purification Room), the Oyudono-no-ma (the Emperor's Bathroom), the Asagarei-no-ma (the Emperor's Dining Room), the Dai Bandokoro (a room for ceremonial meals), and the Oni-no-ma for the emperor's ladies-in-waiting.

A corridor leads from the Seiryo-den to the Shishin-den, and at the corner of the corridor is a glassed screen which lists the annual court events and ceremonies. Wooden stairs also lead from the Seiryo-den into the Totei, the East Yard which is also covered with white sand. In the yard in front of the Seiryo-den are two bamboo trees behind small wooden fencing, the Karatake or Kanchiku (Han Chinese bamboo) and the Kuretake or Gochiku (Wu Chinese bamboo) named after the two ancient Chinese kingdoms of Han and Wu.

Shishin-den   The Shishin-den, also known as the Nanden (Southern Palace Hall) or the Hall for State Ceremonies, is a faithful copy of the original one-story, eighth-century building the design of which was influenced by Chinese architecture. Here, the most important court ceremonies took place, including the New Year audience and coronations. Visitors today approach the building from the south, and the courtyard and the Shishin-den are viewed through the tile-roofed, triple gateway, the Jomei-mon gate, opened only for enthronements. The courtyard is bordered by the tile-roofed Kairo, a double corridor of vermilion posts with a gate on the south, west, and east sides. The grounds of the compound within are covered with raked white sand, meant to reflect the light of the sun and the moon into the palace hall. Appropriately, the west gate is named the Gekka-mon (Moon Gate) and the east gate is the Nikka-mon (Sun Gate).

Within a fence before the steps leading into the Shishin-den are a cherry tree *(sakon-no-sakura)* and a citrus tree *(ukon-no-tachibana)*, bearing names derived from those of the imperial archers and horsemen who once stood guard on either side of the palace entry. (The *sakon* [left] and *ukon* [right] bodyguards, organized into two bodies of archers and horsemen, were originally chosen from among the sons of the regent or chief advisor to the emperor.) The steps leading into the Shishin-den are eighteen in number, corresponding to the eighteen noble ranks within the court hierarchy. (In Chinese lore, the number nine was an auspicious number; by doubling this sum, a greater auspicious state was achieved.) These steps, with white painted ends, have easy risers to facilitate the carrying of the imperial palanquin into the palace buildings. The number of side steps to the Shishin-den remain at the number nine.

The Shishin-den is 108 feet long by 74 feet deep. The eaves project by 20 feet, thereby creating a corridor about the structure. Above the front staircase hangs a tablet with "Shishin-den" written in Japanese script. As with the Seiryo-den, the shutters which are hinged from the top are kept open with rods hanging from the eaves. The steep palace roof is of cypress-bark roofing, forty layers deep, some twelve inches thick.

Within, in the center of the hall, is the 1915 imperial throne created for the enthronement of the emperor Taisho. It is in the shape of an octagonal imperial palanquin painted in black lacquer and surmounted by a golden phoenix 5.7 feet tall with eight smaller golden phoenixes at each point of the octagonal roof. The silken curtains about the throne unit are renewed every spring and autumn. Behind the throne is a nine-panel screen, the Kenjo-no-shoji (sliding screens of the thirty-two Chinese sages), a copy of the original screens of the year 888 by Kose-no-Kanaoka. These copies were done by Hiroyuki Sumiyoshi in the second half of the eighteenth century. The backs of these sliding panels are painted with peacocks and peonies. The empress' throne is placed to the right and to the rear of the emperor's throne and is ten percent smaller.

Jinoza   To the east of the Shishin-den is the Jinoza, a building with a board floor in which affairs of state would be discussed. Further to the east is the Shunko-den or Kashikodokoro, a sanctuary where the sacred imperial mirror (one of the three imperial treasures) was held at the time of the 1915 enthronement. Within are three rooms: the *gejin* (outer sanctuary), the *naijin* (inner sanctuary), and the *nainaijin* (innermost sanctuary) where the sacred mirror was kept during the enthronement period.

Kogosho   The Kogosho (Little Palace) of three large rooms is connected to the Shishin-den by a corridor. This building is a 1958 replacement since in August of 1954 fireworks set off in the Kamogawa river landed on the thatch roof of the Kogosho and burned it down. The building faces to the east and to the palace pond and garden, and its three rooms of eighteen mats each were used for audiences and for receptions. The innermost room is the Jodan-no-ma, the room with the raised platform for the emperor or crown prince. The *fusuma* have scenes of the four seasons and the annual events of court life painted in brilliant colors with broad blue stripes representing clouds at the bottom and top of each scene. Northwest of the Kogosho is a *kemari* (ancient football) field.

Oike-niwa   The Oike-niwa (Pond Garden), the lovely garden to the east of the Kogosho, was created by Kobori Enshu (1579–1647) and reconstructed in the late Edo period. In the foreground is a beach of small black stones, its pond fed by a waterfall, while a stone bridge leads across a portion of the waterway. This attractive garden, designed by Emperor Go-mizuno-o and Kobori Enshu, was the one the emperor Meiji always remembered after his move to Tokyo. Until recently, the water in the garden was carried from Lake Biwa via an underground aqueduct but is now pumped from a well dug solely for the purpose.

Ogakumonjo A corridor leads from the Kogosho to the Ogakumonjo (Imperial Hall of Studies), a six-room structure in the *shinden-zukuri* style. Here the emperor received instruction from his tutors. The hall was also used for the cultivation of poetry and music. There are three audience chambers (*gedan, chudan,* and *jodan*), decorated with pictures of eighteen Chinese scholars by Hara Zaisho and with scenes of birds and flowers of the four seasons, which face the garden. These rooms are of 12.5 mats each and have coffered ceilings and *ramma* (transoms) between the individual rooms. The other three rooms are the Kari-no-ma (Wild Geese Room) with painted *fusuma* by Renzan Gantokan, the Yamabuke-no-ma (Japanese Globe Flower Room) by Maruyama Okyo, and the Kiku-no-ma (Chrysanthemum Room) with paintings by Okamoto Sukehiko. The coffered ceilings are richly decorated. It was in this building that the monthly poetry party was held, imperial lectures were offered, and the New Year's rite of reading took place.

Otsune-goten When the Seiryo-den was held to be no longer proper for the emperor's residence, the Otsune-goten (Everyday Palace), seventy-four by ninety-five feet, was built to accommodate private chambers for the emperor. This building is not open to the public. With some eleven rooms holding a total of 673 tatami, it has the Moshi-no-kuchi (Herald's Entrance) of thirty mats; the *fusuma* are decorated with pine trees and monkeys. It was a room for official business conducted through the court ladies, not with the emperor directly. The Kenji-no-ma is the largest and most attractive of the rooms. Its *fusuma* bear Chinese court scenes painted by members of the Kano School of painters on a gold ground. It was where the imperial regalia would be kept. The three-room audience chamber had a raised platform in its innermost room, the *jodan*.

There are four rooms in the southern portion of the building which were kept for the daily life of the emperor. The two-room Okazashiki is where the emperor received instruction in the composing of tanka, the Ichi-no-ma (First Room) which was a sitting room, and the Ni-no-ma (Second Room) for meeting with other members of the imperial family. Four more rooms were clustered about the eighteen-mat sleeping chamber whose *fusuma* were decorated with bamboo and tigers. Matted corridors surrounded these rooms.

An annex, the Omima (August Three Rooms), was where informal audiences took place, these rooms being decorated with scenes from the ancient Japanese court by the Tosa school of painters. Here, Noh performances could be given on a Noh stage under a separate roof of its own. In addition, Buddhist ceremonies took place in the Omima.

Additional buildings lay beyond these units, primarily for the empress, the dowager empress, and the princesses. The Kogogoten was the living quarters for the empress and was connected with the Otsune-goten by a long corridor. The Jishin-den (Earthquake Hall) was for use by the emperor in times of seismic disturbances and the Osuzumisho (Pure Cool Hall) with a stream running under it was for the emperor's summer evenings. A tea pavilion, the Chosetsu, and the Ohana-goten, a unit for the crown prince (where the emperor Meiji lived before coming to the throne), are also in this area. This inner complex once held the three-room Kenji-no-ma where the imperial sword and jewel were kept. The Higyosha quarters for the emperor's second wife were in this area, known also by its name of Fujitsubo (Wisteria Yard).

The palace kitchens stood in the large open space on the west as one leaves the palace complex, an area now covered with azaleas, moss, and pines. These buildings were removed as a protection against fire at a later date after the move of the court to Tokyo.

Sento Gosho   Separate from the imperial palace is the Sento Gosho, the retired emperor's villa, to the southeast of the main imperial palace complex. Permission to visit the Sento Gosho must be obtained at the Imperial Household Agency in the northwest corner of the palace park. Generally, one must apply two days in advance of the date one wishes to visit the Sento Gosho grounds, although in April, May, October, and November, it is best to apply five days in advance. Tours begin at 11:00 a.m. and at 1:30 p.m. for those over twenty years of age. The Sento Gosho is not open on Saturday afternoons, Sundays, public holidays, and from December 25 to January 5. Tours are conducted in Japanese only. Be certain to ascertain where the tour begins when making reservations, since the Sento Gosho is a good walk from the Imperial Household Agency.

The Sento Gosho was begun by the Tokugawa shogunate in 1627 as a retreat for the emperor Go-Mizuno-o who had as one of his consorts Kazuko, the daughter of Shogun Tokugawa Hidetada. Under the direction of Kobori Enshu, the villa and its lovely stroll garden of eighteen acres around two lakes encompassing two-and-one-fourth acres were completed a few years later. In the meantime, the emperor, discouraged by the interference of the shogunate in his life, suddenly abdicated in 1629 in favor of his five-year-old daughter, the first empress since the eighth century.

Destroyed by fire on various occasions, the Sento Gosho was not rebuilt after the 1854 fire. Today only the nine-acre land-scaped garden, the glory of the Sento Gosho, remains. Lakes, waterfalls, inlets, bridges, tea-ceremony rooms, stones, and huge trees make the Sento Gosho park a lovely stroll garden. To the southeast of the imperial palace buildings and close to Teramachi-dori, the larger of the two lakes has two islands which can be reached by stone bridges, one of which is seasonally roofed with wisteria. The groves of maple and cherry trees in the park have created a small forest in the heart of the city. Originally, a wall separated the Sento Gosho garden from that of the Omiya Gosho (Omiya Palace) of the empress, but this was removed in the mid-1700s and additional stroll paths were added.

It is in the grounds of the Sento Gosho that the Daijosai (Grand Thanksgiving Festival) was traditionally performed by the emperor at the time of his enthronement (until the 1990 enthronement ceremony in Tokyo). The Yuki and Suki Palaces, temporary structures, were erected where the emperor in an overnight ceremony offered prayers and sacred food to the imperial ancestress (Amaterasu Omikami) and the gods and goddesses of heaven and earth, the most important ceremony of an emperor's reign.

Adjoining the Sento Gosho was the Omiya Gosho, home for the dowager empress. Constructed in 1643 by the shogun for the empress Tofukumon-in, the consort of the emperor Go-Mizuno-o and fifth daughter of the shogun Tokugawa Hidetada, she resided here after Go-Mizuno-o abdicated. (He spent many of his long years of abdication visiting his detached palaces, particularly the Shugaku-in of which he was most fond, since he avoided the palace built for him by his father-in-law, the shogun.) Connected to the Sento Gosho by a covered walkway, it too burned in the 1854 fire.

The Omiya Gosho was rebuilt in 1867 for Dowager Empress Eisho, the widow of the emperor Komei and mother of the emperor Meiji. Once separated by a wall from the gardens of the Sento Gosho, the two gardens now form one unit with the north pond with its swift Male Waterfall *(otaki)* overhung with trees and its Female Waterfall *(medaki)* with its more gentle flow of water. A bridge crosses the channel which connects the north and south ponds. The islands of the south pond once held pavilions of pleasure, all now gone. Two tea pavilions exist in the southern portion of the garden, the Seika-tei and the Yushin-tei, the latter moved here from its location at the mansion of the Duke of Konoe in 1884. Today, a reconstruction of the palace stands on its original site and is available to members of the imperial family or special guests visiting Kyoto. The Omiya Gosho is not open to the public, but one may visit the extensive garden (22.2 acres in size) by applying for permission from the Imperial Household Agency.

Appendixes

APPENDIX
1
Getting to Kyoto

RAIL LINES

The Japan Rail Pass is valid on the Japan Rail Line but not on the other private lines mentioned below. Most rail lines have automatic ticket machines and these tickets must be placed in the turnstile, reclaimed, and then finally deposited in the turnstile at the exit. Tickets are also available at ticket offices in the stations if one does not have the correct change for the ticket machine. Long journeys usually require a regular rather than a machine ticket.

Japan Rail   Japan Rail trains from Kyoto Station run in all directions to the north, south, east, and west. Various lines emanate from the station, including local and regular express trains as well as the Shinkansen line. Tickets can be purchased from machines or from the ticket office in the station (language can sometimes be a problem at such offices).

Kintetsu (Kinki Nippon) Line   The Kintetsu Line to Nara has its main entrance on the southwest side of Kyoto Station. Here, trains can be taken to areas in the southern part of Kyoto as well as on to Nara or further south to the Asuka region and to Yoshino. Tickets can be purchased from machines at each station or from the ticket office.

Hankyu Rail Line   The Hankyu Rail Line begins as a subway under Shijo-dori in Kyoto at Kawaramachi-dori. It runs to Katsura (change for

Matsuo and Arashiyama) and on to Osaka. For stations within the general Kyoto area, be certain to take a local and not an express train as you may miss stops.

Keihan Rail Line   The Keihan Rail Line, in a sense, connects three rail lines:

1. The main line operates from its underground (subway) Imadegawa-dori station terminal on the east side of the Kamogawa river and goes south to Uji or to Osaka.

2. Its line to Otsu runs on the surface from its Sanjo-dori line terminal to Otsu on Lake Biwa and from there trains can be taken south to Ishiyama along the Seto River or north to Sakamoto along Lake Biwa.

3. The Eizan Railway operates from the Demachi Yanagi Station at Imadegawa-dori (just above the Keihan subway station of its Osaka or Uji line) to Kurama or to Yase.

The Keihan Rail Line runs on the east side of the Kamogawa river, becoming a subway north from Tofuku-ji Station to the terminus at Imadegawa-dori just below the Demachi Yanagi surface station to Yase or Kurama to the north. To the south, the Keihan Rail Line serves stations in south Kyoto and Uji as well as providing access to Osaka and stations in between.

Keifuku Rail Line   The Keifuku Rail Line serves the western part of Kyoto. One terminal is at the Shijo Omiya-dori intersection from where it departs for Arashiyama. Another terminal for its Kitano Line is at the Nishioji Imadegawa-dori intersection. The Kitano Line runs west to its junction with the Arashiyama Line where one is able to change to an Arashiyama train. These two lines run along the surface, sometimes on city streets.

Kyoto Subway   The efficient subway system runs due north and south through Kyoto under Karasuma-dori from the Kitayama Station in the north to the Takeda Station in the south. Some trains run through to Nara via the subway system and these trains continue on beyond Takeda Station. Tickets are purchased from vending machines at subway entrances, and these tickets are placed in the turnstile at the entrance and then at the exit at one's destination, as described above.

BUS LINES

Kyoto is well served by efficient bus lines that cover all of the major areas of the city as well as locations beyond the city itself. Most lines begin from the bus plaza in front of Kyoto Station, while some begin at the Keihan Sanjo Station on the east side of the Kamogawa river. One enters a bus from the rear and, within the city, pays the set fare that is listed at the front of the bus. Buses are exited from the front where the fare is paid to the driver. A machine behind the driver makes change.

For BUSES GOING BEYOND THE CITY CENTER, one takes a ticket from the machine at the rear entry to the bus. An electric board above the driver indicates the number on the ticket (the point at which one entered the bus) and the fare at the point at which the bus arrived. One exits through the door at the front, paying the driver the appropriate fare on leaving.

LONG-DISTANCE BUSES also leave from the terminal in front of Kyoto Station.

Buses are numbered with one or two digits. THREE-DIGIT-NUMBER BUSES are loop buses within the city of Kyoto, while TWO-DIGIT BUSES start at either Kyoto Station or Keihan Sanjo Station.

Bus stops are marked by a sign with a half-circle for city (green) buses while Kyoto (pale brown) bus stops are marked by a full circle. Such signs indicate the number of the bus route and the times at which buses stop at that position. (Kyoto buses offer longer runs.)

A ONE-DAY PASS for the buses and the subway may be obtained from the Kyoto City Visitors Information Center located in the plaza across from the Kyoto Tower Building.

A map of the bus lines may be obtained at the Japan National Tourist office and is included as an insert on many maps of the city.

AIRPORT BUS

The bus to Osaka Airport can be taken from its starting point in front of the Avanti Department Store across the street from the south side of the Kyoto Central Station.

TAXIS

Taxis may be found at taxi stands throughout the city, but they can be hailed on the street as well. Taxis are metered for fares, and tips are not expected by the drivers. Your hotel can provide you with a card with your destination written in Japanese, a card that you can show the driver—if you are concerned about your pronunciation of Japanese place and street names. A card listing the hotel's name and address can be acquired at the front desk and given to the driver, who will wait and return you to your hotel if you so wish.

APPENDIX
②
General Tourist Information

Each of the sites described within this guidebook lists the hours at which the site is open and whether there is an entry fee. In general, most temples charge a small entry fee to cover the upkeep of buildings and grounds. Shrines, on the other hand, usually do not charge for entrance. Entry fees have not been indicated since they vary.

Imperial palaces and villas (the Old Imperial Palace, the Katsura Villa, and the Shugaku-in Villa) do not charge a fee, but one must register in advance for permission to visit these sites—see below. Virtually all museums, private villas, and gardens have an entry fee.

THE OLD IMPERIAL PALACE, THE SHUGAKU-IN, AND KATSURA VILLA

These three imperial sites require an advanced registration for entry to their grounds. Registration takes place at the Imperial Household Agency Office on the grounds of the Old Imperial Palace just south of Imadegawa-dori to the east of Karasuma-dori—one should bring one's passport with one for identification. The office is closed on Saturday afternoons, all day Sunday, on national holidays, and from December 25 through January 5.

Permission for the tour of the palace grounds can frequently take place the same day, such tours being offered at 9:00, 11:00, 13:30, and 15:00. The grounds of the palace can be visited, but not the interior of the buildings. A separate reservation must be made for the Sento Gosho (the retired emperor's palace), where the lovely grounds and stroll garden remain, even though the original palace structures have been destroyed by fire. This tour is at 11:00 and 13:30 and is in Japanese only.

WEEKENDS AND HOLIDAYS IN KYOTO

Kyoto is a popular venue for the Japanese as well as for tourists; thus, on weekends and national holidays, all sites can be very crowded. Food facilities can be strained at meal times; thus, it might be well to purchase a boxed lunch such as those sold in the Central Railway Station.

National holidays occur on thirteen occasions throughout the year, and on these days banks and public offices are closed. If a national holiday falls on a Sunday, the next day is marked as the holiday. Golden Week (April 29 to May 5) is a period when all Japan seems to be traveling, and advanced reservations for hotels, trains, and public events are essential during this week.

The national holidays occur on:

January 1, January 15, February 11, March 21, April 29, May 3, May 5, September 15, September 23, October 10, November 3, November 23, and December 23.

The *Obon* period of August 13 to 16 also sees heavy travel. Many public functions (museums, etc.) are closed from approximately December 25 through January 5.

KYOTO TOURIST INFORMATION

The Japan National Tourist Office in the Kyoto Tower Building to the north of the Central Station Plaza on Karasuma-dori can answer questions as to any of the sites in the Kyoto area. Maps, brochures, and other information can be readily and cheerfully obtained without charge.

The Japan Travel Bureau, as well as other travel agencies in the buildings around the Central Railway Plaza, can assist in reservations.

MONEY EXCHANGE

Travelers' checks and foreign currency are most easily exchanged at banks. As a courtesy, some of the major department stores, such as Hankyu and Takashimaya, will also exchange travelers' checks for yen, and most tourist hotels can cash travelers' checks as well.

APPENDIX

3

Ceremonies and Festivals

The major festivals or ceremonies occurring at central Kyoto sites are listed below. These events may occur on a date other than as stated since some events take place according to the traditional lunar calendar. Since other events may now be scheduled for weekends for the convenience of attendees, one should check with the Tourist Information Bureau and the events calendars which are issued monthly as to the exact date of the following ceremonies or festivals. Such calendars are available at most hotels and at the Japan National Tourist Office in the Kyoto Tower Building on Karasuma-dori.

The information below was obtained from shrine and temple publications, from the *Kyoto Monthly Calendar,* and from Bauer and Carlquist's *Japanese Festivals.*

Asterisks (*) indicate monthly events that are not listed with each month's festivals.

January
1   **Okera-mairi,** Yasaka Shrine. Devotees attend the shrine to bring home a portion of the sacred fire on which the first meal of the year will be cooked. The action is thought to ward off illness during the new year.
1–3   **Hatsumode.** The year's first visit to Shinto shrines to pray for good luck during the ensuing year. Women often wear their

best kimono at this time. Among the shrines that are most popular for this visit are Yasaka Shrine, the Heian Shrine, and the Kitano Tenman-gu, among other locations.

1–3 **Obukucha,** Rokuharamitsu-ji. Green tea is presented to visitors to ward off illness in the new year.

2–4 **Shinzen Kakizome,** Kitano Tenman-gu. The year's first calligraphy. Children do their first writing of the new year at this shrine in honor of Sugawara-no-Michizane, the patron of writing, of scholarship, and of scholars, who is enshrined here.

2 **Religious service** at 9:30 a.m.

2–4 **New Year's writing** from 10:30 a.m. to 3:00 p.m.

3 **Kyogen** performances and calligraphy demonstrations from 1:00 p.m. to 2:30 p.m.

8–12 **Kanchu Takuhatsu,** Shogo-in. One hundred monks start on their first begging walk of the year.

8–12 **Toka Ebisu, Gion Ebisu, and all Ebisu shrines.** Ebisu is the patron of business and good luck. (He is one of the Seven Gods of Good Fortune, and thus he is very popular with merchants and businessmen.) Stalls are set up for the sale of various items. The following are some of the main events of Toka Ebisu held at the Gion Ebisu Shrine:

8 **Shofukusai** (Festival for Happiness). A Shinto service is held from 2:00 p.m. to 3:00 p.m. and then the festival begins. Bugaku is offered as well *kagura* (sacred dance to traditional music) performed by the *miko* (young women of the shrine staff), and *mochi* (rice cakes) are made—all to please the gods.

9 **Yoi-Ebisu Bugaku.** Performances are offered throughout the evening.

10 **Hon-Ebisu** (Main Festival of Ebisu). A service is held at 2:00 p.m. in honor of Ebisu's first taking up residence in this shrine on this date.

11 **Nokori Fuku** (Remaining Luck). From 2:00 p.m. to 4:00 p.m. and again from 8:00 p.m. to 10:00 p.m. *Miko* (female shrine attendants) distribute to those present the sacred *mochi* which was made on January 8.

9 **Ho-onko,** Nishi Hongan-ji. Annual service in honor of Shinran, founder of the Jodo Shinshu sect of Buddhism.

11   **Shobo Dezome-shiki** (Fire Brigade Parade), Okazaki Park. Over two thousand firemen and one hundred fire vehicles (including helicopters) perform fire drills and rescues using ladder trucks and helicopters. Antique fire vehicles form part of the parade.

15   **Seijin-no-hi** (Adults' Day, a national holiday). A coming-of-age celebration for those who have reached their twentieth birthday. Celebrated by municipalities and individual families as well as at certain shrines and temples.

15   **Toshiya** (Archery Contest), Sanjusangen-do. A traditional archery contest under the rear eaves of the rear platform of the temple from 8:30 a.m. to 4:00 p.m. No charge to temple visitors who have paid their entrance fee.

21 (monthly)   ***Hatsukobo,** To-ji temple. First service of the year in honor of Kobo Daishi. Monthly fair held on the temple grounds.

25 (monthly)   ***Tenjin Matsuri,** Kitano Tenman-gu. First service of the year in honor of Sugawara-no-Michizane. Monthly fair on the temple grounds and precinct.

February

2–4   **Setsubun.** The day of the celebration varies according to the lunar calendar. This festival marks the final day of winter. It is celebrated by driving demons away by throwing beans (*mamemaki*) throughout the house and about the temple. *"Oni wa soto, fuku wa uchi!"* ("Out with evil, in with good fortune,") is the cry which accompanies the scattering of the beans. The festival is celebrated at most temples and shrines among which are the following ceremonies:

2-3   **Mibu-dera.** On **February 2** at 1:00 p.m., *yamabushi* (itinerant "mountain" priests) and *chigo* (a boy who serves the gods) hold a religious procession about the temple grounds. At 2:00 p.m. thousands of pieces of wood that have been donated by devotees are set aflame to protect the people from illness or misfortune. On **February 3,** Kyogen is performed eight times from 1:00 p.m. to 8:00 p.m. by members of the temple district to exorcise demons.

2   **Tsuinashiki** (Ceremony to Chase Devils), Yoshida Shrine. A very popular festival in which Hossoshi, in a strange costume and wearing a golden mask, appears with a halberd and sword. He and his associates, carrying torches, chase away a pair of red and green devils. An evening bonfire and stalls selling charms and food make this evening into a partial fair at which some attendees wear masks and colorful costumes. From 6:00 p.m.

3   **Okame Setsubun,** Senbon Shaka-do. Okame is the round, cheerful-faced deity whose mask is very popular. She is considered the patron of business and prosperity and, as a onetime living person, she was associated with this temple. At 3:00 p.m. well-known citizens of Kyoto wear an Okame mask as they scatter beans from the temple Hondo.

3   **Setsubun,** Shogo-in. The itinerant mountain priests *(yamabushi)* gather at their headquarters for a ceremony in which a large log is burned as an invocation.

3   **Oni Horaku** (Devils' Dance), Rozan-ji. 3:00 p.m.–4:00 p.m. In a ceremony with a thousand-year heritage, three devils (a red one representing greed, a green one representing jealousy, and a black one representing complaints) dance to the accompaniment of drums and conch shells. After a lengthy dance, they are chased away by the scattering of beans. A fire is lit as an invocation.

3   **Setsubun,** Kitano Tenman-gu. At 1:30 p.m. Kyogen is presented at the Kagura-den (Hall for Sacred Dances) of the shrine. Afterwards, a group of geisha offer dances and then conclude their performance by scattering beans to ward off evil.

March

1 to April 3   Doll Display, Hokyo-ji. A display of dolls from the fourteenth to the nineteenth century and costumed mannequins. From 9:00 a.m. to 4:00 p.m. Fee.

3   **Hina Matsuri.** The traditional Girls' Festival when dolls were displayed on five- or seven-tiered stands, particularly dolls representing the emperor and empress and their court. The

day was also known as "Peach Blossom Day" since a bloom of the peach tree often decorated the display.

14–16   **Nehan-e** (Commemoration of Buddha's Death and Attainment of Nirvana). This important Buddhist celebration is held at many temples.

20–May 24   **Treasury Opening,** To-ji. The temple treasures are on view. 9:00 a.m. to 4:00 p.m. Fee.

21   **Shunbun-no-hi** (Vernal Equinox Day, a national holiday). A holiday reputedly begun under Prince Shotoku in the 600s. Today, it marks respect for growing things in nature and, as a portion of the *higan* Buddhist ceremony, families often visit their family graves.

21   **Izumi Shikibu-ki,** Seishin-in. A memorial service for Izumi Shikibu, a famous Heian-era poet. A nine-foot-tall tower is erected as a memorial in this small temple in the Shin Kyogoku shopping area.

April

1–18   **Kano Chakai** (Cherry-viewing Tea Ceremony), Heian Shrine. Daily from 9:00 a.m. to 4:00 p.m. Fee. At noon on April 16, court and other traditional dances are presented on a stage in front of the Daigoku-den in order to please the gods.

1–30   **Miyako Odori,** Gion Kaburenjo Theater. The annual spring "Capital Dances" by geisha. Fee. Tea ceremony may be enjoyed for an additional fee. Performances daily at 12:30, 2:00, 3:30, and 4:50 p.m.

4   **Go-o Taisai,** Go-o Shrine. Karate and the recitation of Chinese poetry to please the deities.

8   **Hana Matsuri** (Flower Festival). Birthday services in honor of the birth of the Buddha featuring a baptizing ceremony called *kanbutsue.* In all temples.

10   **Hirano Jinja Sakura Matsuri,** Hirano Shrine. A festival celebrating the cherry blossoms and featuring a parade of costumes said to go back to Heian times.

14   **Shunki Taisai,** Shiramine Shrine. Heian-period football *(kemari)* is played in Heian costume after religious services.

15   **Heian Shrine Festival.** Kagura dance is performed to *gagaku* music.

15–28   **Kyo-odori,** Minami-za Theater. Springtime geisha dance performances. Fee.

17   **Yoshida Matsuri,** Yoshida Shrine. Court dances in early costumes to please the gods. 9:30 a.m.

21–29   **Mibu Kyogen,** Mibu-dera. A very popular performance of Kyogen skits by devotees of the temple is given from 1:00 p.m. to 5:30 p.m., five performances daily and then until 10:00 p.m. on the last day.

29–May 5   **Golden Week:** A series of national holidays when the Japanese travel to popular resort areas and tourist-oriented cities and towns.

29   **Conservation Day,** a national holiday. A holiday which replaces the former Emperor Hirohito's birthday holiday.

May

1–4   **Nenbutsu Kyogen,** Senbon Emma-do, Inno-ji. Kyogen performances have taken place at this temple since the fourteenth century. Performances at 7:00 p.m. the first two days and from 2:00 p.m. to 6:00 p.m. on the last two days. Admission free.

1–4   **Shinsen-en Kyogen,** Shinsen-en. Kyogen as performed by devotees of the Shinsen-en temple. Performances from 1:30 p.m. to 6:00 p.m. the first two days and from 1:30 p.m. to 10:00 p.m. the last two days. No charge.

1–24   **Kamogawa Odori,** Pontocho Kaburenjo Theater. Springtime geisha dance performances. Fee. Tea ceremony available for an extra fee.

2   **Ochatsubo Dochu** (Parade of Tea Jars). From Kennin-ji to Yasaka Shrine. Each spring, the shogun required the tea dealers of Uji to present him with the first tea leaves of the season. The leaves were packed in large ceramic jars, and on this occasion, such jars are paraded from the Kennin-ji to Shijo-dori and on to the Yasaka Shrine in remembrance of this past event.

3   **Constitution Day,** a national holiday. *Yabusame* horseback archery performed at Shimogamo Jinja from 1:00 p.m.

5   **Jishu Matsuri,** Jishu Jinja. Noon. Procession of one hundred children in samurai costumes leaves Kiyomizu-dera at 2:30 p.m. *Rei-taisai* prayer ceremony.

5   **Kodomo-no-hi** (Children's Day, a national holiday). Formerly known as "Boys' Day." Cloth carp are flown from poles and various martial arts displays take place, particularly at the Budo Center in Okazaki Park.

15   **Aoi Matsuri** (Hollyhock Festival), Shimogamo and Kamigamo shrines. An imperial messenger in an ox cart, his suite, and some three hundred courtiers start from Kyoto Gosho at 10:00 a.m. and arrive at the Shimogamo Shrine at 11:40 for ceremonies. They leave there at 2:00 p.m. and arrive at the Kamigamo Shrine at 3:30. During the Heian period, hollyhocks were thought to ward off thunderstorms and earthquakes; thus, these leaves are worn on headgear, are on the carts, and are offered to the gods as well. Reserved seats can be obtained at the Imperial Palace at the start of the procession.

18   **Yoshida Reisai,** Yoshida Shrine. *Yamato-mai* traditional dances are offered to the gods at the shrine on this date.

21   **Gotan-e,** Nishi Hongan-ji. Memorial services for Shinran Shonin, founder of the Shinshu Jodo sect of Buddhism.

June

1   **Kaminari-yoke Taisai,** Kitano Tenman-gu. A festival to honor the god of thunder. Protective talismans are distributed. From 4:00 p.m.

1–2   **Kyoto Takigi Noh,** Heian Shrine. In the light of burning torches, Noh performances begin at 5:30 p.m. (Postponed in case of rain.) Fee.

5–6   **Oda Nobunaga Service,** Honno-ji. Services for the assassinated fifteenth-century civil head of state. Ninja show and flamenco guitar. Temple treasures are on view at 2:00 p.m.

5   **Eisai-ki,** Kennin-ji. A memorial service in honor of Priest Eisai who brought tea seeds from China and popularized tea drinking in Japan.

8   **Iris viewing,** Heian Shrine.

9–12   **Toki-ichi** (Pottery Fair), Senbon Shaka-do. A service in appreciation of used pottery held at 2:00 p.m. on June 10. Pottery sold at reduced prices.

12   **Yatsuhashi Ki Matsuri,** Honen-in. *Koto* music in honor of Yatsuhashi Ki and his contribution to the *koto*.

15   **Aoba Matsuri** (Green Tea Festival), Chishaku-in. A group of *yamabushi* (itinerant mountain priests) hold a religious service in honor of Kobo Daishi on the anniversary of his birth. 9:00 a.m. to 4:00 p.m.

15   **Yasaka Matsuri,** Yasaka Shrine. Performances of the *azuma asobi* shrine dance. 10:30 a.m.

25   **Gotanshin-sai,** Kitano Tenman-gu. The monthly celebration and fair held in honor of Sugawara-no-Michizane. On this occasion, a large ring of miscanthus (Japanese plume grass) is installed around the main gate with anyone passing through it guaranteed freedom from any summer epidemic. The shrine art treasures are on view. About fifteen hundred festival stalls. From 9:00 a.m.

30   **Nagoshi-no-harai,** various temples. A service to purify people of the sins that they may have accrued during the first six months of the year. If one passes through the miscanthus ring which is set up on the shrine grounds and eats *minazuki* (rice pudding) and red beans, one can then face the torrid and humid summer months with equanimity. Ebisu Shrine, 6:00 p.m./Heian Shrine, 4:00 p.m./Kamigamo Shrine, 6:00 p.m.

July

7   **Seitai-Myojin Reisai,** Shiramine Shrine. The Tanabata celebration when the Princess Weaver Star and the Cowherd Star cross paths. The story was taken from a Chinese fairy tale of the separation of two lovers. At this shrine, a traditional folk dance *(komachi odori)* is performed by young girls in sixteenth-century costumes. The festival begins at 3:00 p.m., while the dances begin at 4:30.

7   **Tanabata Matsuri,** Yasaka Shrine, Kiyomizu-dera, and Jishu Shrine. Same as above. At the Jishu Shrine, *kokeshi* dolls are blessed in hopes for a good marriage.

7   **Mitarashi Matsuri,** Kitano Tenman-gu. Prayers for improvement of artistic skills.

10   **Omukae Chochin** (Welcoming Lanterns: the beginning of the Gion Festival). Traditionally costumed celebrants carrying lanterns on long poles welcome the three sacred *mikoshi* (portable shrines) of the Yasaka Shrine and accompany them

on a procession through the center of the city. Three traditional dance groups perform when the procession stops at City
Hall on Oike-dori at 6:10 p.m. and then back at the Yasaka
Shrine on the return at 8:40 p.m. The procession moves from
the Yasaka Shrine along Shijo-dori to Kawaramachi-dori to
Oike-dori to Teramachi-dori, and then back along Shijo-dori
to the shrine.

10   **Mikoshi-arai** (Cleansing of the Main Mikoshi), Yasaka Shrine.
The main *mikoshi* for the chief deity of the Yasaka Shrine is
carried on the shoulders of young men to the Shijo Bridge over
the Kamogawa river. Here the chief priest of the shrine purifies
the *mikoshi*, after which it is returned to the shrine by the young
men. 7:00 p.m. to 8:30 p.m.

13–16   **Gion Bayashi.** The Gion floats are parked in their respective
neighborhoods. Traditional music is performed on each float
in the evening. On June 15 and 16, many homes traditionally
display their family treasures.

13–15   **Obon,** many temples. The welcoming home of the spirits of the
deceased for their annual visit.

16–17   **Yamaboko Junko** (Procession of Floats), Gion procession.
Leaves Karasuma-shijo at 9:00 a.m. and passes through Shijo-
dori, Karasuma-dori, Oike-dori, and Shinmachi-dori ending at
around 3:00 p.m.

17   **Shinkosai** (procession of *mikoshi*), Yasaka Shrine. At 6:00, 6:30,
and 6:40 p.m. the three sacred *mikoshi* carried on the shoulders
of young men, each following a different route, arrive at Shijo
Teramachi where the *mikoshi* remain until July 24.

24   **Hanagasa Gyoretsu** (Procession of Flowered Sunshades), Yasaka
Shrine. A colorful procession of many geisha, traditional
dancing groups, and children, all in ancient costume featuring
flowers. Various dances are performed in the Yasaka precincts.
The procession starts at Teramachi-Oike at 10:15 a.m., reaches
Teramachi-Shijo by 11:00, and arrives at the Yasaka Shrine by
11:25 a.m.

August

Rokusai Nenbutsu Odori (Nenbutsu Prayer Dance), various
temples at various dates. This traditional religious dance,

attributed to Kuya, dates back more than a millennium. It can be observed at Mibu-dera on the second Sunday of the month at 8:00 p.m., and on the following day at 8:30 p.m. On the third Sunday, it can be seen at 8:30 p.m.

1   **Gion Hassaku,** Gion Hanamachi. A ceremony in which *maiko* (apprentice geisha) and geisha show gratitude to their seniors. 11:00 a.m.

4   **Kitanosai,** Kitano Tenman-gu. A memorial service in memory of Emperor Ichijo. 9:00 a.m.

7–10   **Manto-e** (candle lighting), Rokuharamitsu-ji. Lighting of human-shaped lanterns and religious service to welcome back the souls of the dead during the *Obon* period. From 8:00 p.m.

7–10   **Rokudo-mairi** (Pilgrimage to Rokudo), Rokudo Chinno-ji. A part of the *Obon* ceremonies. According to tradition, the entrance to the Six Regions (Rokudo) of the nether world is located in the area of the Chinno-ji temple. Legend relates that the temple bell resounds some ten billion miles, as far as the other world. Thus, thousands crowd into this area to ring the temple bell to call the souls of their dead back to earth for *Obon. Obon* continues until August 16 when the fires on the five hills about Kyoto light the souls back to the nether world.

8   **Rokudo-mairi,** Senbon Shaka-do. Welcoming services for ancestral spirits. The Shaka image in the main shrine is shown on this occasion.

8–9   **Kamogawa Noryo** (night stalls along the Kamogawa river). Along the western side of the Kamogawa river between Oike-dori and Shijo-dori, some two hundred stalls are set up for sales from 6:00 p.m. to 11:00 p.m. A folk-song concert and stage events take place.

8–10   **Toki Matsuri** (Pottery Fair), Gojo-dori. Stalls selling ceramics at a discount line both sides of the street to honor the deity of pottery who is enshrined in the Wakamiya Hachiman Shrine on Gojo-dori. The fair runs from early morning until night.

Second Sunday   Yuzen Washing, west bank, Kamogawa river. A once-a-year event held at Sanjo-mon when the final process of washing excess dye from Yuzen fabrics takes place as a reminder of a practice used before pollution laws forbade use of the river for this purpose.

9–16   **Manto Kuyo** (ceremony of lantern lighting), Mibu-dera. Some eight hundred lanterns are lit in the corridor to the Hondo (Main Hall) to welcome back ancestral souls. *Nenbutsu Odori* on August 9 at 8:00 p.m. and on August 10 and 16 at 8:30 p.m.

9 and 16 Rokusai Nenbutsu Odori, Mibu-dera. Teaching Buddhist doctrine through a one-thousand-year-old ceremony in which a dance in colorful costumes teaches by means of entertainment. Kyogen is also performed. Free.

14–16   **Manto-e** (candle lighting), Higashi Otani Cemetery. Beginning at 6:00 p.m., each of the thousands of graves in the cemetery are lit with a candle to welcome back the souls of the dead.

15   **Manto-e,** To-ji. Service to welcome back the souls of the dead.

16   **Daimonji Gosan Okuribi** (The lighting of fires on the five hills surrounding Kyoto to help guide the souls of the dead back to the nether world). At 8:00 p.m., the fire in the shape of the character for *dai* (great) is lit on the eastern hill, Nyoigatake. The fires on four other mountains to the west and north (Myoho, Funagata, Hidari Daimon-ji, and Torii) are also lit at this time.

20   **Rei-taisai,** Goryo Shrine. *Obon* dances.

23–30   **Jizo-bon** A children's festival in local residential areas (i.e. Nishijin, among others) when lanterns are lit, games are played, and parties are held all in honor of Jizo, the patron deity of children.

September

14   **Mantosai,** Hirano Shrine. Hundreds of paper lanterns illuminate the inner precincts of the shrine from 6:30 p.m.

15   **Respect for the Aged Day,** a national holiday.

15   **Konpira Kushi Matsuri** (Comb Festival), Yasui Konpira-gu. An exhibition of old combs is held, and women in costumes of the past parade at 1:00 p.m. Religious services are held for old, used combs brought to the shrine and a "Black Hair Dance" *(Kurokami Odori)* is held.

15–November 24 (Showing of the Treasures of To-ji). The temple treasure house is open from 9:00 a.m. to 4:00 p.m. Fee.

Third Sunday   Hagi Matsuri (Bush Clover Festival), Nashinoki Shrine.

A two-day festival in which a haiku contest is held on the first day from noon to 3:30 p.m. Fine paper tablets with *tanzaku* poems inscribed upon them are hung on the bush clover, all dedicated to and for the pleasure of the shrine deities. On the second day there are religious services in the morning. This is followed, after 1:00 p.m., by traditional dances, flower arrangements, and Kyogen plays. An open-air tea ceremony is also held.

22 or 23 **Higan** (Autumn Equinox, a national holiday). On this day, the sun sets in the due west, the location of the Buddhist Western Paradise. Thus, temples hold services for the dead during this period and families tend the graves of their deceased. ("Higan" means "other shore" in reference to the land of the dead.)

21 **Rei-taisai,** Shiramine Shrine. Noh plays by firelight at 3:45 p.m. and 6:00 p.m. Free.

22–23 **Shinkosai,** Seimei Shrine. Abe-no-Seimei (921–1005), the noted Heian-era scholar of astrology, is enshrined here. On September 23, the *mikoshi* holding his spirit is taken through the streets around the shrine by girls in traditional garb, a boys' band, and decorated horses. The procession lasts from 1:00 p.m. to 5:00 p.m.

October

1–5 **Zuiki Matsuri,** Kitano Tenman-gu. A harvest festival to please the gods so that the harvest will be plentiful. A thousand-year-old festival begun by the emperor Murakami (reigned 946–967). The roof and other portions of the shrine *mikoshi* are decorated with *zuiki* (taro), pumpkin, and other vegetables. The *mikoshi* is placed in a temporary shrine at Nishioji-Shimodachiuri. On October 1 at 1:00 p.m., there is a procession of young men carrying three ordinary *mikoshi* on their shoulders around the shrine and then to the *otabishi* (temporary location) where they will remain until October 4.

2 **Kenchasai,** tea ceremony at the *otabishi* at 10:00 a.m. with explanations by a noted tea master.

4 **Kankosai,** a procession to return the *mikoshi* to the shrine held from 1:00 p.m. to 5:00 p.m. The *zuiki mikoshi*, covered with vegetables, also returns.

5   **Goensai** (Last Festival). Eight young women in ancient costumes perform religious dances at the shrine from 3:30 p.m.

All month   **Treasure viewing,** To-ji. The treasure house is open from 9:00 a.m. to 4:00 p.m. daily.

1–15   **Treasure viewing,** Ninna-ji. The Ninna-ji treasure house is open from 9:00 a.m. to 4:00 p.m. daily. Fee.

5–December 20   **Autumn treasure viewing,** Jotenkaku Museum of the Shokoku-ji. The museum is open from 9:00 a.m. to 4:00 p.m. Fee.

8–November 15   **Autumn Exhibition,** Ryozen Rekishi-kan. Exhibit of Meiji-era personalities and activities. 10:00 a.m. to 4:30 p.m. daily. Fee.

9–13   **Treasure viewing,** Toji-in.

10   **Sports Day,** a national holiday.

10   **Shuki Konpira Taisai,** Yasui Konpira-gu. Konpira, a half-dragon, half-fish demon, is the patron saint of travelers. At 1:00 p.m., a parade of children in samurai garb accompany the demon.

Mid-month to early November   **Kamogawa Odori,** Pontocho Kaburenjo Theater. Geisha dances weekdays at 12:30, 2:20, and 4:10. On Sundays and national holidays at 12:00, 1:40, 3:20, and 5:10. Fee. Additional fee for tea ceremony. All seats reserved.

16   **Inzei Amida Kyo-e,** Shinnyodo Temple. An annual recitation of a rare sutra which was brought from China by the monk Jikaku Taishi Enju (Ennin). From 9:00 a.m. to 10:30 a.m. A rare mandala, the *jodohensozu*, is on display.

19–21   **Hatsuka Ebisu Taisai,** Ebisu Shrine. An annual festival in which a dancer portrays Ebisu and performs a joyous traditional dance on a temporary stage in the shrine grounds. Many stalls on the evenings of October 19 through October 21 enliven the scene.

19   **Funaoka Matsuri,** Kenkun Shrine. A parade of boys in medieval armor portraying Oda Nobunaga's soldiers as they marched into Kyoto to take control of the government in the 1500s. Exhibition of cultural assets from Nobunaga's household. From 11:00 a.m.

22   **Jidai Matsuri** (Festival of the Ages), Heian Shrine. A procession which illustrates the costumes of residents of Kyoto from the earliest days (794) to the Meiji period of the late nineteenth century. Reserved seats available on Oike-dori. One of the three great processions in Kyoto each year. There are thousands in the parade, all in costume. Starts from the Imperial Palace at noon and reaches the Heian Shrine by 2:20 p.m.

26   **Unagi Hojo-e,** Mishima Shrine. Autumn prayers for eels eaten during the year and a release of eels into the shrine pond. 2:00 p.m.

29   **Yokosai** (Ceremony of Poem Recitation), Kitano Tenman-gu. A recitation of the twenty best poems selected from all over Japan. Read by eight descendants of Sugawara-no-Michizane dressed in costumes of Michizane's time. The event recalls the occasion when Michizane wrote a poem to the emperor while in exile. 3:00 p.m.

November

Early November   A period when the color of the autumn leaves are at their height. Some of the more attractive areas at this time of year are Kiyomizu-dera, Shinnyo-do, Zenrin-ji/Eikan-do, and Nanzen-ji.

1 and 3   **Tea Ceremony,** Nijo Castle. From 9:30 a.m. to 3:00 p.m., tea ceremony is conducted for the public in the Seiryu-en garden of Nijo Castle. Fee.

1–10   **Gion Odori,** Gion Kaikan Theater. Reservations needed for the dance performance by geisha. 1:00 and 3:30 p.m.

1–15   **Meiji Era Exhibition,** Ryozen Rekishi-kan. The museum is open from 10:00 a.m. to 4:30 p.m. Fee.

1–24   **Viewing of temple treasures,** To-ji. Treasure house open daily from 9:00 a.m. to 4:00 p.m. Fee.

1–30   **Viewing of temple treasures,** Zenrin-ji/Eikan-do. Treasure house open from 9:00 a.m. to 4:00 p.m.

1–30   **Shichi-go-san** (Festival for seven, five, and three-year-old children). November 15 is the date for the celebration for children of three (boys and girls), five (boys), and seven (girls). Parents take them to the shrine for blessing, the children often dressed in traditional garb. The following shrines are particular sites for parents and children: Yasaka Shrine, Kitano Shrine, Ebisu Shrine, and Heian Shrine.

1 to December 20   **Viewing of temple treasures,** Shokoku-ji. Autumn exhibition at the Jotenkaku Art Museum. 9:00 a.m. to 4:00 p.m. Fee.

3   **Culture Day,** a national holiday.

5–15   **Ojuya,** Shinnyo-do Temple. A ten-day recitation of the *nenbutsu* in remembrance of the ten-day recitation by Ise-no-kami Tadetani. Nenbutsu service 5:00 p.m. to 7:00 p.m. from November 5 through November 14. On November 5, the service runs from 9:00 a.m. to 5:00 p.m. On November 11, a tea ceremony is held at 9:00 a.m. Procession at 2:00 p.m. on November 15. The Inner Hall is open from 9:00 a.m. to 5:00 p.m. Fee.

Second Sunday   Kuya-do Kaizanki, Kuya-do Temple. Dancing *nenbutsu* service in honor of Kuya.

21–22   **Opening of the Honmaru Goten** (castle keep), Nijo Castle. Special opening of the Honmaru Goten of Nijo Castle from 9:30 to 3:30. The one time a year this palace is open to the public.

21–28   **Ho-onko,** Higashi Hongan-ji. Memorial services all week for Shinran Shonin, founder of the Jodo Shinshu sect of Buddhism.

23   **Labor Thanksgiving Day,** a national holiday.

26   **Ochatsubo Hokensai** (Annual Grand Tea Ceremony), Kitano Tenman-gu. Tea ceremony by major tea masters in memory of Hideyoshi's great tea party held at the Kitano Shrine in 1587. At 11:00 a.m., a service in which the new tea is dedicated and tea containers from famous collections are placed before the gods to please them. Tea ceremony by four major teahouses follow all day long. A display of many kinds of traditional confections from 10:00 a.m. to 3:00 p.m.

December

1–25   **Kaomise** (Kabuki dramas), Minami-za. The climax of the Kabuki year. The most famous and capable Kabuki actors offer samples of their best performances in the traditional grand style.

2–13   **Gion Odori**, Gion Kaikan Theater. Dance performances by geisha.

10   **Shimai Konpira** (Last Service of the Year), Yasui Konpira-gu.

Konpira is the patron of voyages. One can have one's name inscribed on a votive stick which is then placed in a "treasure ship" as protection in future travels and for "sailing" into the new year. The shrine's collection of *ema* (votive tablets) are also shown this day.

13 **Ofuku Ume,** Kitano Tenman-gu. *Mochi* (rice cakes) made from plums (Japanese apricots) taken from the shrine trees. The sale continues through December 20, and if these *mochi* are eaten on New Year's Day, health and happiness will be ensured throughout the new year.

Third weekend   Shimabara Sumiya, Shimabara Kaburenjo Theater. *Mochi* pounding for the making of rice cakes for the New Year festivities takes place in the demonstration hall. Singing and dancing by geisha and *maiko.* 10:30 a.m. and 1:30 p.m.

21 **Shimai Kobo** (Last Service of the Year), To-ji. A special service at the end of the year for Kobo Daishi and the monthly fair are held.

25 **Shimai Tenjin** (Last Service of the Year), Kitano Tenman-gu. Last service of the year for Sugawara-no-Michizane and the monthly fair are held.

25 **Ominugui-shiki,** Chion-in. The abbot of the Chion-in polishes the image of Honen with a pure, white silk cloth during the service. The prayers offered on this day are meant to eradicate the sins of the past year. 1:00 p.m.

31 **Omisoka** (Grand Last Day), Chion-in, To-ji, Myoshin-ji, Kiyomizu-dera, Shinnyodo, etc. All old debts are paid and the business and house put in order for the end of the year. At midnight, the temple bells toll 108 times to symbolize the 108 failings of mankind.